Dear Meaghan
I took a bath geth
you this book
          lots of love
                [signature]
                xxx
                2013

LOST *for* WORDS

Other books by Hugh Lunn:

LOST for WORDS

AUSTRALIA'S LOST LANGUAGE IN WORDS AND STORIES

Hugh Lunn

ABC
Books

For Ken Fletcher
R.I.P.

 The ABC 'Wave' device is a trademark of the
Australian Broadcasting Corporation and is used
under licence by HarperCollins*Publishers* Australia.

First published in 2006 by ABC Books for the
AUSTRALIAN BROADCASTING CORPORATION.
Reprinted by HarperCollins*Publishers* Australia Pty Limited
ABN 36 009 913 517
www.harpercollins.com.au

HarperCollins*Publishers*
25 Ryde Road, Pymble, Sydney, NSW 2073, Australia
31 View Road, Glenfield, Auckland 0627, New Zealand
A 53, Sector 57, Noida, UP, India
77–85 Fulham Palace Road, London W6 8JB, United Kingdom
2 Bloor Street East, 20th floor, Toronto, Ontario M4W 1A8, Canada
10 East 53rd Street, New York NY 10022, USA

ISBN 978 0 7333 1759 0

Cover and internal design by saso content & design pty ltd
Set in Palatino 10/16.5pt
Printed and bound in Australia by Griffin Press, Adelaide

12   11 12

CONTENTS

Acknowledgements

I wish to thank the many people who donated words and phrases for this book, especially: Sam Aherne; Rob Allen and Megan Surawski; Sandy, Jenny and Thomas Armstrong; Sid Ash; Malda Bertram; Tom Biggs; Tim Campbell and Josie Heinz; Keith and Yvonne Chalk; Carleen Corrie; Cathy Creagh and Kenny Fletcher; David and Lyndell Cronin; Joan Dash; Elizabeth Dawson; Glenys Dean; Robert Deveridge; Johnny Duncan; Jim Egoroff; Brian Francis; Anne-Marie and David Hunter of Daisy Hill and their friends (Carole Cherry, Louise Leach, Anne Ferguson, Peter and Carmel Casey, Susan and Paul Lambert, Gil and Bev Wright, Bruce and Cathy Mawhinney, Peter and Di O'Donnell); Anne Lawrence; Lynda Litz; Judith and Alice Lunn; Carol-Ann McVinish; Maureen Meggitt-Lorne; Lesley Park; Heather Patrick; Jim Pisanos; Lynda Robertson; Tania Ruscoe; Daisy H. Smith; Tom Thompson; Janice van der Horst; Mrs T.C. Walters.

Introduction

- -

Language tells us who we are: because we are the words we use.

If we adopt the language of another society we lose our rights of memory in our own kingdom.

The first time I realised Australia had lost its lingo was when I was writing a memoir about growing up in the 1940s and 50s. To capture the era, I had to remember the phrases and words we used back then because most of them had disappeared from view.

Readers wrote from all over Australia surprised that their parents had spoken just like mine in Brisbane. And they recalled other phrases that I'd forgotten: **It's snowing down south; I'd know his hide in a tannery; he's all mouth and trousers.**

Reading their letters, I too experienced the intense joy of remembering.

And so I began collecting every old turn of phrase that came my way, scribbling them down on scraps of paper and tossing them into an old leather school port which someone had thrown out on the footpath for a council rubbish collection. I kept the port in a tiny, fireproof brick room for sixteen years because I treasured this little collection; I could see that succeeding generations of Australians had not inherited what was rightfully theirs: a rogue-ish, rich, direct, expansive, expressive language.

Speaking at an all-boys school, I described to more than 100 how some galoot had … A boy put up his hand to ask: 'What was that word you used? Galoo?'

'Will someone tell this galoot what a galoot is?' I asked.

But no one could.

They'd never heard of the word. But they were very, very interested to know of its existence.

These boys all, of course, knew what a nerd was, what a wimp was, what a wuss was. They could easily converse in the truncated, sarcastic, dismissive form of conversation now common at dinner tables all over Australia: **In your dreams, as if, you wish, bring it on, get a life, Puh-leese, Hello! Hello! I was, like, Oh My God!**

Absolutely.

Unlike me when I was at school, these boys did not have to learn their poetry and times tables 'off by heart'. But they were still rote learning: every morning and every evening they were absorbing the culture and idiom of American television programmes, computer games, and films. A sort of cargo cult worship, always passively waiting for more to arrive on our airwaves.

How long since you saw someone in a TV sitcom on our screens reach out across the coffee table and say, 'Excuse pigs without tails'. Or heard a TV character tell someone to drop by: 'Just toot and come in - you know, the Egyptian Pharaoh.' Or a woman say: 'Now **she** was an education'.

Of course, the English language is always changing. That's what makes it so evocative and is one of the reasons why it has come to so dominate the globe. But whereas overseas foods have arrived to join, expand and enrich our menu, the tongue of telly has stunted our slang. So that shades of meaning have almost disappeared.

Change isn't good if it happens in only one direction. That's called being subsumed.

The influx of American television could have added to our language, making it richer in nuance and colour. But instead it has taken over what we had, and inhibited expression. 'You'd do a lot with a stick and a bucket of eggs!' or 'Don't just stand around like a spare groom at a wedding!' has been reduced to: **Get real!**

As in George Orwell's *1984*, most people are now content to offer a few stock phrases, which have replaced a whole plethora of words and sayings.

Whatever.

Tell someone who cares.

Get over it.

Get a life.

At the same time as the language of the people has become impossibly simple, higher education has made the language of politics and the bureaucracy impossibly complex. The candid, plain-speaking colourful lingo we once spoke has been displaced by evasive obfuscating gobbledegook which has taken over government and bureaucracy.

As in the Communist Revolution in China, this politically correct language has added lots of syllables, but no sense.

I was in China in 1965, even before the Cultural Revolution, and everyone was expected to attend **struggle meetings** to learn their **revolutionary tasks** to defeat **running-dog capitalist-roader class enemies**. Everyone repeatedly used these terms so as not to require re-education.

In Australia forty years later, if you don't **negotiate, liaise, consult, provide leadership** and claim **the ability to mentor and form partnerships with appropriate key stakeholders and mitigate against sub-optimal outcomes and issues**, then you won't even get interviewed for a public service job.

Orwell predicted the lying 'doublespeak' would arrive by 1984, but what arrived was triplespeak: '**At the end of the day going forward the peak body umbrella group will take up the challenges in the wider community to initiate consultation and embrace diversity.**'

Why then have they added all the syllables?

To put it in the Australian vernacular: **So the pushy people get the cushy jobs**.

This book is not Banjo Paterson or Bazza McKenzie or the bush, but rather the language of 1950s urban-dwelling Australians.

It is not exclusively Australian; but it is how we spoke.

It is not a list, and is therefore not meant to be exhaustive, or, I hope, exhausting. I have grouped the contents of my port into themes and stories: and, just for fun, I wrote a fifteen-episode wireless serial called *Lost for Words*.

Some of the phrases in this book are still around. Every so often a newspaper headline writer dusts one off like a museum exhibit and puts it up for display. But generally they have fallen from favour and you just don't hear them in conversation any more.

As we used to say, **more's the pity**.

One night at a speech in Gympie, Queensland, I mentioned how we had lost our language. A woman stood up and said no, that's wrong, we haven't lost our language: 'We gave it away.'

So this book and its sequel — *Words Fail Me: a journey through Australia's lost language* — is a small attempt to ask for it back.

I wanted to write it down before it became extinct. To try to keep it partof us, and to delight all those who are Australian … and all those who can remember.

If you have some old word or phrase from the way we used to speak and don't want it forgotten, please send it to me at:

PO Box 4017
St Lucia South, Qld 4067

Or

hughlunn@hughlunn.com.au

And maybe one day it will live again.

Hugh Lunn
www.hughlunn.com.au

Chapter one

SOLD *into* SLAVERY

We'll duck into the paper shop on our way. I'm going to buy Myrtle a Casket Ticket. You never know your luck till a dead horse kicks you.

LOST FOR WORDS EPISODE I: *An Outing*

Most Australians in the 1940s and 50s and early 60s listened to serials on the wireless in their lounge room. One of the kids would kneel in front of the wireless, bathed in the green glow, and turn the white needle around to the right station to catch the family's favourite radio serial.

Then, as the valves warmed up, a voice would crackle through the speaker …

'This is Episode 1 of our new radio serial, **Lost for Words,** *the story of Bert and Grace and their trials and tribulations bringing up a young family after Bert returned from the War.'* The music would rise and the reading begin …

Grace is sitting at her dressing table putting her face on, getting ready to take three of her kids — Morris, Delma and Ima — to visit their Aunty Myrtle.

'Dearie me, I look like the wreck of the *Hesperus*,' she announces to herself. 'I look like a high wind in a mattress factory. I look like I've been dragged through a bush backwards. It's a good job I scrub up well.'

Grace usually got around the house in a floral dress with untidy hair, no make-up, her petticoat and bra straps showing. But to attend church or a wedding or for an outing, she would put on her Sunday best.

Grace snaps shut her compact and pops it into her enormous handbag, which has two handles and sits on her wrist like a giant navy blue leather pillow.

'Kids! Get a wriggle on, or we'll be late.'

'I'm coming, Mum.'

'So's Christmas. Shake your feathers. Make it snappy! What's keeping you? Get a move on!'

'I can't find my windcheater! It's been stolen.'

'It must be there somewhere. Use your eyes instead of your mouth.'

'It's not in my room. Someone's taken it!'

'You can't see for looking.'

'But I've looked everywhere.'

'Then use big eyes.'

'But I still can't find it, Mum!'

'Perhaps it's up in Annie's room, behind the clock.'

'It must be lost!'

'Where did you lose it?'

'If I knew where I lost it, it wouldn't be lost.'

'No giving cheek! I'll say a prayer to St Anthony.'

'Oh, here it is.'

'Come on, slowcoach.'

'Oh jings, now I can't get the zipper to work.'

'Take your time and hurry up! Don't shilly-shally, will you, or we'll miss the tram. Shake a leg. You kids are strung out like Brown's cows. If you don't get cracking this instant, I'll light a fire under your tail. Morris, have you washed your face?'

'Of course, Mum.'

'Let me see. Yes, a lick and a promise by the looks. Your ears are so dirty we could grow spuds in them.'

By this stage, Grace is done up like a sore toe. 'I'm going to play the duchess at Myrtle's,' she tells the kids. 'That's why I'm wearing my blue charmeuse and my pearls. Or I could wear my midnight satin trimmed with shallots. I've never been a fashion plate, but I can put on the dog as well as anyone.'

They troop down the front stairs, past the gerberas, gladioli, mother-in-law's tongue, ochna, fishbone ferns, oleander, and azalea.

'We'll duck into the paper shop on our way,' Grace says. 'I'm going to buy Myrtle a Casket Ticket. You never know your luck till a dead horse kicks you.'

Finally Grace and the kids clamber onto the tram to go to her sister-in-law Myrtle's, saying: 'We haven't seen her in a month of Sundays.'

When they arrive at Myrtle's front gate, Grace whispers to the kids, 'Now, mind your Ps and Qs.'

'What's a P, Mum?' asks little Ima.

'A great relief. With my Woolworths bladder it is.'

'Mum, I'm busting to go! I need a widdle!'

'Morris, haven't I always told you to go before we leave? Not that I can talk. Well, ask Aunty Myrtle when we get in, and make sure you pull the chain. And be on your best behaviour, remember, be courteous, or you'll get the wooden spoon.'

Some mothers carried a wooden spoon on visits, and they would rap the child on the knuckles or the bum to keep them in line.

No one ever went visiting empty-handed. Usually people 'brought a plate', which meant bringing some food to contribute to the event.

Grace presents Myrtle with a home-baked cake, saying: 'I made it from scratch.'

Myrtle takes a peek in the cake tin and says: 'Well, Grace, it's almost as good as a store-bought one.' This is said in jest, because they both know, as everyone does, that homemade cooking or sewing is invariably superior.

The kids are told to be still and quiet while the ladies have a good old natter in the Genoa lounge chairs, which can hardly be seen under the arm protectors and antimacassars, which prevent the velvet upholstery on the back of the chair from being stained by hair oil (Macassar oil).

'Stop fidgeting, stop jiggling,' cautions Grace. Children were always being accused of fidgeting. For some reason, staying still, as if you were very old and immobile, was desirable, and considered good manners. This was excruciatingly boring, but outings were for the enjoyment of the adults, not the children. In most things, the grown-ups' enjoyment took precedence over the kids'.

'While you're on your feet, Morris,' says Aunty Myrtle, 'do fetch me a serviette from the table, there's a dear.'

Morris hands over the serviette.

'Aunty Myrtle,' pipes up little Ima, 'will you fetch me my glass?'

Grace and Myrtle snort in disgust at this audacity.

'What are you, a cripple?' says Myrtle. 'You're big enough and ugly enough to get it yourself! I'm lost for words.'

So Ima gets up and is standing exactly between Aunty Myrtle and Grace, blocking their view.

'Ima,' says Grace. 'Who do you think you are, the glazier's daughter? Move out of the way. And shut your mouth, are you trying to catch flies? And, Morris, don't talk with your mouth half full, fill it up! And don't point with the cutlery, and keep your elbows off the table. It's unseemly. And Delma, stop licking the knife. I didn't know we had a sword swallower in the family. Get your hands out of your pockets, Morris, or I'll sew them up. And, little Ima, stop sniggering, it's common.'

Then Grace turns to her sister-in-law: 'Now, Myrtle, you know I'll be doing the books for Janice's new dress shop, don't you?'

'Fancy,' says Myrtle. 'That will be fun. Janice is such a sweetie. She's an unclaimed treasure.'

'Aunty Myrtle, what's an unchained pleasure?' asks little Ima.

'Little pigs have big ears,' replies Myrtle.

'Yes,' says Grace, standing up. 'Now, small fry, we're sick of the sight of you. Get out and entertain yourselves. Run along and go exploring the neighbourhood. But keep your wits about you.' (That was the 1950s' equivalent of Stranger Danger.)

Then the women settle back for a private chinwag. Married women seemed to have hundreds of names for men who were charming, risky, dangerous, and, as you'd suspect, attractive and alluring.

Grace: 'Yes, I'm surprised some dapper dan hasn't arrived and swept Janice off her feet.'

Myrtle: 'Alfie was sniffing around, but all he got from Janice was advice on how to tie a cravat.'

Grace: 'Oh, that Alfie, he's a snazzy dresser, isn't he?'

Myrtle: 'Yes, a snappy dresser, and a handsome devil. Easy to see he's been to charm school. He must have kissed the Blarney stone.'

Grace: 'He's a bit of a rogue, though, don't you think? He's done alright for a ne'er-do-well.'

Myrtle: 'He did get in with the wrong crowd for a time there. Still and all, he's certainly a wag, a card, funny as a circus.'

Grace: 'And a bit of a scoundrel. Don't forget, Myrtle, a man can laugh a woman into bed.'

Myrtle: 'Alfie can put his shoes under my bed any day of the week. He always has a smile on his dial.'

Grace: 'But don't you think he's a bit of a rough diamond?'

Myrtle: 'A fancy dan.'

Grace: 'All mouth and trousers.'

Myrtle: 'Alfie does talk a lot of palava, a lot of malarky, but then he's always been a bit of a rascal.'

Grace: 'But he is a bounder, I've heard.'

Myrtle: 'Flash Jack from Gundagai.'

Myrtle pours Grace another cup of tea.

Grace: 'Yes, well they say his brother, Clem, is a bit of a stinker.'

Myrtle: 'Some say Clem is lower than a snake's belly.'

Grace: 'Yes, he married that girl Enid, then shot through on her, left her stranded with all those kids, and ran off with the woman from the bakery. She wouldn't say boo.'

Myrtle: 'That Enid is a saint. She won't hear a word against him.'

Grace: 'He's led a charmed life, that's for sure. He's never got what was coming to him, and he deserved it, I'm sure.'

Myrtle: 'Not a nice man, a real so-and-so.'

Grace: 'A grub. A bit too seedy, you couldn't guess what he gets up to.'

Myrtle: 'Clem's a real creature. He's nothing but a hood.'

Grace: 'And he thinks he's crash hot.'

Myrtle: 'Crooked as a dog's hind leg.'

Grace: 'A real mongrel.'

Myrtle: 'A vile creature.'

Grace: 'He charmed the pants off her.'

Myrtle: 'I could tell you a thing or two about that!'

Grace: 'Well, he always thought he was a killer diller.'

Myrtle: 'Get the stance he put on outside the pictures on Friday. He's got no shame.'

Grace: 'He's got more front than a rat with a gold tooth.'

Myrtle: 'Yes, he is a lovely article.'

When the kids arrive back, Grace is cross: 'Who do you think you are, the Scarlet Pimpernels? I've been looking for you up hill and down dale, you will-o'-the-wisps. We were about to send out a search party.'

Then it is time to go. 'Put your skates on, kids,' Grace says. 'We can't live on fresh air — I'll duck into the butcher shop on the way home. And I don't want to hear you asking the butcher again what his sign means. He's told you a thousand times, it's not *No Expecting*. The sign says *No Expec-tor-at-ing*. It means no spitting in the shop. He should have a sign up: *No Giving Cheek.*'

What Mum said

A woman arrives at the school fete all dolled up to the nines in a crisp white cotton dress, stiletto heels, rouge, a picture hat, and pearls. She starts sashaying around the coconut ice and toffee stalls, where all the mothers have been working in the heat since daybreak.

As the woman glides past, Mum leans across to one of her kids and whispers loudly: **'What you see when you haven't got a gun!'**

If you were having an argument and Mum didn't believe something she'd say: **'That's a lot of hoo-haa!'** or **'That's a load of old tripe.'** Tripe was the white spongy stomach of an animal that you tried to eat for tea. It was the worst meal your mum ever gave you. She tried to smother it with white sauce, but it was still like eating spongy castor oil.

If she was amazed by something that happened, your mother would say:

'**Now that tickles my fancy.**' Or, '**That takes the cake.**' Conversely, '**That's been done to death.**'

If you said Mum's dumplings **went over a treat** Mum would answer: '**Flattery will get you everywhere**'; but when she felt she was being ignored or not taken account of, she would say: '**Don't mind me.**'

If the kids kept saying 'She won't let us,' or 'She always makes us,' Mum would intone threateningly: '**She's the cat's mother.**'

If she came home and found you sitting in her favourite chair, she'd call you a **cuckoo**.

When Mum got rid of a pet — the dog or the drake or the goat or the rooster — she would always say cheerfully: '**It's gone to a farm.**'

Mothers were somehow able to convince their daughters that they would be the **hit of the fancy-dress ball** wearing her old dressing gown and a Mexican hat. It's **just what your grandmother ordered!** And they could convince their sons that they were the **star turn** at the school concert when singing out of tune.

When she was proud of her daughter's acrobatics or face pulling, a mother would say: '**She's a bit of a trick.**'

If her son helped her out around the house she'd say: '**Buggerlugs, what would I do without you**? **Your blood's worth bottling.**'

Mothers were strong and positive. If you were panicking about schoolwork, she would tell you to **show some gumption**.

But if you let her down, you knew you'd gone **beyond the pale** when she announced: '**That's red hot.**' And she was very disappointed when she shook her head and said: '**Anyone who leans on you is leaning on a dead stick.**'

Sometimes, mothers got the blues too, though. Then they'd say:

- **If it's not one thing, it's another.**
- **I'm all at sixes and sevens.**
- **I was left like a shag on a rock.**
- **I must have the patience of Job.**
- **I'll have to grow mean bones.**

Mother's advice

Mothers gave their best advice when you were catastrophising — thinking up the worst scenario and expanding it, working yourself up into a knot.

- Never borrow sorrow from tomorrow.
- Never worry worry until worry worries you.
- No use crying over spilt milk.
- We'll cross that bridge when we come to it.
- The longest night has a morning.
- It's a long road that hasn't got a turning.
- You're not happy unless you have something to worry about.
- These things are sent to try us.
- Never mind, we'll survive.
- We'll just have to make do.
- Uncertainty is worse than reality.
- To be brave is not to be without fear, but to overcome it.
- There is no disgrace in being even the least when all are great.
- The way to a friend's house is never long.
- Don't make yourself hard to love.

IN THE KITCHEN

Never put the good carving knife under the boiling water — you'll only blunt it.

If you are carrying an overly full cup of tea, you won't spill any into the saucer as long as you don't look at it.

Always take the pot to the kettle, not the kettle to the pot — presumably to reduce the risk of scalding.

On cold winter nights, put a metal fork or spoon into a glass bowl before you pour boiling water into it: the metal absorbs some of the heat, thus preventing the bowl from cracking.

If a pot of milk on the stove has bubbled up and is about to spill, blow on

it; that's the quickest way to stop it boiling over.

Jam came in tins, which you opened with a can-opener. Mum advised: never open a jam tin and leave the sharp lid sticking up, because, once, a girl leant across the dinner table and sliced open her face on the exposed lid.

If a flower arrangement is not working, add some yellow flowers to make it pleasing.

GOOD ADVICE

Never put anything smaller than your elbow in your ear — very young children, upon hearing this, would then try to put their elbow in their ear.

Let your food go down before you start swimming. Because if you swam on a full stomach, you would get a cramp and drown. If all the kids were going swimming, Mum might yell out: 'Don't come back drownd-ed.'

- A pound of knowledge outweighs a pound of gold.
- Two wrongs don't make a right.
- Wish in one hand, spit in the other, and see which fills up first.
- If wishes were horses, beggars would ride.
- Don't wish your life away.
- If the girl down the road puts her head in the fire, that's no reason for you to!
- I always praise the boys in front of the girls, and I praise the girls in front of the boys.
- God helps those who help themselves.
- One good turn deserves another.
- Keep your head down and your bum up and you'll stay out of trouble.
- He who sups with the Devil needs a long spoon — stay clear of trouble-makers.
- Don't trust anyone with your money, not even me.
- Always tell the truth, that way you only have to remember one story.
- But if someone asks you a question and it's none of their business, then you're allowed to tell them a lie.
- A man will be criticised but he will not be laughed at.
- If you haven't got something nice to say about someone, don't say anything at all.
- If someone asks you what you paid for something, just say: 'I paid too much.' This will always be acceptable.

ADVICE TO DAUGHTERS

Deportment — mothers talked about it, to try to stop girls slouching around. Women would even send their daughters to a Deportment School where they learnt to walk gracefully. Good posture was: **stomach in, chest out, shoulders back**.

- Never wear glittering jewels, or pearls, before midday.
- Never comb or brush your hair at the dinner table or in a restaurant.
- To make hair grow thicker, hold each lock tightly between your fingers

and singe the ends with the flame of a match. (This was a silly idea, and didn't work.)

- Never ask a woman what her dress cost. It's rude.
- Mothers would tell their daughters that only tarts and Italians had pierced ears. For some reason, Italian girls were able to have their ears pierced without losing their virginity. But for every other girl, pierced ears were a sure sign that they were **damaged goods**.
- At night-time, never wear mauve. Always wear a colour that shows up.
- When a girl wore a gown with green spots to the ball, no one asked her to dance all night. But when she wore a pale blue dress, she was asked for every dance.
- Always get dressed up. If you don't, the other girl will, and she'll get the boy even though you're just as well-heeled as she is.
- Strapless evening gowns must be worn with gloves above the elbow.
- Short sleeves must be worn with gloves just below the elbow.
- Short-wristed gloves are to be worn only with long sleeves.

- Every time you sigh, you lose a drop of blood from the heart.
- When it comes to older men, the advice to daughters is clear-cut: 'Lunch, dear, but never dinner.'
- Don't mistake the shadow for the substance.
- If you like him, take him to meet your friends and see if he's still the one for you.
- But never introduce your donah to your pal — never introduce your sweetheart to your best friend, because she might well run off with him.
- Marry in haste, repent at leisure.
- On marriage, start as you mean to finish.
- There's more fish than them what is swimming about — when your sweetheart has just given you up.
- In a few months' time you'll be beating them off with a stick.
- And if you wouldn't listen to her, your mother would say: 'You'd better take my advice now, because I won't be around when you're my age.'

Mother's work

Mothers were expected to be **houseproud**. If the house was in **a real state**, then she was in **a real state**.

'We'll have to **tart the place up** before the visitors arrive,' your mum would say. 'Let's get this house **shipshape and Bristol fashion**. I want it **spick and span**. This place has gone to **rack and ruin**. The lounge room looks like a **Chinese pakapoo ticket**. The dining room is **like a pigsty**. It's like a **den of iniquity, a house of ill-repute**.'

She would then **Hoover the floor**, in between **pinning up a frock** or **running up a skirt** on her **Singer sewing machine**. Then she would lift the wet clothes out of the **copper** and onto lines held up by **clothes props**. As she did so, Mum would tell her **brood**: '**It doesn't take me all week to do one hour's work**.'

'Anyway, it's **clean dirt**,' she would often say.

If a visitor saw a cockroach, she would explain: 'They fly in out of the palm trees.' Or 'the council must have just cleaned the drains.'

As work piled up, a mother would announce: 'I'm sick of being the **wood-and-water joey** for everyone else.' This literally meant the person who had to fetch the wood and water, but what she meant was that all the menial and difficult jobs were left for her. Then she would add: '**There's life in the old girl yet. Lucky I've got broad shoulders**.'

SOLD INTO SLAVERY

With three or more children, and no labour-saving appliances, many mothers felt **put upon**. And they had many ways to express the fact that they couldn't absorb any more. She might warn she was going to **blow her top** or have **a nervous breakdown** or a **hissy fit**.

Occasionally, a younger child might be sent along to the convent with an older school-age sibling, to be babysat by the nuns if a mother with a lot of children needed a break.

Mothers would refer to themselves as **general dogsbody** or **chief cook and**

bottle washer or **slave no. 42**, saying 'I'm working my fingers to the bone.' No wonder mums looked forward to **Endowment Day** when the government gave mothers (not fathers) some money for each child.

If you asked her to do something for you at such a time your mother would say:

- Who was your slave last week?
- What did your last slave die of?
- Kill the old ones off first.
- I'm one step from grumpy.
- I'm at the end of my string.
- I'm at the end of my tether.
- I'm waiting on you hand and foot.
- I'm being dragged from pillar to post.
- Not this little black duck!
- Not on your life!
- You can whistle for it.

Home sweet home and the fire's out — that's what your mother would say when the family got home after a day at the beach and everyone was tired, sunburned and **grizzly**. While everyone else in the family could have **a lie down** or a cool bath, she had to cook dinner, just like on every other day. Thus, mothers often recalled a stanza of poetry said to have been written for a housewife's tombstone:

Don't cry for me now,
Don't cry for me ever;
I am going to do nothing,
For ever and ever.

Chapter two

UNCLAIMED TREASURES

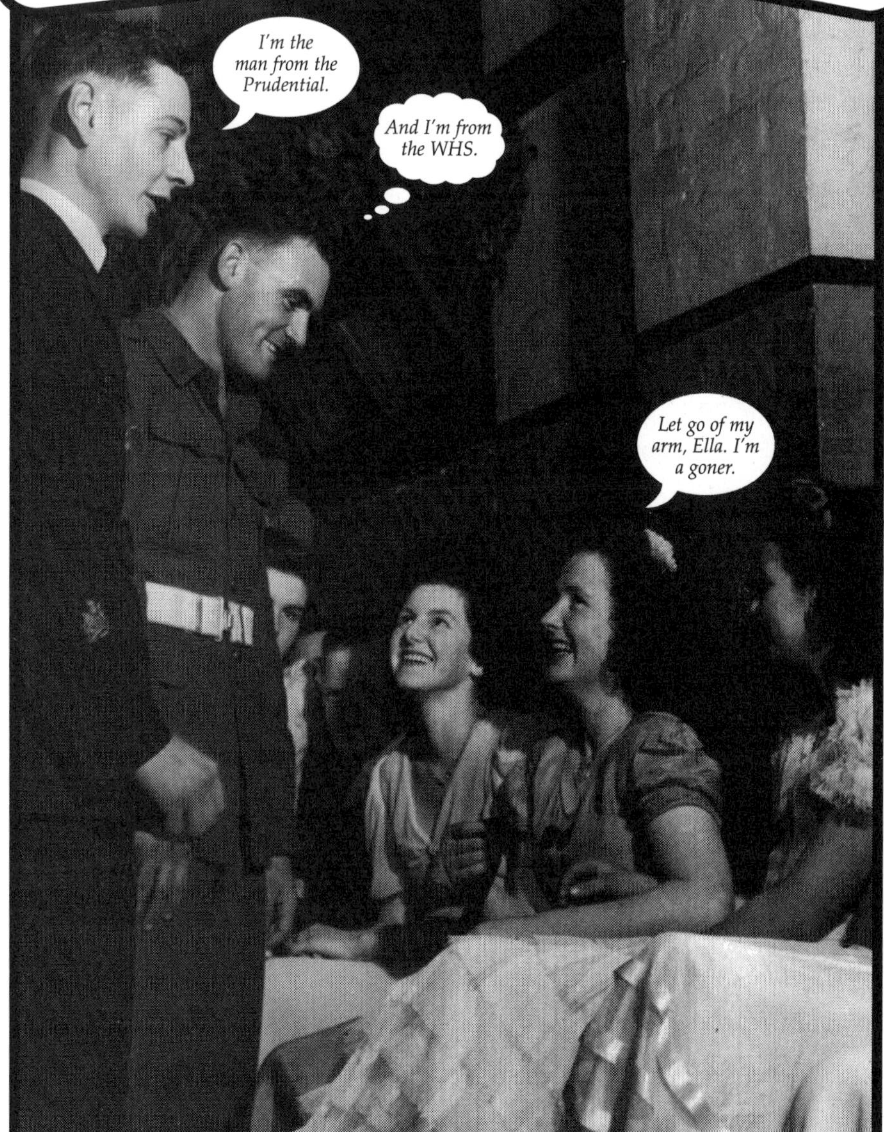

The birds and the bees

‛*Look not upon a maiden lest her beauty be a stumbling block to thee.*’
There were a lot of **stumbling blocks** around in those days.

THE WHITE-ANTER

He **took a shine to** her and now he’s **carrying a torch** for her — unrequited love, she doesn’t know.

He’s gone **gaga** over her.

He’s **a goner** — a bloke referred to himself as ‘a goner’ when he had fallen head over heels in love.

He thinks she’s **the be-all and end-all.**

She’s a **dish**, **dishy,** so he’s been **itching** to say hello to her. In fact, he’d **crawl over broken glass** to meet the **sheila**.

His pal replies: ‘**Strike while the iron is hot**.’

Finally, the boy gets the girl. They are **smooching** at the bus stop. They are **cavorting** and **carousing** and **canoodling** and **pashing**. **As sure as eggs** she’ll have a **lovebite** on her neck next morning.

Now they’re **joined at the hip** — **sweethearts** who are always seen together. They are now **an item**. They **get on like a house on fire**, **get on famously**. They even write love letters to each other, and on the back of the envelope they inscribe **sealed with a loving kiss,** or, shortened, **SWALK.**

But the bloke didn’t listen to his mother’s advice: Never introduce your **donah** to your **pal**. He introduces his girlfriend to his best mate, and his mate starts **giving her a smooch** behind his back.

His mate is a **white-anter**.

White ants hide away under ground and inside the wooden stumps of your house. They are so clever, they eat away all the timber, but leave a thin skin of wood or paint on the outside to hide their work. You think all is **fine and dandy** until suddenly your house falls down, and your girlfriend marries your best mate.

THE OLD SHEIK!

When some old man got a young girlfriend late in life, women would mutter: **'No fool like an old fool'** — thinking that the girl must be a **tart** and **only after one thing**: his money. They knew that now he would have to **fork out** to give her the best things money could buy.

But the man's mates would admiringly call him **the old sheik**.

Some would say: 'Good luck to him. In my case, **the wheel of that wagon is well and truly broken**.' Or another might say: 'I don't know how he does it. All I've got now is **a dried flower arrangement**.' Or: **'Ain't love grand. He must think all his Christmases have come at once.'**

SHARKS IN THE SEA

She certainly knows how to **play up to** a man.

She's leading him **up the garden path ... and over a cliff** — she's fooling him with a series of lies. She's been **kicking her heels up** while he is out of town. So she's **in the market** for a lover, a spouse, a boyfriend.

Also she is **on the market** because she's got **bedroom eyes**. She's **making eyes** at other boys. **Making goo-goo eyes. Making calf eyes.**

She's being faithful to him, but only **after a fashion**.

He's unhappy: **'Jealous-y is a curse-y,'** say his friends.

But where there's smoke there's fire. He was right all along. She gives him the **heave-ho, the big A**, ending the affair, ending **the big romance**.

She used to **go with** him, but now she's **gone** on some other bloke. He's heartbroken, so his friends try to cheer him up by saying **there's plenty more fish in the sea**, or **there's still a lot of sharks in the sea**. But among themselves they worry. They say **he's proving hard to place**. He's **a dud**.

ON A PROMISE

It could be you that you **took a bit of a shine to** a girl. Next thing you had to do was **fall for the girl,** and when you **fell for her** you fell for her **like a ton of bricks**.

The girl tells her girlfriend: 'I don't really **fancy** him.'

But the friend replies: 'Well give him to me. **I'm feeling frisky. He can put his shoes under my bed anytime**.'

So the girl changes her mind and from then on she really **takes to you**.

Then you might tell your mates: '**I'm on a promise**.'

WHS

Girl arrives home from the dance and complains to her mother: 'It was awful, he belongs to the **WHS**' — the wandering hands society.

When he first saw her across the dance floor, he said to his mate: '**Hubba-hubba-ding-ding, look at the legs on that thing**.' He reckoned she was **a bit of alright**.

There were plenty of **smackeroos** but then he was **all over her like a rash, going the grope**. All night she was telling him: '**Keep your hands to yourself**.'

Yet all evening he was trying to: **Win on, Flash on, Crack on, Race off, Get on to, Get her into the cot**. He was **slobbering all over her**. Then he put **the hard word** on her.

'Mum, **he propositioned me!**'

'Are you sure he propositioned you, or did he propose to you?'

'I know what he did, Mum! The **two-timer's** already got **a lady friend** who he's **shacked up** with.' (If a man and a woman lived in the same house or flat, but weren't married, they were **shacked up**, or **living in sin**.)

He was **only after one thing**. He tried to **take advantage** of her. He said, 'I'm not a **sex wreck**, but I'd like you to be my **passion pet** ...'

When she declined, he **ditched** her.

He was only after **a bit of skirt, a bit of nooky, a bit of hanky-panky**.

LOST FOR WORDS EPISODE 2:
Mean Bones

Lost for Words. **The story of Bert and Grace and their trials and tribulations bringing up a young family after the War.**

Grace, wearing a ballerina-length dress and high heels, was pushing the carpet sweeper over the hall rug. The little red contraption on a broomstick was full of bristles that rolled over the carpet pile, brushing the grit and rubbish into the canister.

'I'm the meat in the sandwich,' she complained to herself. 'I'm in a real pickle. Lord knows I've tried to work a way around it.'

Just then, Bert came marching up the path after work in the factory. Under his breath he was pacing out an old ditty:

Left, left, left right left,
I had a good job and I left, I left, I left right left.
Serves me right, right,
I had a good job for twenty-five bob
and I left, I left, I left right left.

With the last step he reached the front door. 'Home is the hunter, home from the hill. I'm exhaustipated.'

'Darling,' said Grace. 'Guess where you're taking me tonight?'

'Blanket Bay,' Bert replied curtly, dropping his briefcase on the floor and walking straight into the bedroom.

Bert always dressed up in suit trousers, white shirt and tie, and carried a briefcase to work. The briefcase did not hold documents or law briefs or paperwork. It held his crib and his work clothes — a set of clothes almost identical to those he was wearing, but older and more worn. He had never become accustomed to being a factory worker. So anyone who watched him swing on the strap on the tram every morning, and every night took him for a solicitor or, at the very least, a bank clerk. Bert liked it that way. In the air force, flying Lancaster bombers over Germany, he had enjoyed the uniform, the responsibility and the homesickness. He had gone through London museums, stood in front of Henry VIII's many suits of armour — ranged from boyhood to death — and marvelled at how tall the king had been. In Ireland he had picked three four-leaf clovers, which were even now pressed in his old RAAF logbook, hidden at the back of the linen press. Bert had always looked forward to coming home after the War and starting a career. He had never pictured for himself this endless future: standing eight hours in a noisy factory gluing veneers together, his ankles swelling, his deafness becoming more profound.

'It's a Christmas do at "Frocks by Janice",' Grace said, interrupting Bert's melancholy thoughts. 'It's going to be like a fete.'

'A fate worse than death,' came Bert's reply from the bedroom. 'Wild brumbies wouldn't drag me there. I don't go to just any dogfight. I noticed that Janice had put up all her Christmas *desecrations*. She's got more twirls than you could poke a stick at. That shop is chock-a-block. You can go on your Pat Malone. It sounds about as interesting as a scone recipe, but I suppose it's good for women and kids.'

'Yes, Bertie, Janice certainly knows how to dress a window. What she suffers for her art! And she *has* given me a part-time job doing her accounts. Come on, it's her gala opening, dear.'

'You mean galah opening. About as exciting as a budgerigar convention. Why would she want me to go?'

'Don't be such a stick-in-the-mud, Bert. There's no show without Punch. Cyril and Myrtle will be there. It's going to be a big turn-out.'

'Yes, Myrtle's bound to have Cyril in tow, as usual,' said Bert, as he walked out of the bedroom in shorts, short-sleeved checked shirt and sandals. 'So every man and his dog will be there. What you're saying is I have to knock off work to carry bricks. There ought to be a law agin it. It'll be another all-night sufferance.'

For the first time, Bert noticed Grace's rig-out: the rouge, the lippy, the face powder, the hair newly set, and, finally, the crepe dress in 'Thenard's blue' that was always saved 'for best'. 'Is it going to be another Iced VoVo and cordial party?' he asked.

'You can't go dressed like that, Bert! It's going to be very swish. I've laid out your suit on the bed. Come on, get dressed, or we'll be late.'

'I am dressed,' replied Bert. He was getting testy. 'And I'll get changed when I'm good and ready.'

'Cyril will be in his suit.'

'Well, that's his funeral. Heavens to Betsy, it's enough to drive a man to drink.'

'Janice is putting on a big spread. It's shaping up to be a pleasant evening.'

'You mean yet another bunfight,' Bert replied, resignedly returning to the bedroom. 'You women are in cahoots. We're becoming social butterflies. This is the second time we've been out this week. We haven't done that in donkey's ages; not since little Ima came along. I've always said Myrtle keeps poor Cyril on a short lead, but now I can see I'm leg-roped as well. I don't understand it though. *Why* are we going?'

Bert waited, then said to himself, 'But answer came there none.'

Bert was putting on his tie clip when Grace walked into the room.

'It's no use, Bertie,' she said, dropping both arms loosely by her sides as if they were broken, a dead giveaway that he'd better give her his undivided attention. 'I've been hit for six. I'm having a bad streak. It's all gone haywire. The whole thing's a shemozzle. I've made a boo-boo. It's all gone to pot. It's a shambles. It's cock-eyed. I've tried to bite my tongue, Lord knows I've tried. I'm that cheesed off with your sister-in-law. She's the fly in the ointment. It's always tit for tat with her. I don't know if I can face her again. Not by myself.'

'Aha! she cried, as she waved her wooden leg!' said Bert. 'Now we're cooking on gas. That's why it's so vital I come along to this shindig tonight. What's Myrtle done this time?'

'Well, I've had my eye wiped,' Grace said. 'Myrtle has been helping her sister by minding their boy — and,' she added, as if to explain everything — 'he is an only child.'

'His Nibs is spoilt rotten,' added Bert.

'Yes, Myrtle's sister certainly mollycoddles him,' said Grace.

'It's the fate of the only child to be ruined,' said Bert.

'His mother is like a hen with one chick.'

'She's making a rod for her own back.'

'Spare the rod and spoil the child.'

'He's a real Little Lord Fauntleroy.'

'She's too protective. Won't let him out of her sight.'

'Are they hoping he'll join the Vienna Boys Choir?'

'You shouldn't handle children with kid gloves.'

'It's not healthy to treat him like a little tin god.'

'They think he's Boy Wonder, that's for sure.'

'Well,' said Bert, 'what has all this to do with you? With us?'

'Myrtle thinks it's a crime, the way that child is being brought up,' began Grace. 'Myrtle was minding the boy last week, and he went missing. The mother came home and had a pink fit, so Myrtle came and got me and we sent out a search party for him. When we finally found him he was at the paint shop sitting up like Jacky eating a chocolate, totally oblivious to all the fuss he'd caused. It was the first time he'd ever got out. The first time he'd had fun. Myrtle's sister gave her what for. They had words. And now the sister wants to keep the boy so close to her that she's started telling him the bogeyman will get him if he leaves the house. The poor child is scared witless, he hides under the bed. Myrtle doesn't feel she can say anything, being family and all that, and until this they'd never had a cross word between them. And blood is thicker than water, so she asked me to have a word to her sister — to tell her she's got to stop scaring the boy, and just take to him with a belt if he doesn't do what he's told.'

'Give him a clip over the ear,' added Bert.

'Yes, give him a good hiding,' said Grace. 'And I'm to tell her to let

the child roam a bit, or he'll never learn by experience. It's like with dogs, you've got to allow them to learn to be street-wise. And, Bertie, I promised Myrtle I would. Tonight at Janice's party!'

'And you want me along to back you up,' said Bert.

'It sounded simple when Myrtle asked me, but now I think about it, how can I face her sister, and tell her to loosen the apron strings? But Myrtle is relying on me to speak up. And I did promise!'

'F'crying out loud, Grace, I'm lost for words. Is it Tree Week and you're the sap? This isn't your problem. Tell Myrtle you are going to mind your own business and she should mind hers.'

Grace wiped her eyes, picked up her compact and sat down in front of her large dressing-table mirror.

'I'll have to grow mean bones,' she said to herself.

FALLING PREGNANT

Mothers liked to see their daughters marry young, before they tripped and **fell pregnant**. Mothers knew that, when it came to an unwanted pregnancy, the world criticised the girl, not the boy. No one ever talked about **unmarried fathers**.

Question: 'Punctuate the following sentence: fun fun fun trouble.'

Answer: 'Fun period fun period fun no period trouble.'

So, before women's liberation and feminism, a girl was on her own if she **got herself pregnant**. She was then **up the duff** with **a prawn in the dilly**, **a bun in the oven**, **up the spout**, **in the family way**, **infant-icipating** until the baby **came along**.

No one seemed to really think that the bloke had to take any responsibility, except in jokes about a **shotgun wedding**.

A girl even had to be careful if she got engaged too many times. She might then be considered **shopsoiled** — meaning she started to lose her **character** and **good name**, and acquire, in their place, **a reputation**. A girl who said she wanted to have children was **getting clucky**.

Yet none of this was talked about openly. If a girl started talking about **love-**

making, her mother would probably stop her short with: '**Don't bring the bedroom into the lounge room**.'

In newspaper reports of divorce cases, '**misconduct**' was used as a euphemism for adultery.

In the 1930s, 40s and 50s, if both the man and the woman wanted a divorce, one of them would have to agree to put on a charade in order to be caught in the act of adultery by a witness.

So the husband might book a room at a cheap hotel, and the witness would arrive at the appointed time to see the man and a lady friend in the room. The bed would be turned down, and folded on the bed would be an **eau de Nil nightgown** and a **pair of men's striped pyjamas**: enough evidence for the court to draw all the right conclusions. They were obviously **having relations**.

The witness could then honestly describe all of this in court, and it could be reported word for word in the Sunday tabloids for all to read.

No one appeared to know much about sex. A woman told me how, in the 1950s, her Brisbane Catholic girls' school held a dance in conjunction with a local Catholic boys' school. The girls' dresses were inspected beforehand, for modesty. For once, boys and girls could mingle and talk on the dance floor. As the boys and girls enjoyed their new-found freedom and chatted animatedly, the nuns patrolled inside the hall and the Christian Brothers patrolled outside.

On Monday morning, the head nun got up at assembly and went crook. She said: 'There was too much oral sex taking place on the dance floor.'

No one laughed.

No one knew what she was talking about.

Women never talked about 'breasts'. Females were said to have **a bosom**, as if it was singular. If a woman had a very large bosom, a man would say **she could rest her cup of tea on her bosom**. Nor did anyone openly say that women menstruated. If it was ever mentioned it was done so in code: She's got her **period**, or, **the Curse**, or, **the communists are in control**, or **the red flag is flying**.

References to what went on between lovers were vague. If a young man asked at tennis: 'What's the score?', an older woman might whisper: 'Forty love. Fifty if I catch you.'

Fathers warned their sons: **'Remember, son, in the end it's the personality you have to live with**.'

Confirmed bachelors

The country seemed to be full of bachelors after World War II. Probably nowadays it would be established that many such men were suffering post-traumatic stress syndrome. People often said of these bachelors: **'He hasn't been himself since the War**.'

These men referred to their part in the War as being **involved in a bit of a scrap**, or **a show**.

Because the War was so recent, conversations everywhere often included the phrases **before the War** and **since the War** and **for the duration**.

One bachelor called Turner lived in a backyard shed, a few doors from my parents' cake shop. He occasionally came in for a meal. The bottom of his right leg was missing, and in place of a foot he wore a sort of large horseshoe, attached with iron rods. It made a terrible thump when he walked. Everyone respectfully called him 'Mr Turner'.

Women in the public service had to give up their jobs once they got married. So there was no question about it: the man at that time felt he had to be the breadwinner. There are many reasons for a man never marrying, but back then some men could never get **the necessaries** together to go about supporting a wife and large family. So they became lodgers, and rented rooms in houses and flats.

Such men were eventually labelled **confirmed bachelors** — men who had dinner in pie shops. They were aged 40 to 50, unmarried, no girlfriend; a man who your mum would say was not the marrying type. He was **set in his ways** — sitting there **like a lonely little petunia in an onion patch**, or **like a shag on a rock**.

The men themselves called it **batching, living like a dicky bird** or **living like a mopoke**. Such men were also known as **orphans, lodgers** and **strays**. They would often say: '*I haven't spoken to a living soul all day*.' And if they had no job to go to, and so could sleep in and stay up late, they were said to **keep gentleman's hours**.

However, if a bachelor was very much older, a lonely old man, he would be known as an **old codger**, an **old cove**, a **silly old coot**, **a local yokel**, **a local identity**, or **a death adder**.

If a bachelor was from out of **the mulga**, he might be called **a bushwhacker** or **a bit of a hard nut from out of the scrub**.

Confirmed bachelors would listen to the races on their **tranny** or read **potboilers** or **penny dreadfuls**, or paperback **westerns**, which were called **deadwood dicks**. Or they might listen to **gramophone** records (big 78s) of famous speeches. One lodger I knew listened to recordings of a Christian preacher who ended each segment with '**It's in the book!**', meaning the Bible.

But they didn't live well. Mothers would say of these men: 'He's **living off steam**,' or 'Arthur is **living very comfortable**, he **likes the comforts of home**, he **likes his creature comforts**', which was a kindly way of saying he and his house are in a complete mess.

Then there were the **unclaimed treasures**: lovely, gentle, unmarried women.

STRAYS AND BLOW-INS

The suburbs were full of stray dogs and cats, and also men described as **strays** who would enjoy the family life of relations or neighbours. They were also often called **blow-ins**, because they were like a stray fly that always arrived just as you were dishing up lunch. The cook would of course invite him to partake with the family. But a blow-in could also be anyone who turned up unexpectedly at mealtime.

Because most people didn't own a car, or a telephone, friends kept in touch by letter. '**Barring an accident**, we'll be there on Saturday week.' Or, 'I'm arriving tomorrow, **please God**.' Or they would simply drop in. People you hadn't seen for months or years would turn up, unannounced, uninvited, at your back door and say: 'Yes, **I'm still in the land of the living**. I'm still **alive and kicking**.' And the householder would say: '**It's been a long time between** *drinks!*' Everyone knew you couldn't keep in constant contact, so there was no overhanging guilt or embarrassment.

If someone who was certain of a big welcome did **pop in**, they were called a **do-drop-in**.

THE POOR RELATION

In an era of limited government welfare, most people felt a degree of responsibility and fondness for all their kinfolk. Including **the poor relation**.

This was a relative who lived in near poverty and could turn up at any moment, in need of a bed, a feed or just a welcoming face. They might be put up on a veranda, a sleep-out or a room attached to the shed out the back. In any case, they were welcomed, but their arrival was sometimes — even if silently — resented.

Thus you might say: '**I don't want to be treated like a poor relation**.' Or, 'It's a scandal: **he treats her like a poor relation**.'

- My brother is coming to live with us, so I'm lumbered.
- **I don't want charity.**
- The poor blighter, he's such a worrywart.
- **I don't want to make a nuisance of myself.**
- A change is as good as a holiday.
- **If you could see your way clear.**
- He's down on his uppers.
- **Thanks a bunch.**
- Misery loves company.
- **I've been hanging on like grim death.**
- He's stony-broke.
- **You just can't win.**
- It's a crying shame. He was never left anything in the will.
- **I'm not interested in dead men's boots.**
- Where there's a will there's a relative.
- **He'll die of old age before he hears from me.**

Chapter three

FATHERS

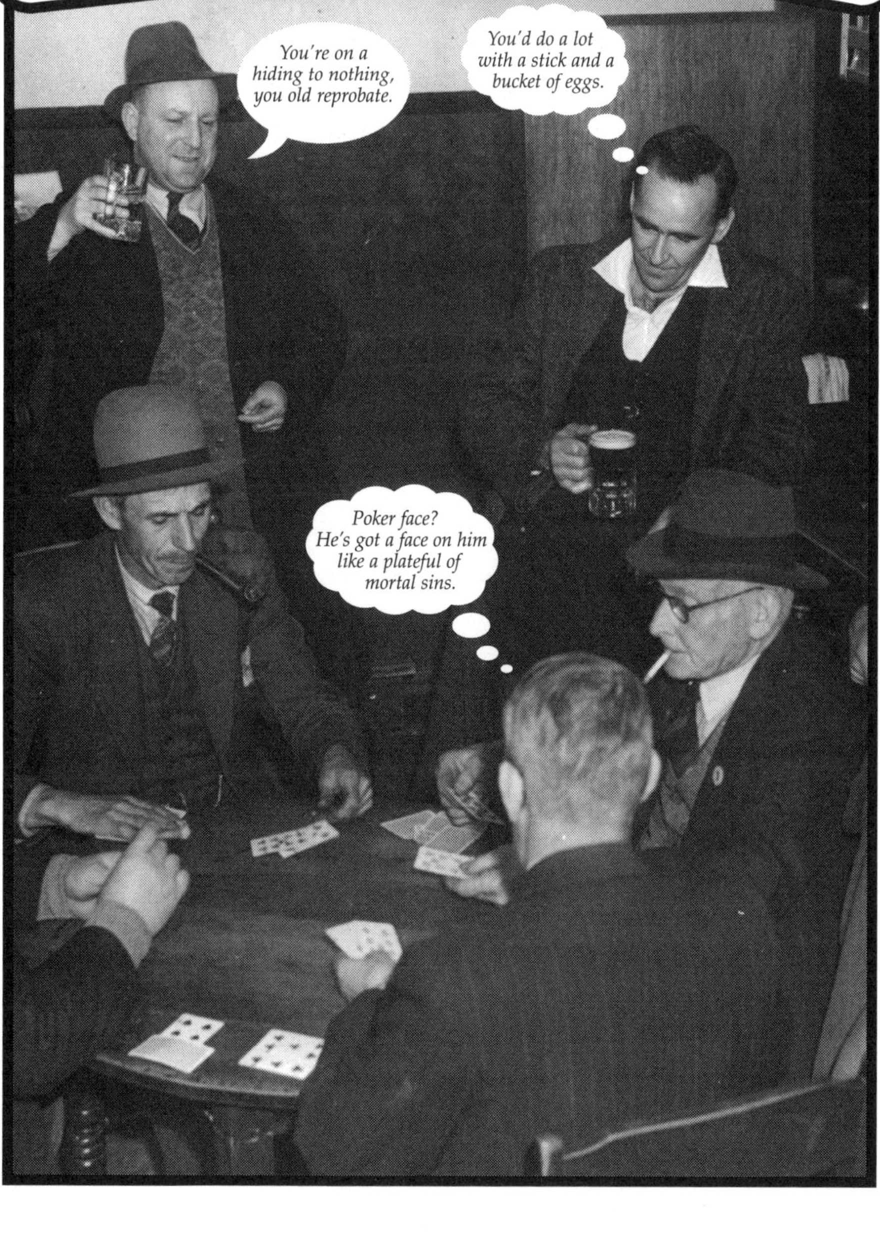

LOST FOR WORDS EPISODE 3:
Playing snooker

Lost for Words. **The story of Bert and Grace and their trials and tribu-lations bringing up a young family after the War.**

Bert is at the back door, talking to Grace, his missus.
'Mother, get the girls over for a hens' night. I'm off to see a man about a dog.'

'But you swore blind you were staying home tonight, Bert,' says Grace. 'You know my sister is coming. You promised you'd stay in.'

'Look, snooks, I don't want to argue the toss. Kevin is waiting. It's the big match tonight against those couple of easybeat brothers Alfie and Clem. I'm off like your grandfather's trousers, off like a bride's nightie, off like a bucket of prawns left out in the sun.'

'But ...'

'You can complain till the cows come home, till you're blue in the face, it won't stop me. I am sorry I'll miss your sister. I clean forgot about it, Grace.'

'I'll forgive you. Thousands wouldn't. You're off the hook. This time. I don't know why you spend so much time up at that club, Bert.'

'It keeps me out of mischief. You must agree with that.'

'Alright, dear, but you'd better put on your good strides, you can't go out looking like something the cat dragged in.'

'Greetings and salutations, Kevin, you old bastard, how's tricks?'

'Fine, Bert, you old reprobate. You're full of beans tonight. What's your wife up to?'

'She's got her sister over.'

'Has Gracie got a sister?'

'She's got three of the buggers well. One of them is a bit of a battleaxe.

A bit of a dragon. She's got a face like a plateful of mortal sins. Those old girls can go at it hammer and tongs — they can talk nineteen to the dozen. They can go at it like one thing.'

'Hold on, Bert, don't look now, but that girl behind the counter, Vera, she keeps giving me the glad eye.'

'She's a pushy bird, Kevin, a real pushy dame. Nothing flash but.'

'I'm not complaining. The manager told me that she's a two-pot screamer: she'll get very friendly after a couple of drinks.'

'She's not my cup of tea well, Kevin. If she didn't have an Adam's apple, she wouldn't have a figure.'

'What's that got to do with the price of eggs? She scrubs up well, Bert.'

'You mean she's a scrubber. She wears all her money on her back.'

'I reckon Vera is a sight for sore eyes but. She would pass muster anywhere in Sydney.'

'Kevin, she used to be a good sort, a real looker. But I reckon now she's gone to the pack, gone off the boil, she's let herself go. She's an old boiler. She's as rough as bags. As rough as guts. Rough around the edges. Forget about her.'

'She's a real dag but. She's a bit of a trick — she'll have you in stitches.'

'First time I've heard you mooning over a girl, some highfalutin' sheila. And I notice you've put on your best clobber, Kevin.'

'I tell you she's a real goer.'

'So was my missus. And I got stuck with her; I had to marry her to get rid of her. Forget about this bird.'

'I think Vera is a good sort and a bit of alright.'

'Kevin, take it from a man of experience, Vera is a crook sort and a bit of a bat. Not much chop and not much acumen either. And I've met her mother. I was working in the backyard a month ago, and Old Ma Johnston came out and gave me what for because of the racket I was making. The old bag. The silly old goat. I told her, you can't make an omelette without breaking eggs. And you know what they say, Kevin: "When you fall in love with a girl, have a look at her mother, 'cos in 20 years' time that's what she'll look like."

'It's alright for you, Bert, you married the girl of your dreams, you've already got Gracie. I'm still looking but.'

'Such is life without a wife ... and Hell on earth with one. The trouble is, Kevin, my missus holds the whip hand.'

Bert and Kevin are having a beer before they play snooker against Alfie and Clem. They like to badmouth the competition, have a dig, sling off, slag off at them.

Neither likes Alfie.

'That Alfie, he's travelling on high octane — he's looking for trouble, Kevin. He's a bit of a mug lair. Never wears a white shirt, as a rule. He's a blowhard who's always telling porkies. He's a cocky bastard who won't cop any criticism. A smart alec.'

'Is he a fighter, Bert?' asks Kevin.

'I think he's fairly up for it. He's certainly the type to say "Whacko" and go for it.'

'He's too cocksure, Bert. I don't trust him. He's got a face like a water rat and about as long as a minute. He's an Oilcan Harry — a flashy dresser, a bit of a spiv, the way he ponces around in that cravat. He's always taking the micky. Having a lend of me.'

However, Bert doesn't mind Clem: 'But Clem's not a bad sort of fella, Kev. And don't worry, he'll tell you where to get off. He's a good judge of a schooner — he's smart. He's the full bottle on income tax. But he's so mean he wouldn't give you a cold if he had one. Watch out he doesn't fleece you, or he'll skin you. Cunning as a shithouse rat.'

'That's a lot of tommyrot, Bert. Anyone with half a brain knows how to do a tax return. Clem's all talk. He doesn't know shit from clay. He wouldn't know his fist from his fingernail. He doesn't know his arse from his elbow. He wouldn't know a bee from a bull's foot. He's worse than useless. I'll tell you what, he couldn't drive a wooden horse. He can't cut the mustard. He can't even spell his own name. He's a blinking idiot. If you asked him how he was, he'd be stuck for an answer. He doesn't know if he's coming or going; doesn't know if he's Arthur or Martha. He always likes to have two bob each way. He hunts with the hounds and he runs with the hares. And he's not a footballer's elbow. He wouldn't know how to pour sarsaparilla out of a boot if the instructions were printed on the sole.'

'Take my advice,' says Bert, shaking his head, 'don't rub him up the wrong way. It's hard to get a handle on him. He looks a real square in a penguin suit, but I reckon there's no flies on Clem. You can see where they've been but. Now, Kevin, we're going into this snooker game on a wing and a prayer. Don't shoot your bolt and fail to finish on like you did last week. But don't take too long over your shots either. Keep your trap shut and she'll be apples. Last week we were caught on the hop and Clem caught you napping. You'll have to pull your socks up.'

'You're spot-on, Bert. Now, if we're going to beat this pair, we'll have to go all out but. We've got to get some scores on the board. If I just roll up my sleeves we'll have this game shot to ribbons. We'll be laughing. We'll be home and hosed. Remember, Bert, we're not playing for a sheep station.'

'Look at them over there. That Clem, what's his caper? He's got a look on him as though he's just licked shit off a thistle.'

'He always looks like that. He's got a head on him like a twisted sand-shoe.'

'Yeah, like a dropped meat pie.'

'Like a half-sucked mango.'

'Like a diseased rice pudding.'

The snooker match begins with Bert saying: 'Come on, Kevin, we'll have to gird our loins and sally forth. Don't louse it up.'

Bert quickly sinks a red and a blue.

'We're going great guns here, Kev.'

'You saved our bacon, Bert. We're even-stevens.'

'Yeah, it's as close as all get out.'

'She'll be jake.'

But then Kevin misses a shot by a mile.

'You scared the pants off me, Kevin! You didn't come within cooee of that green ball!'

'Righto, righto, keep your shirt on.'

Bert sits down and drops his head. 'I certainly drew the short straw when I got you as a partner, Kevin.'

'Well, who do you think I am? Mandrake? My cue is skewiff. It's out of true. Out of whack. It's cactus, stuffed, buggered, it's wonky, it's cruddy. It's got a lean on it like a fern tree gully dunny. I'm on a hiding to nothing here, Bert.'

'You're the biggest whinger in Christendom, Kevin.'

'Well that's my excuse and I'm sticking to it.'

'Don't dingo on me now, mate. Here, I'll have a crack at him. The rotten dog of a mongrel. Never say my mother bred a piker. Look, we're still in with a show well.'

❧

'It's all gone to pot, Bert. We've only got two chances now: Buckley's and none.'

'We're up shitter's ditch, Kevin.'

'Yes, up shit creek without a paddle in a barbed-wire canoe.'

'It's all over bar the shouting.'

'We got done like a dinner, Bert.'

'Yeah, I'm gonna kick the first dog I see.'

'Look at those two. I'm jack of them. I'm jacking up. *You're a tinny bastard. You'll keep, Clem!'*

❧

'Hail the conquering hero comes!' shouts Bert's wife, Grace, as Bert arrives home at midnight.

'Not this time, love. I'm browned off. I'm cheesed off, duck. I'm fed up. We were bushwhacked, we got beaten like a dozen eggs.'

'Bert, I'm lost for words.'

Drunk again

When Dad was getting ready for a drink he'd say:

- A beer wouldn't go astray.
- My skin is cracking.
- I've got to see a man about a dog.
- I'm off to wet my whistle.
- I'm off to wet m'gills.
- I'm off to see the wizard.

And there were several traditions to be followed:

1. First eat a plate of mashed potato, or drink a glass of milk.
2. Never drink alone: **Drinking with the flies**.
3. Never knock one back: **Better your belly burst than good liquor be wasted**.
4. **Avoid wowsers** — they not only didn't drink, but they didn't approve of others drinking (or gambling **for that matter**).
5. If you were in a circle of thirteen workmates at the pub, you would each take it in turns to buy everyone a beer. When it was your turn to shout, you were **in the chair**. If you couldn't keep up drinking glass for glass, the others in the circle would say **you're dragging the chain** and you would have to catch up. You weren't allowed to **sit on a beer** (drink it too slowly).

Blokes would ask: 'What's your poison?'

- Grog
- Plonk
- Mother's ruin (gin)
- Turps (**on the turps** or **on the hops**)

FULL AS A TICK

- He hit the bottle every Friday night
- Then he was half-tanked
- Then shickered
- Then crissed as a picket

- Worshipping the spirits
- Paralytic
- Full as a carpet snake that swallowed a wallaby
- Cut
- Blind
- Legless
- Stoned
- Plastered
- Blotto
- Pie-eyed
- Soused
- Sozzled

- Had a skinful
- Full as a butcher's dog
- Full as a butcher's hook
- Full as a state school
- Full as a state school hat rack
- Full as a Catholic church
- Full as a fat lady's stockings
- Full as a boot
- Full as a tick
- Drunk as a skunk
- Drunk as a lord
- Three sheets to the wind
- He was well oiled by the time we arrived
- He was well away
- Been out on the tiles

HAIR OF THE DOG THAT BIT YOU

- I've got a mouth like the bottom of a cocky's cage.
- I've got a mouth like the inside of a Greek wrestler's jockstrap.
- He's had a touch of the sun (he drank so much he's throwing up).
- He's having a bad turn (he's drunk too much, but if he **took a bad turn** it meant he had a heart attack).
- He's got an eye like a dead mullet.

A pastor was walking along when he saw one of his parishioners drunk in the gutter with a pig snuffling at his feet. The pastor shook his head and declared:

You can tell a man who boozes
By the company he chooses.

So the pig got up and slowly walked away.

Bludgers and offsiders

BLUDGERS

If there was one thing Australian men couldn't stand back in the 1950s, it was a bloke who **bludged on the job** and got out of work.

Such men were called **lazy buggers** or **bludgers**.

It would be said of such men:

He wouldn't work in an iron lung — he'd get out of breathing if he could. Some victims of the polio virus had to spend the rest of their lives lying on their backs with all but their heads inside a huge, pressurised iron machine, called an iron lung, which did their breathing for them.

He's **a blister** — he always turns up after all the hard work has been done.

He's **swinging the lead** — someone **hanging off the end of a shovel**, **not pulling his weight, not doing a tap**, not doing **his fair share**. Whenever you turned around, he was **having a blow** (having a breather). If the workers quite liked him they might add: he's **a nice bloke but pretty tired**.

He's **a gunna** — a colleague who's always going to (gunna) get around to doing a job, but never does.

Men who didn't work hard, who **skived off** and left the others **in the lurch**, found it hard to **hold down a job**. If they kept dodging work, then the others would say he was **for the high jump** (going to be sacked). Particularly if he was a **pain in the gut**. He might apply for a new job but if his **reputation went before him**, he'd probably **get a knock-back**.

Such men were said to have **a lot of gall** and always had **a string of excuses as long as your arm**.

They were said to **live the life of Riley**. They were always trying to **get in for their chop**.

And they were often seen as incompetent: 'He wouldn't know **which side was up**.' Or, he's **all over the shop** — you don't know what he's going to do or say next.

Still, this **sponger** was better than the worst workmate, a **scab** — the one who worked during a strike.

OFFSIDERS

In the days when most men did **heavy work**, a working man would wear a **dozer hat**. It had no bash, no band and a floppy brim. He would flog the dog with it, chase the cows with it, or lift a hot billy out of the fire with it.

It was considered indestructible.

Important workers were always referred to as the **top dog**. This was the name given to the top sawyer in a pitsaw. He stood on top of the log and guided the saw that was wielded by the man in the pit who did all the work. This man was the bottom dog, who, in days gone by, would go blind from constantly looking up into the falling sawdust.

The top dog always needed a good **offsider** to help him, particularly if he was **flat as a tack** and **up to his eyeballs** with work, **pushing it uphill** and needed to **strike a blow**. A man didn't want to **bust a gut** shifting heavy loads or rounding up cattle all by himself. Men were always **flat out**. But they also said: 'You'd be **flat out** proving that' — meaning it's impossible.

Many men would do more than just **hold their end up**. They would **play above their weight**, and do more than their fair share of the labour. **How did you do that? The Egyptian way: hard work and perseverence**.

The term **offsider** came about in the days when bullock teams hauled giant logs out of the bush, before World War II. When a bullock team was stuck in a rut, they sent a man around to the other side to flog the bullocks, to get them to pull harder. He was called 'the offsider'.

To coordinate when they wanted to throw a heavy weight, a man and his offsider would say, '**Hockey one, hockey two** ...' then throw it on 'three'.

Before starting work, men would spit on one hand, rub both hands together, then take up their axe or pick or shovel saying, '**No rest for the wicked**.' They **whacked up** frames in a **hell of a hurry** and always said, '**I can't** complain' or '**It's no good growling**' or '**We'll have to carry on rewardless**' — this originated in World War II, a jocular turn of phrase from the motto '**Press on regardless**'.

They knew no one would listen to their complaints anyway, so would add: '**It might look like fun but it's no picnic.**'

If the job had fallen behind time they might say, '**Crikey, we'd better get cracking then**' and '**Kick on**'. If they were going to have to work late, they'd say, '**It'll be another midnight sufferance!**' If someone said it couldn't be done, a good worker would always reply: '**Well it won't be for the lack of trying.**'

If either man had to take leave he would no doubt say: '**I've got to see a man about a dog.**'

And the other would reply: '**Don't take all day then.**'

The only boss these men admired was one who was a **straightshooter** — who said what he thought and didn't **mince words**. You liked this person because you knew where you stood with him; he was never guilty of going behind anyone's back, which was **a cardinal sin** at work.

A boss men liked was the **Chief Powwow** of the foundry. A boss they didn't like was a **bigwig** or a **big shot**.

If you mixed with the bosses you were **hobnobbing**.

Resting your bones

People were always having a sleep in the afternoon. It was endemic. Mothers had **a nap, a cat nap**, or **a good lie-down** after lunch, before all the kids got home from school. Workers had **a spell**.

Grandparents had **a kip** and uncles had **a snooze** and could doze off in their chair at anytime. Fathers **put their feet up, rested their bones** or **caught forty winks** or had **a camp**, and would fall asleep on Saturday afternoon with the form guide across their bellies and the **trannie** blaring out the cricket or the races.

Babies went **ta-tas**, while kids just **flaked out** where they fell.

Lazy people were said to **loll around** or **lie about** and be examples of **slothfulness**. If you pretended to be asleep to get out of work you were **lying doggo**.

There was no television to watch, no video games to play, no Internet, no computers, no stereos. Families would have a piano but not a record player, and with no other thing to make a noise except the Victa mower, summer afternoons were made for snoozing. In hot climates where houses were built on stumps, most people kept a squatter's chair or a cane chair on the dirt under the house, because it was the coolest place in summer.

When it was time to go to the **Land of Nod** you **hit the sack** or **hit the hay**.

If they had a big day coming up, girls would say: '**Wake me early in the morning, Mother, for I'm to be Queen of the May.**'

If you were **dead to the world**, despite kids playing in the house, it was said you could go to **sleep on the edge of a razor blade**. If you slept in you were a **sleepyhead**. To wake you up, parents called out, '**wake up, Australia**' or '**Rise and shine, your King and country need you**' or '**Up guards and at 'em**' or '**Get the duck's meat out of the corner of your eyes**'.

When fathers **surfaced** they would most likely say: '**That nap has done me the world of good.**'

Everyone wore pure wool, checked dressing gowns, with piping, and a silky cord round the waist. If worn by a man, there were cigarette burns down the front. If worn by a woman, there were breakfast stains, probably some egg yolk from the **jaffles** she made for the family that morning.

Boys wore pyjamas and girls wore **shorty pyjamas** or **baby doll pyjamas**.

How many hours sleep do we need?

Nature allows five,
Custom seven,
Laziness eight,
And wickedness eleven.

The gee-gees

Racehorses were known as **neddies** and **gee-gees**, but **the gee-gees** were the races. The suburbs, as you walked around, seemed alive with the sound of race callers.

Someone having a bet on a race was said to be **having a flutter on the gee-gees**. Or **investing a pound**. Punters loved to believe that backing horses was actually investing their money, rather than gambling it away. Even if they were betting their **bottom dollar**.

Punters had lots of rules at the races:

1. **Odds on, look on** — don't back a horse that is odds on, just watch the race.
2. **Never put your shirt on a roughie** — a rank outsider.
3. **Weight stops a train** — any horse, no matter how strong, or fast, or better than its peers, can easily be handicapped out of a race.

Break any of these rules and you would **lose your shirt** and end up **stony-broke**. What everyone was searching for was a **dead cert** — a horse that could not be beaten. These usually finished **stone motherless last** (a long way back). Particularly if you'd put your money **on the nose** (backed it to be first past the post).

Backing racehorses was so widespread before poker machines and casinos that betting odds became part of everyday language. **Ten to one** it'll rain tonight. **Two to one** he won't turn up.

The best thing about the races was the exciting seven-words-a-second broadcasts that echoed from nearly every wireless on a Saturday afternoon: *Round the corner into the straight and as they straighten up for the home turn with two furlongs to go the whips are out. You can put your glasses down, it's London to a brick on Bernborough ... the rest are beaten all ends up.*

Fathers used to advise their sons: '**The only way to make money out of a racehorse is to follow it around with a shovel.**'

LOST FOR WORDS EPISODE 4:
Trouble at work

Lost for Words. The story of Bert and Grace and their trials and tribulations bringing up a young family after the War.

After two weeks' holiday, Bert is back at work, feeling a bit down in the dumps. As Grandma used to say, 'It's back to porridge and auld (old) clothes.' At the end of the week, the foreman, Simpson, calls him in.

'Look, Bert,' says Simpson. 'You've been dragging your feet all week. You're falling down on the job. As soon as the siren went, you made a beeline for the canteen, and you haven't struck a blow since lunchtime. You just won't knuckle down, will you? You'd better sharpen up or we'll think you've got duck's disease: your tail's too close to the ground. You're dragging your bum. Loafing on the job. Where's your get-up-and-go?'

So Bert goes home to his wife, Grace.

'Bert! Why the long face?'

'Things are crook in Tallarook,' he says.

'And there's no work in Bourke and they're not eat'n' in Leeton,' adds Grace. 'Tell me all about it.'

'I've just been chipped. Simpson, the foreman, is on my hammer. He's on my back. He tore strips off me today. He says I'm NBG: no bloody good. That we've got to get some scores on the board. I should have told him to get the shit off his liver, or that I don't give a hoot. I should have told him to go to blazes. I should have said, "If you think I care then you've got another think coming." I should have told him he could stick it. The spiteful bugger.'

'Don't worry, love,' Grace replies. 'You're just collar proud. Grandma always said we were collar proud if we'd just had a holiday and weren't settling down to work. You're like the draughthorse who's been spelled in a good paddock and now the collar just seems too tight for your neck. It's chafing.'

'Well, I'm really browned off, Gracie. In fact I'm cheesed off. I've had a gutful. I've been pushed from pillar to post. I wasn't born to be a wage slave. I can't help it if the orders keep coming in dribs and drabs. I've a good mind to toss it all in. Blow it! They'll just have to box on without me.'

'But needs must when the Devil drives, Bert. You don't want to go putting a spoke in the wheel, a spanner in the works. You'll have to get off your dinger or you'll lose that job and we won't be able to pay the rent.'

'Yes, dear heart, 'nuff said,' says Bert. 'By hook or by crook I'll keep the job. I'm the breadwinner, I know I've got to bring home the bacon. I go to work to put bread and butter on the table. But the trouble is it's Rafferty's rules at work. Anything goes; nothing is done according to Hoyle. They never let the right hand know what the left hand's doing. No wonder it's all jerry-built. And you know I'm a perfectionist, duck. I don't know how I got roped in to do this job. Only this morning, Kevin said, "Jump on the other end of this" and it was a load of 100 sheets of veneer, 350 pounds no less, and between us we just managed to lug it up to the warehouse. And then I was just having a spell when Kevin had the cheek to say, "On with the motley! Lend us a pound" and together we gave this pallet the heave-ho and pushed the whole thing across the floor. I'm not a navvy.'

'I know you've been working your fingers to the bone trying to keep your end up,' says Grace. 'Why don't you go over Mr Simpson's head and explain to the boss that you're too young for light work and too old for heavy work?'

'Oh, it's not worth the candle, he won't listen, he's a head case,' replies Bert. 'I'm the low man on the totem pole. I tried to talk to the bigwig. I got as far as the office and the secretary palmed me off. I said to her, "I speak to the butcher, not the block," but she wouldn't let me past. Today I tried to catch the boss's eye at smoko, but he gave me the bum's rush. He gave me short shrift, the cold shoulder!'

'Now Bert, the boss is probably worried about the strike everyone's been talking about.'

'Well, I'm sick of being his whipping boy. I used to be his blue-eyed boy when I first joined the firm. And do you know, the whole time Kevin and I were carrying that veneer, Simpson was standing there, holding up the doorframe, smirking, and he says, "When do Laurel and Hardy arrive?" He was aiming it fairly and squarely at me. Trying to goad me. You wouldn't read about it. *He's* the bludger. While we've all got our nose to the grindstone, he wouldn't put his shoulder to the wheel and do a hand's turn.'

Grace interrupts: 'Well, dear, cream always rises to the top.'

'So does scum,' says Bert. 'What a shirker, he's always trying to get out of work, and makes sure he leaves it to everybody else. He'd do a lot with a stick and a bucket of eggs. The big oaf. He's always standing around like a spare groom at a wedding. He's about as useful as tits on a bull, as useless as a two-bob watch.'

'Language, dear, remember little pitchers have big ears,' says Grace, pointing to the five kids doing their mensuration at the kitchen table.

'Well, Simpson's up to no good, I'll wager. It wouldn't surprise me if he's been tickling the Peter. He's just the sort who'd tickle the till when nobody's watching. He's got shifty eyes. I reckon he's been half-inching his way through the factory filching anything he can lay his hands on. If he isn't pinching stock, I'm a monkey's uncle. His attitude is bugger you, Jack, I'm alright. He's always looked after number one. He's all over the boss like a rash, the brown-noser. To my mind, he's the one who has been swanning around all week, showing off. I wouldn't pee on him if he was on fire.'

'But you don't want to annoy Mr Simpson, dear. Isn't he a big man?'

'He couldn't fight his way out of a paper bag, a brown paper bag, or even a wet paper bag. He couldn't pull the skin off a custard or a rice pudding. What a lazy joker. Imagine Simpson saying I've got duck's disease! Why, I've been as busy as a blue-arsed fly all week. I'm like

Errol Flynn sword-fighting the pirates as they appear on the deck. I'm working my guts out.'

'Why don't you ask that nice young Mr Dawson to help you?'

'Too late, love. He got French leave.'

'He's gone to France?'

'No, dear heart, he's done a bunk. He shot through without giving notice.'

'What a pity, he was so well brought up. And a good dancer. I wonder where he is now. The last time I saw him it was at the firm's Christmas party. If only we'd saved the Christmas bonus instead of spending it on our holiday.'

'Well I'd say it got too hot for him to handle. He was doing more foreign orders than any of us. Why, I reckon he's probably opened a furniture shop with the items he made at work. I've only ever made that console for you, and the sideboard for Aunty Rose, and they were from offcuts anyway.'

At work on Monday, Bert's mate Kevin is called in to see the big boss.

'We've got a big order in, Kevin,' says the boss. 'Now we'll need two good men or a dozen footballers for this job. So we'll use our apprentices but I want someone to be overseer. Who can you recommend?'

'Bert Mason is your man,' says Kevin. 'He's a good stamp of a man, a good egg. He'll be there when the whips are cracking.'

'Bert,' says Kevin. 'There's a big order in. Can you be the overseer? You'll have to box clever on this one.'

'Too right, mate,' says Bert. 'Kevin, I'm lost for words. How come this has happened?'

'I just went in to bat for you with the boss,' says Kevin. 'I put in a good word for you. Now let's get cracking.'

'Kevin, you come up trumps every time. Thanks.'

Bert wheels a crate of veneer through the yard when he surprises the apprentices lounging around a stack of frames.

'Do you work here?' one of the lads asks Bert.

'No,' says Bert, 'I'm just carrying bricks. Now, you there with the hair on, what are you doing?'

'I'm helping Jack.'

'And what's Jack doing?'

'Nothing.'

'Old habits die hard. Well, brains trust, I'm going to pull rank and throw my weight around. You nincompoops can't just sit around here loafing, contemplating your navel all day. Get those crates shifted. Let's get this show on the road. Come on, pal, put your back into it. Use a bit of elbow grease.' And to another who is taking his time, Bert says: 'Don't make a welter of it, sport. Come on, step on it. You're puddling along there. Just get the job done quickly.'

'But Mr Simpson said we should ...'

'Well Mr Simpson has given you a bum steer,' says Bert. 'Don't bother about Simpson, lads. He's not a bricklayer's elbow. He's just a crawler who sucks up to the boss. He's just a shitkicker Mr Nobody. Don't worry if he goes crook on you, he's got no power or authority. I wouldn't listen to him any more. He's been given his marching orders.'

'But we shouldn't have to lift these heavy weights,' says one lad.

'Look, sonny, don't argue the toss. You're wasting everybody's time. It's either heads or tails, and for you it's tails. Don't try to make it a complicated thing. Just get on and do the job you've been told to do, and you'll have it shot to ribbons in no time.'

Superstition

If anyone was digging in the garden and a kid asked what they were doing they always, *but always*, said: '**I'm digging my way through to China.**'

It was always China, never anywhere else.

If they were having a run of bad luck, they would always say **I must have killed a Chinaman**. Presumably Europeans did not understand the Chinese culture and saw them as mysterious and mystical and able to invoke curses. Certainly every Australian refused to claim victory early in a sporting contest, or even over a cold or disease, always fearfully saying: '**I don't want to tempt the Chinese gods**.' These gods would punish you for your proud, boastful ways. It was similar to saying: 'I don't want to **put the mockers on** myself.' But different from **put the kybosh on**, which meant someone had deliberately stopped some event or relationship.

Every kid at school thought that if you swallowed tomato seeds, they would grow in your stomach and gradually a green tomato bush would come out of your mouth or ears.

If you didn't want something bad to happen, you crossed the first two fingers on your right hand and said: 'Fingers crossed he doesn't find out,' or 'fingers crossed it never happens.'

To prove that you were telling the truth you licked your right index finger and then made a quick cross over your heart and said: 'Cross my heart and hope to die.' You then had to hope it didn't happen.

To show someone was a lunatic, and should be in the asylum, you rolled your right index finger around next to your temple and then pointed at the person.

A bit like pointing the bone.

If a man was impatiently waiting for a tram, to make it hurry up he rolled a cigarette — if he had **the makings**, which were a tin of tobacco and cigarette papers. The tram was sure to arrive just as he was about to take the first drag on his **durry**. Smoking was only allowed in certain train carriages or in the back half of the bus, behind a thick black line painted on the ceiling. Basically, apart from the front of a bus, you could **suck on a fag** anywhere else, any time.

Cigarette smoke filled the air in picture theatres, restaurants, offices, houses, planes, doctors' waiting rooms, airports, bus stops, train stations, supermarkets, foyers, rest rooms, corridors and lifts.

If you didn't want it to rain, you took an umbrella.

If you saw one snake by itself you knew you should be careful, because it meant you had a secret enemy around. Though if your mother thought you were worried, she would say: **'Bosh! That's an old wives' tale.**' However, if she saw one fly come in the house, she immediately predicted an unexpected visitor.

An extra teaspoon on the saucer? 'Oh, there's going to be a wedding!'

Tiny specks of tea leaves floating in your teacup? Visitors.

If you drank weak tea you'd have ginger-haired kids.

Two married women making a bed? One will fall pregnant.

If you ate in the toilet, you were **supping with the Devil**. Teachers told kids this to try to instil hygienic practices. Some churches condemned playing cards as **the Devil's playthings**.

When you suddenly shivered for no reason, **someone just walked over your grave**. If you started to tell a story, and forgot what you were going to say, **it must have been a lie**. If your mother dropped something on the floor, and you picked it up for her, she would say: 'You'll get **a pleasant surprise** ... when you get to school tomorrow.'

A hot ear? Your mother would say, **'Your ears are burning, someone is gossiping about you.'**

Itchy nose? Scratch it and then **shake hands with a fool** (the closest person to you) for luck.

Itchy palm? Left hand to pay out, right to receive.

If two people said the same word at the same time, they had to link **pinky fingers** and make a wish, while saying the name of a poet. If either of them said 'Shakespeare' they had **speared the wish**, and it would never come true.

Some people started a new month with the refrain: **A pinch and a punch for the first of the month**. Others said **hares and rabbits** or **rats and rabbits**. It made the month lucky for you, but only if these were the very first words you spoke.

If giving a purse or a wallet as a gift, you had to put a coin into it first, so it would start out with money, and thus always carry money.

Whenever you **pulled an ugly face** your mother would warn you to stop 'or **the wind will change and you'll be stuck with it**'. Children believed this implicitly. Some mothers told their children that if they stared hard into the bush they might see a fairy: 'They use flowers, like the crepe myrtle blossom, to make their frocks.' Certainly fireflies at dusk do look remarkably like mischievous dancing fairies.

Some mornings you would find that a ring of mushrooms had appeared on the lawn overnight. This was called a **fairy ring**, because it was said the fairies used the mushrooms as chairs at their dances. And if you were sceptical, you would eventually become convinced. Because when the mushrooms had long decayed away, in their place appeared an extra-green ring of grass which stayed there for years. It was said that it was **fairy dust** that created this ring. But real sceptics said the whole thing was created by one mushroom in the middle which exploded, sending spores and fertiliser out in a circle to enrich the soil.

A mysterious little ditty mothers would say to daughters:

Warm hands, cold heart, dirty feet.
Cold nose, warm heart, dirty feet.

If children wanted it to stop raining after school they would chant:

Rain, rain go away,
Come again
Another day.

If it was a lovely, bright, safe evening they would sing:

Moonlight,
Starlight,
Bogey won't be out tonight.

You could wish on the first star that appeared:

Star light,
Star bright,
First star I see tonight,
Wish I may,
Wish I might,
Get the wish I wish tonight.

❧

Next time you wish upon a star, make sure it's not a satellite was said after the first satellite, the Russian Sputnik, went up in 1957.

❧

Girls avoided having a curl on their forehead because it would label them as having a terrible temper, as the chant went: 'There once was a girl, who had a little curl, right in the middle of her forehead; when she was good, she was very, very good, but when she was bad, she was ... horrid!'

Little girls would ask their mother: 'Who am I going to marry?' So the mother would count the buttons on the child's dress, marking them off with **tinker, tailor, soldier, sailor, rich man, poor man, beggar man, thief**.

The last button was the occupation of her intended.

Or, the mother would peel an orange in one continuous strip, and the girl would toss the peel on the kitchen floor. The shape gave the initial of the name of the man she would one day marry. It was always O for Oliver, S for Sandy, C for Cyril or D for Derek.

You just couldn't get an orange peel to form the letter H.

Tricks

Entertaining was very simple and cost nothing.

To play a trick on a small child, a man would pinch the child's nose between two fingers, then show the tip of his thumb held between the fingers and announce he'd **stolen their nose**.

A trick adults played on kids was to ask: 'Do you want to play **fifty-two card pick-up**?' Kid said 'Yes'. Adult threw the whole pack in the air and kid had to then pick them all up.

Strip jack naked — a game everyone talked about, but no one had ever played!

To trick your mother, you would eat your boiled egg, and then upturn the eggshell in the eggcup and take it back to your mother, saying: 'I couldn't eat it.' She would then crack the shell and feign surprise when it was empty.

To scare people, you would blow into a paper bag, walk up behind them, and burst the bag. The victim usually leapt a foot off the ground.

Bosses would send apprentices on wild errands: a baker might send a boy off to the builder's for 'a bag of sand for the sand cakes'. Or the boy might be sent to the store for 'a long weight'. He would arrive at the shop and say: 'I've been told to come here for a long weight.' He would be told, after a long wait, that it was being used, and to come back later.

When you started whinging about how tough things were, someone in the family would sarcastically start playing an **imaginary violin**, imitating the sentimental music in silent movies, to show they felt no sympathy.

To show someone you didn't care, you put both hands up to your nose, thumb to nose, thumb to little finger and waggled your fingers like playing a trumpet. Or you would thumb your nose at them, by resting your thumb under your nose and then flicking it out at them. If you felt you'd done something smart, you would exhale on the fingernails of your left hand and polish them on your shirt.

In any gathering there was sure to be someone who could entertain the children by wriggling their ears while leaving their head and face still.

A great trick played by every child was to ask a younger one: 'The word ornithorhynchus, do you know how to spell it?'

When they said they couldn't, they would ask you to tell them the spelling. And you always answered: '**I-T**.'

Parents recited this little ditty to babies:

Clap handies,
Clap handies,
Till Dad-dad comes home.
Dad-dad's got money,
And Mummy's got ... none!

Using fingers, they recited a little rhyme:

Here's the mother's knives and forks,
Here's the mother's table,
Here's the mother's looking glass,
And here's the baby's cradle ...

or

Here's the church and here's the steeple,
Open the doors and see all the people.

At some point at school, most boys would start making fake money by putting a penny or a shilling under a sheet of paper and rubbing a pencil on the top. The raised relief picture of the coin would magically appear on the paper. It was like being a counterfeiter.

Girls would make a '**chatterbox**': a square of paper folded up in such a way that it made a little pyramid which you fitted your fingers into. This was opened and closed with the fingers, magically revealing, and then hiding, the inner folds. A different colour was painted on each of the four exposed leaves of paper, a different number was written on each of the inner folds, and then a riddle or joke was written under each of the inner folds. Holding the **chatterbox**, you invited your friend to choose a colour. You'd twist the chatterbox with each letter spelt out, for example b-l-u-e. The person then chose a number from the inner leaves, and you then counted it out with movements of the fingers, one-two-three-four-five. The person then chose another number from those visible, and you unfolded this fold, to reveal the joke or riddle.

In some parts of the bush, locals would sneak up on newlyweds in the middle of the night (a fortnight after the wedding) and bang kerosene tins and **billy cans** outside the window to wake them up. They called themselves **tincanners**.

The following poem was sometimes recited by the tincanners on the Queensland side of the New South Wales border:

The bulldog ant at close of day,
When the ringtail possums sing,
Canters down to the billabong,
To temper his well-worn sting.

The emu sits in the blue gum tips,
And suckles its hungry young.
The echidna smooths its silken coat,
With the tip of its fork-ed tongue.

The mosquito picks his canine teeth,
With the bones of the night's repast,
And folds his head neath a fluffy wing,
As a black snake brushes past.

How to keep a secret

If you failed to keep a family secret and **spilled your guts**, your mother would accuse you of being *a balsam seed*: you only have to touch the balsam plant lightly and all the seeds spill out.

So there were four rules to keep secrets safe.

Rule 1. Don't go up to people and say: 'I've got a secret and I'm not telling,' because they'll soon wheedle it out of you by saying, **'Fess up.'**

Rule 2. Be prepared with some quick replies: **'Never you mind**.' Or, **'You tell me then I'll tell you then we'll both know!'** Or, **'Suck it and see**.' Or, **'Not telling**.' Or the sort of replies mothers kept up their sleeves for deflecting curious little kids and **nosy parkers**:

What's in that packet, Mum?

It's a wigwam for a goose's bridle.

Where did that baby come from, Mum?

Ask no questions and you'll be told no lies.

Mum, why did you marry Dad?

Ask a silly question and you'll get a silly answer.

Fathers had their own, more whimsical ways of replying to keep their secrets safe.

- Where are you going, Dad?
- **I've got to see a man about a dog.**
- Where is the dog?
- **That's for me to know and you to find out!**

Or he might say: **I'm off to see the Wizard**. That was guaranteed to stump even the most curious child.

- What are you shopping for, Dad?
- **This, that and the other.**
- When will you be back?
- **Your guess is as good as mine.**
- Where did you go, Dad?
- **I went there and back to see how far it was.**

Rule 3. A secret is only fun if you share it, but the other person must believe it is a secret.

'This is between you and me and the gatepost, strictly speaking, I know I'm telling tales out of school, but this is bigger than Ben Hur, I hope he doesn't twig, I don't think he's cottoned on yet, but here's the drum, I'll give you the good oil, a little bird told me, in fact a little dickybird told me, mum's the word, keep your trap shut, keep it under your hat, this is on the QT, it's hush hush, just quietly between you and me, don't say a dickybird.'

Rule 4. Don't complain when your secret becomes known to all.

I should have kept my trap shut. I shouldn't have blabbed. **The Devil made me do it**!

Cracker night

For a fortnight every year, Australian shops were full of fireworks leading up to the evening of November 5, **Guy Fawkes Night**.

The rest of the year, you just couldn't buy fireworks at all.

Since fireworks were called **crackers**, Guy Fawkes Night was known by kids everywhere as **cracker night**. And when you saw how excited people got, you could understand why, for example, if someone went crazy people said he'd **gone crackers**. Or, if an event was a smashing success it was **a cracker**.

Whole streets got together on cracker night and pooled all their fireworks. But Protestants and Catholics celebrated separately. Protestant grown-ups would make a huge bonfire on a spare allotment and burn an effigy of Guy Fawkes while reciting:

> *Please do remember the fifth of November,*
> *With gunpowder, treason and plot.*
> *I see no reason why gunpowder and treason*
> *Should ever be forgot.*

Because Guy Fawkes was a Catholic who had tried to blow up the British Parliament in 1605, Catholics were not supposed to join in the celebrations. But who could resist the colours, the skyrockets, the fire and explosions? So Catholics had their own little cracker night in the backyard without a bonfire.

But everyone had at least these crackers:

- **Bungers**, also called **penny bungers** because of their price — as big as a man's middle finger, red, with a white wick at one end. After you lit one you threw it as quickly as possible, like a hand grenade. Deafening explosion! Boys used penny bungers to blow up people's letterboxes. If you lit one under an upturned can it would be blown way above the treetops. Sometimes bungers wouldn't go off, so you broke them in the middle to expose the gunpowder, then lit it to send fire fizzing out from your hand.

- **Double bunger** — the wick was in the middle. One end would explode, sending the bunger elsewhere. Several seconds later it would explode again. There was even an ice-cream called **the double bunger** which had two wooden sticks instead of one.

- **Catherine wheels** — nailed to a tree, when lit they spun around emitting spectacular coloured flames.

- **Fizzer** — a cracker that just petered out.

- **Flower pots** — several small bungers tied together into one.

- **Golden shower** — sprayed out golden sparks all over the yard.

- **Jumping jacks** — small bungers tied together like a concertina. When each one exploded the cracker jumped somewhere else and exploded again, and then again, a dozen times. No one could predict where it would land next.

- **Roman candles** — fired out a beautiful white light.

- **Skyrockets** — rockets on long sticks, usually launched from a milk bottle. They landed all over town, occasionally setting a house on fire.

- **Throwdowns** — when you threw them on the ground they exploded. Great for annoying people.

- **Tom Thumbs** — lots of tiny green and red crackers knitted together with string, like the vest on an American Indian chieftain in a film.

Injuries from explosions, and the odd house fire, led to cracker night eventually being banned in Australia.

Whistling

The only way to get a cab was to stand on a corner and whistle. In the 1950s all men could whistle loudly. The cabbie heard you because there was no airconditioning, so all the cabs had their windows wound down and the drivers rested their right elbow on the open window.

Kids stayed in contact in the bush by whistling.

It was quite normal for a man to whistle a tune while walking or working, so they were very good at it. Some women confessed they would surreptitiously follow a man because they liked how he whistled and they wanted to hear the song to the end.

Men whistled in various ways: with two fingers in their mouth; through the centre of their teeth; out the side; through pursed lips; and some would cup both hands together and whistle by blowing between their thumbs. They controlled the volume by opening and shutting their hands.

Chapter five

DUNDERHEADS and RATBAGS

Artists and merchants

In the Australian lingo of old, if you wanted to warn friends off someone, you added **merchant** or **artist** to your description of them. 'An artist' was very good at what they did, and 'a merchant' was so called because it was what they did for a living.

He's a **bull artist** — tells **porkies** (lies).

Bullshit artist — not simply a **bull artist**, but a real **skite**.

She's a **lurk merchant** — always pulling **swifties** on people.

He's a **con artist** — someone who cons you out of money.

A **hold-up merchant** — someone who just takes your money.

Grog artist — a drunk.

A **speed merchant** — a very fast runner.

A **bash artist** — a big-hitting cricketer.

An **intercept merchant** — one who plays offside in rugby league when he can get away with it, so he can intercept a pass. Usually from New South Wales!

Dunderheads and ratbags

The one thing nobody was short of in Australia, before the modern era of political correctness, was words and phrases for putting a person in their place.

There was no mucking around with polite euphemisms designed to lessen the blow. Back then we didn't say someone was in need of a **more sustainable direction**, or was **organisationally challenged**, or was **indulging in inappropriate behaviour**, or required some **team orientation**, or **lifestyle choice realignment**.

DUNDERHEADS

A person who knocked over a tray of newly cooked meat pies was a **clumsy clot** or even a **dunderklumpen** or a **bumbleton**. Though **you stupid galoot** was the phrase most favoured for **a bloody idiot**.

Unfortunately, that wonderful word **galoot** has now completely disappeared from modern Australian language. I used it a couple of years ago in a talk to 100 Grade 10 students and one boy put up his hand.

'What's that word *galloo* mean?' he asked.

'Would someone please tell this galoot what a galoot is?' I asked the class.

Everyone looked at me blankly.

Immediately I commented on **what a pack of drongos** and **what a mob of big galahs** I was dealing with. But they hadn't heard of those phrases either.

Such put-downs were usually said to someone lower down the totem pole who had made a silly mistake: a **silly billy**, or a **silly dick**.

It got very personal, so you had to be robust to **cop it sweet**.

The teacher at school, the parent at home, or the boss at work did not hesitate to call you **a numbskull**, or, worse still, **a nincompoop**. Or else you were **as silly as a two-bob watch, silly as a wheel, dumb as a doorknob**, and **as thick as two short planks to boot**. The insults available were almost endless — all waiting to be used on someone you didn't like, or who had **upset your equilibrium**. You could call them **a dope, a silly duffer, a dunderhead, a dumbcluck** or **a buffoon**. Or, better still, **a goose**, if you considered they had made a fool of themselves.

Yet still up your sleeve were the almost onomatopoeic words like:

- Nong
- Ninny
- Dud
- Dingbat
- Twit
- Nitwit
- Drip
- Sook
- Dill
- Right Charlie
- Oaf ('You bloody oaf') — clumsy or stupid.

Your victim might be:

- Three plates short of a picnic
- One thermos short of a picnic
- A few sandwiches short of a picnic
- A few crumbs short of a picnic
- A few bricks short of a load
- A couple of rungs short of a ladder
- A shingle short
- Or, simply, something's missing in the upper storey
- Or, not the brightest crayon in the box, or not a full packet of bickies.

A bit of a no-hoper was a slightly sympathetic way of saying someone was trying, but not succeeding. (Today they would be dismissed as 'a loser'.) Many insults included the word 'dead', with all that that implied. A person who failed to act in the way required could be called a *deadhead*, or *a deadbeat*, or just a straight-out *dead loss*.

BIRDBRAINS

The head was a good place to start for insulting terms. Someone you didn't like could be: *a blockhead, a knucklehead, a pinhead, a scatterbrain*, or *a boofhead* (which could be shortened to *a boof*). Boofhead was a cartoon character, tall with a big head. He was supposedly thick and dull, but in his innocence he often made telling comments which got to the kernel of the matter, much like the jester in a Shakespearean play.

You could be called *face-ache, fartface* or *fungus features*.

Inside the head was no better. You could be called *a lamebrain, rattle brain, shit-for-brains, spaghetti-for-brains* (if you made everything more complicated than it really was) or, if you were considered none too bright, *birdbrain*. If foolish, *you must have rocks in your head*.

And worst of all: *You wouldn't have a brain to begin with*.

If someone described you as *a double-ended broom-handle* you were *worse than useless*.

RATBAGS

Beware those who didn't go along with the status quo and spoke out against the system. Such a person was *a firebrand* (or worse still, at the height of the Cold War, *a self-confessed communist firebrand*). If they were having an effect they were *a troublemaker*; if not, they were dismissed as *a ratbag*. Or worse still, *a total ratbag*.

If someone was *a God-botherer* or a *Bible-basher* (that is, a religious fire-brand), they were *a crank*.

At the absolute worst, ratbags were known as *stirrers*. There was said to be one of these in every town. Thus '*He's the local stirrer*' was often heard all over Australia. He was someone who was forever complaining and trying to get others to complain as well.

However, conversely, if a person agitated from the sidelines without getting involved, they were *a knocker*, *a nark*, *a whinger*, or *a miseryguts*. Today they'd be called a conspiracy theorist.

Whereas someone who stood up for what he believed in was *a rooster*, or, if he were short, *a bantam rooster*; someone who *had a go*, and *took up the fight*.

If you quietly but consistently stood outside the accepted dress codes, you were *a nonconformist*.

If you were considered a harmless eccentric then you were *an odd bod* or a *local identity*.

DINGOES

If you didn't speak out, or act on your beliefs, you were, totally illogically, said to be *a dingo* or *a squib*.

Anyone who was a coward back then was a *dingo*, or, worse still, a '*dirty dingo dog*'. If a friend or relative hadn't supported you, or backed you up, then they had *dingoed on you*. If they'd informed on you, that was *a dingo act*.

Not paying your way could quickly lead to a person getting a bad reputation as having *short arms and deep pockets*. If you wouldn't readily *dub in* when it was your turn to shout, you were *a cheapskate*.

If you asked for money from others you were **a cadger** who usually greeted people with the words: **'If you could see your way clear ... only to tide me over'** (lend me some money).

Similarly with cigarettes: you would try to **cadge** a cigarette.

You might be called **a sponger** or **a scrounger** and it would often be said that a man was **sponging off society**. Your mates would have to **put the acid on you**, to get their money back.

The Australian language of abuse wasn't always easy to figure out.

Sometimes a phrase could have both a good and a bad connotation. **'A couple of reprobates came into the shop'** would mean they looked like criminals. But **'How are you, you old reprobate?'** was an affectionate way of greeting an old mate.

'You old bastard' was very friendly and warm and said to a close friend; but 'You **dirty bastard'** was unfriendly and aggressive.

Miserable sods

- **He gives me the tray bits**.
- She gives me **the willies**, the **jimjams**, the **creeps**.
- **I'd know his hide in a tannery** — if you really hated the sight of him.
- **She's very petty** — 'petty' was one of the very worst words you could use to describe a person. Worrying over **trifles** was frowned upon by a society that had seen long lists of their dead from wars, and had seen disease ravage their children.
- To **stand on her dig** — she wouldn't **give any ground, stuck to her guns**. But if she was being totally unreasonable, she would be said to be **standing on her dignity**.
- She's **a nasty piece of work** — had mean or cruel things to say about others. Or, as the woman walked away, your mother might say: **'She's not a very nice piece of work.'**

- He's **all sweetness and light** first thing in the morning, but don't ask him to do anything after eight at night.
- He's **hail-fellow-well-met** — like **a real go-getter**. This could be a criticism meaning he is insincere and possibly **a shyster**. On the other hand, it could be used to describe a friendly good-humoured bloke, or one going places.
- He sticks **like a burr to a blanket**, or **like a burr to a horse's tail** — hanging around too much, **like a bad smell**.
- **Who does he think he is? King Farouk?** — a man wearing large black sunglasses (in an era before sunglasses were standard). Wearing sunglasses anywhere but at the beach was considered to be showing off.
- **Pop** — an old man. Could be derisive.
- **Listen pal, sport, brains trust** — what you said if you didn't like someone or were annoyed with them.
- **A bit dodgy —** not **ridgy-didge**.
- **Goody-two-shoes** — she's too sweet, don't trust her.
- **She's a real Pearl Pureheart** — another goody-goody.
- **A ne'er-do-well**
- **The cunning old wretch**
- **That wretched man**
- **The miserable sod**
- **He always thinks his sheep are the blackest**
- **A bad egg**
- **Snowdropper** — someone who pinches ladies' underwear off people's clothes lines!

Then there were the people who, while not wicked, were not to be **aped**.

- **The Spoiler** — she finds it irksome to see other people happy. So, for example, she will reveal the surprise birthday party plans, and then affect dismay that she's **let the cat out of the bag**. Or she always manages to spill beetroot juice on your fresh tablecloth, or break your best teacup, or drop cake crumbs onto the carpet and then walk on them. When she gets up from the table, there's always a mess where she was sitting.

- **A Flash Harry** — he's usually up to no good, **involved in a bit of skulduggery**. He's **up to putty**. He's **got more front than Woolworths**, is **not backward in coming forward**. He's had a **colourful past**; which means he has done a lot of things, some of which he shouldn't have. He **could sell refrigerators to the Eskimos**, but he **can't lie straight in bed**. He's **so crooked he could hide behind a corkscrew**. You **wouldn't trust him as far as you could throw him**, or **as far as you could spit**. He would **get away with murder**. He is **as guilty as heck, as guilty as sin**, or **as guilty as all get out**. He's had **more luck than a fat priest** — he's never had to do much, never worked hard, never done physical work. If he has **too many irons in the fire**, he will finally **get his comeuppance, come to no good** and be **hung out to dry**. Your grandmother would say of him: **he's born, but he's not buried**. By this she meant he has done some wrong, but he is still around, so his evil deeds can still catch up with him.

- **A badly bred boy** — that's what your aunt would say about a disrespectful shop assistant who displayed **rank bad manners**.

- **She's no better than she ought to be, and a lot worse than she should be** — an enigmatic statement a grandmother would make about a woman she didn't like. Such a woman would also be described as **very forward**. It was difficult to make out what was meant, but it was clear that the woman was not in favour, and her virtue was in doubt, if not easy.

- **That child has a pretty ordinary background** — other people's backgrounds (their parents and close family) were always being discussed. This took up a lot of conversation, perhaps because people did not move around too much so people knew each other's relations.

The know-all

- -

So nice of you to drop by. You're a godsend. I'm in need of a friend. I feel like threepence worth of Heaven help me.

I was in the neighbourhood. What's wrong?

Oh well, it's a very sad story. It all started when my cat, Oliver, came home ill from the cattery.

That's a very narrow description.

Well, yes. Is it? It was awful. To look at him, it would make your navel curl.

It strikes me you are dwelling on this too much. Have you been neglecting the cat?

I suppose I'm just an average cat-lover.

Average. Oh. The average person is quite imbecilic when it comes to looking after pets. Most people are so ignorant it isn't funny. What sort of grains does he eat?

Grains? I never fed him grains.

Really? Oh dear.

I just gave him fish and meat. I've always fed my cats that way.

Just as I thought. And this is the first time you've had a problem? Well, you've been living on borrowed time. Skating on thin ice. Where does Oliver usually sleep?

On the end of my bed, as a rule, or on the veranda.

Worse than I thought. What liquids does he drink?

Just the usual. Water.

From the tap no doubt. No wonder. And how have you treated this recent illness?

I took him to a veterinarian ...

To a vet! You're really scraping the bottom of the barrel. They're not worth a crumpet.

Well he charged like a wounded bull.

You're a tiger for punishment, aren't you?

So I was taking Oliver twice a week ...

You're a glutton for punishment!

This veterinarian is very well respected. He's as sound as a bell.

He just wants to sell you every new-fangled product that's on the market. Why would you trust a vet? What would a vet know?

Well, it was a serious illness.

All the more reason to avoid the vet. Don't you know that when a vet is trained, his knowledge is narrowed down rather than expanded up?

No, I didn't know that.

Haven't you ever heard of positive vibrations?

No, never, what are they?

Don't you ever read?

I've never read about positive vibrations.

You'd better bone up on them. If you use the earth's vibration, you can cure yourself, with no doctors or vets or those poisons they call medicines and vaccinations.

Well, it's too late for Oliver now. You see, he died this morning.

Don't you believe in the afterlife?

LOST FOR WORDS EPISODE 5:
Sourpuss

Lost for Words. **The story of Bert and Grace and their trials and tribulations bringing up a young family after the War.**

In the RSL club, June and Alma are chatting while washing glasses at one end of the bar. Vera is at the other end of the bar putting out the peanuts, trying to ignore the two of them.

'What's eating Vera tonight?' asks June.

'She's cheesed off. Browned off,' replies Alma.

'She looks a right sourpuss.'

'She's down in the dumps; miserable as a bandicoot.'

'Why the long face?'

'She's had a gutful. She says she's been kicked in the teeth.'

'Vera! Is there any undercurrent, dear?' calls out June.

'Don't bother her, June,' says Alma hastily. 'She's like a bear with a sore head. She'll get over it.'

But June would not be hushed.

'Vera, darling, did you get out of the wrong side of the bed this morning?'

'Take no notice of her. She'll get cool in the skin she got hot in. She'll cool off in the juice she cooked in.'

'Vera, you've got a face as long as a wet week! Don't trip over your bottom lip.'

'Don't rub it in. Let her go, June.'

'Vera, lend me your face to fight a bulldog.'

'Now she's really ticked off.'

'A bit on the sulky side? We've got the sulky, Alma, all we need now is the horse.'

'Now you've done it, June. She'll be really surly.'

'In the doldrums, are we? Feeling a bit down in the mouth?'

'She's been a sad sack most of this week.'

'Have you got the umps, Vera? Got the mugwumps?'

'Look, June,' says Alma. 'She's been out of sorts ever since that Kevin was supposed to take her out for Sunday dinner, and he never showed. Now he's even stopped coming to the club.'

'Vera! You look like you've lost sixpence and found a penny.'

'Don't tease her, June. Vera's set her cap at Kevin.'

'Don't be such a spoilsport, Vera. Don't be a wet blanket. I can't think of anything more disheartening and sobering than a wet blanket, can you? And your rouge is smudging, dear.'

'If I were her, I wouldn't be that upset. Kevin's really an old fusspot. And he's got a face that would curdle cream.'

'Well then, she should stop her bellyaching. I've never known such a grizzleguts.'

'She won't hear a word against him. Even though he's made her the laughing stock of the district.'

'Come on, Vera, buck up. Chin up.'

'That won't stop her being toey, testy, cranky, stroppy, snaky and crotchety.'

'Oh fiddlesticks! I tell you, Alma, misery loves company. Besides,

Vera has always had a shirking temperament.'

'Don't be so narky, June.'

'Alma! Why are you picking on me? I'm not creating a song and dance because my boyfriend, who I never had in the first place, gave me up! I've still got my boyfriend, so is there a bit of jealousy in the camp?'

'I'm just saying you could be more sympathetic.'

'Are you trying to say I'm the termagant shrew? It's all my fault, is it, Alma? Are you saying I'm a bit of a tartar, a harridan? Well the boot is on the other foot! I'll tell you what, Alma, I'm lost for words!'

Chapter six

MY WORD

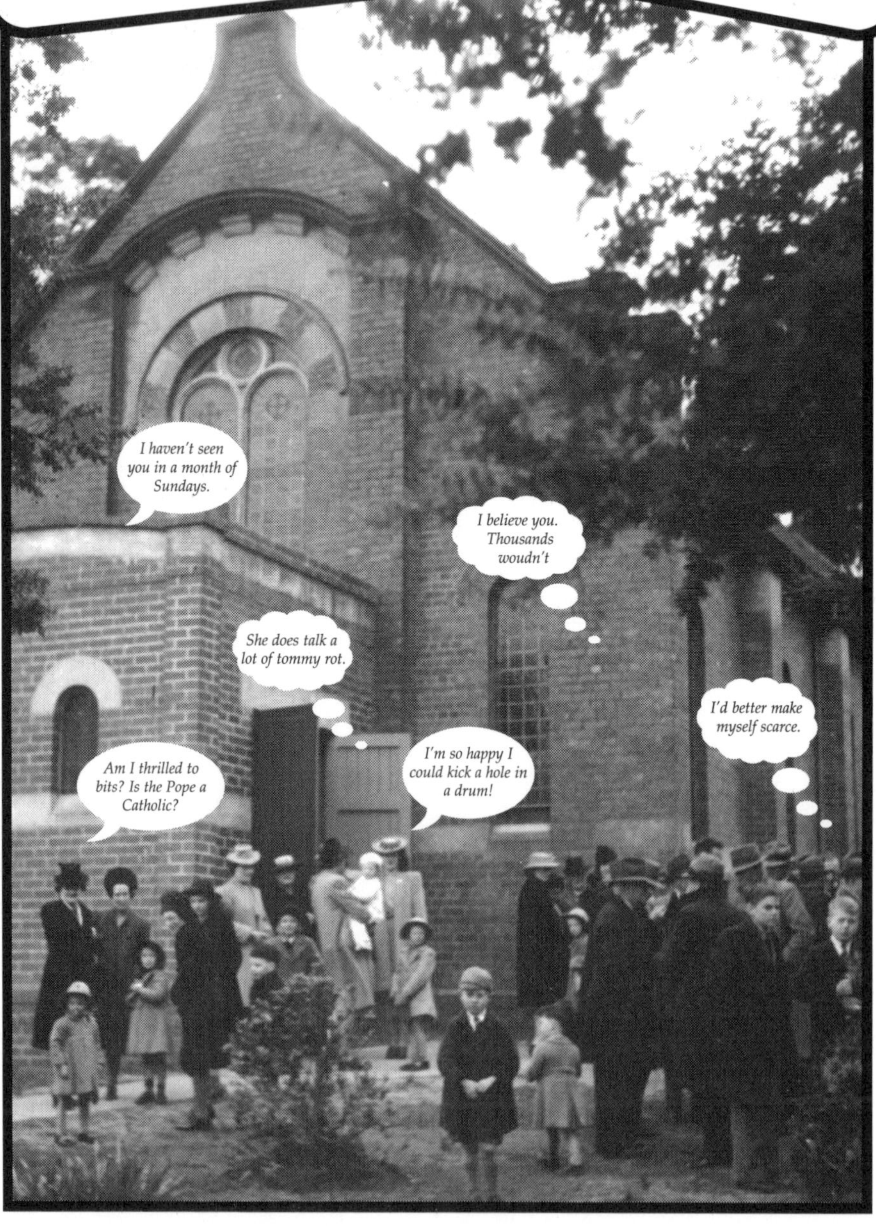

Heavens to Betsy

Once upon a time, Australians spoke a rich, evocative, expansive, euphonious, metaphoric, enthusiastic language. While this inventive tradition continues today with a few, a large slice of the Australian population now finds it simpler to constantly repeat the same few words and phrases, used ad infinitum in movies and the American TV sitcoms which dominate the nation's evenings.

Here are just a few old Australian alternatives to some of these words and phrases.

Absolutely!

- Too right
- Too true
- Is the Pope a Catholic?
- Can a duck swim?
- That's dead right
- I reckon!
- I'll say!
- You bet
- You betcha!
- Blood oath
- My oath!
- My colonial oath!
- For sure
- You can say that again
- No risk
- My word!
- Good on you
- Sounds right
- Dead set
- Righty-ho

- Right you are
- Okeydoke
- Alrighty
- Exactly!
- Fair enough
- Correct-o-mundo!
- You're on the money

Yessssss!!!!!
- I'm so happy I could kick a hole in a drum!
- Thank Heavens to Betsy!
- Ripper!
- Beauty!
- Pearler
- Mighty!
- Hold onto your hat!
- Grouse
- I'm over the moon

Way to go!
- That's the best suggestion to date
- That's the ticket
- That's the shot
- You're on the right track
- Now you're cooking on gas
- You're going great guns
- Your blood's worth bottling
- She's jake
- She's apples
- She's sweet
- She'll be right

Bring it on!

- Fire away
- Let her rip
- Have a bash
- Give it a burl
- Give it a whirl
- Have a lash
- It's in the bag
- It's shot to bits
- It's shot to ribbons

Oh my God!

- Fancy that!
- Love-a-duck!
- Holy cow!
- Jesus wept!
- Stiffen the wombats!
- Strike me pink!
- Strike me pink, yellow and blue, I'm an Irish cockatoo!
- Strike me handsome!
- Strike me lucky!
- Strike a light!
- Stuff me with the rough end of a pineapple!
- Hell's bloody bells!
- That's a turn-up for the books!
- Struth!
- Blow me down!
- Cripes!
- Golly!
- Good golly gosh!
- By George!
- Well that takes the cake!

- Wouldn't that rot your socks!
- Holy moly!
- Holy dooley
- Goodness gracious me!
- Dearie me!
- Heavens to Betsy!
- Heavens above!
- Well I'll be buggered!
- What the dickens!
- What the blazes!
- What in blue blazers!
- Cripey crows!
- Shiver me timbers!
- Wouldn't that blow a hole in your nightie!
- My goodness!
- Glory be!
- Well I'll go *he*!
- Well I'll be!
- Well I'll be a monkey's uncle!
- Well I never!
- What's the world coming to?

Whatever

- It's your funeral
- Go for your life
- Suit yourself
- Search me
- Fair enough
- It's a free country
- Any obs?
- Same diff
- What's the diff?

- And what have you
- More fool you
- I couldn't give a hoot
- That's my story and I'm sticking to it
- I'll believe you, thousands wouldn't
- And the rest!
- I'm buggered if I know
- Blowed if I know
- Takes one to know one
- Your guess is as good as mine
- That's as clear as mud

Tell someone who cares / Build a bridge and get over it

- Cheer up
- Buck up
- Chin up
- Look after yourself
- Take care
- Hurts, doesn't it?
- That'll hurt you
- You'll get all that sort of thing, if you live long enough
- Bully for you
- I couldn't give a Continental
- I couldn't give a tinker's curse/cuss
- I couldn't give a rat's
- Don't take offence, but ...
- Serves yourself right
- Tough luck
- Tough titty
- You don't say
- Come off the grass

Hello? Hello?
- Are you one sandwich short of a picnic?
- Do you get my drift?
- Wakey-wakey!
- Sharpen up!
- Wake up, Australia, Tasmania's floating away!
- Rise and shine, your King and country need you!

Get a life / Get real
- Come off the grass
- You're on the wrong track
- For pity's sake!
- You're still wet behind the ears
- Pull your head in
- Go jump
- Go take a running jump at yourself

In your dreams / You wish
- Easier said than done
- Pigs might fly
- Pull the other one, it plays 'Jingle Bells'
- Tell me another one
- I don't want to pooh-pooh your idea, but ...
- I wasn't born yesterday
- I didn't come down in the last shower
- I'm not stupid
- Tosh
- A load of hogwash
- Eyewash
- That's all very well and good, but ...

- That's a half-baked idea
- Wake up to yourself
- You don't say!

As if

- Sod off
- Rack off
- Fat chance
- My foot!
- Bugger that for a joke!
- Be buggered!
- No fear
- Like Hell
- Come off it
- Come off the grass

I'd like to see that

- Talk's cheap
- Big talk, no action
- Go ahead, and see how far you get

Oh puh-lease

- What a lot of hooey!
- What a load of piffle!
- What a lot of malarky!
- Spare me days!

Enough already

- Getting back to normal ...
- My uncle ...
- Harking back ...
- Apropos of nothing ...
- In my day ...
- I mean to say ...
- No dice

I don't think so

- Perish the thought
- All the same ...
- Still and all ...
- Not on your Nelly
- Not in a fit
- Not in a pink fit
- Not for all the rice in China
- You've got the wrong end of the stick
- By the same token ...
- ... and laugh!
- Leave well enough alone
- Least said, soonest mended
- Cheese it!
- Let's start with a clean slate

It's all gone pear-shaped

- It's just not my week
- I must have killed a Chinaman
- It's gone bung
- It's on the blink
- It's all gone to pot

- It's a dead loss
- Up to putty
- You just can't win
- All bets are off

*

Excuse me?

- Well pardon me for living
- Don't mind me
- Don't give cheek

*

It's a no-brainer

- It's a cinch
- It's as easy as pie
- It's money for jam
- It's money for old rope
- It's a doddle

*

The modern **I hear what you say** used to be plainly **You're wrong**. And what used to be **Get your arse into gear** is now **Just do it**.

There seem to be no modern versions of the gentle exclamation **It just doesn't seem right**. Or, **Muggins here** — meaning I'm a mug for doing this job, but I'm going to do it anyway because I feel a sense of obligation. Or the old Aussie plea, **Fair's fair**. Or, **Not bad**, meaning pretty bloody good.

Thankfully, the practice of blatantly labelling people has **gone out with straw hats**. For example, in the Brisbane suburb of Dutton Park when I was a boy there once was an institution called **The Blind, Deaf and Dumb School**.

*

Mid last century was also a time when we did not know that mental illness was basically an altering of chemicals in the brain, or that, in many cases, the illness is related to the number of neurons being produced in different parts of the brain. So there wasn't much sympathy in the language for those who suffered.

- She's a bit dotty
- She's gone slightly potty
- She's a real scatterbrain
- Her brain is addled
- He's lost his marbles
- He went berko (nutty *or* angry)
- He's got bats in the belfry
- She's a bit whacky-the-noo
- Gone in the head
- As nutty as a fruitcake
- As mad as a hatter
- As mad as a March hare
- As mad as a meat axe

- He's gone crackers
- He's round the twist, bonkers, nuts, off his rocker, away with the fairies, and cracked in the head. He's a hard case, loony, a loon, a lunatic, a cot case, a basket case, a fruit loop, a fruitcake, a crackpot, a screw loose, and is out of his tree
- He's dropped his bundle
- The white van will come to take you away *or* The men in white coats will come to take you away

Whereas if someone was just angry, they were:
- As mad as a cut snake
- As mad as a meat ant
- As mad as a packet of bungers

Mrs Kerfoops

It was the **done thing** for women to use an imaginary name when they couldn't be bothered saying, or remembering, the name of an acquaintance they were talking about. This usually meant they didn't like the person.

The most popular of these names was **Mrs Kerfoops**: 'I hear old Mrs Kerfoops is having a bit of trouble with that salesman bloke she calls her husband.' Or, 'We'll have to ask that Mrs Kerfoops; she's the **full bottle** on sponge cakes.'

Such names were also readily available to use for someone whose name momentarily escaped you: 'That awful woman down the road, you know, **Mrs Foggabolla**, was up complaining about the kids again today.' Or, 'The head-master reckons old **Mrs McGillickhay** had better stop keeping her six children at home all the time.' Or, '**Old Spundulicks** has been down pinching our eggs out of the henhouse again.'

Then there was: **Old Chisel Whiskers**; **Old Stocking Top**; **Old Frogabolla**; **Old Hoojar**; **Old Hoot-me-flute** who lives down the creek; **Old Thing-a-me-tight** down the road. Men might say there goes old **Hoppy-go-fetchy**, or there's old **Dot-and-carry-one** (if he had **a gammy leg**). Sometimes the **old codger** would be called a **local identity**.

If your mother was unimpressed by some fellow she'd say: '**Who's he when he's at home**?'

When you asked your mother what the name of something was, and she didn't know — or she wasn't going to tell you — she would answer: '**Hurdy-gurdy-gongolope**' or '**Tri-anti-wontigon**.'

If it was a person, she would simply say: 'He's **a fellow of my acquaintance**.'

When men talked of someone who didn't matter to the story, or whose name they couldn't remember, they called him **Whatchamecallem** or **Thing-a-me-bob** or **Thing-a-me-jig** or just plain **Thingo**. Or else it was **Whosits** or **Whatsits** or **bloody Whatsisname**. Or, **I struck a chap** on the tram tonight.

If he was a **perfect stranger** and you didn't **know him from Adam**, or you **wouldn't know him from a bar of soap**, you called him **Joe Blow**, or a **bod**: 'Some bod wants to know the time', or a **joker**: 'Who's that joker in the safety zone?' Or joker could be used to describe someone who did not stand out in any way: **an ordinary joker**.

Whereas a **clown** was a stranger who always **mucked things up**: '**Some clown put this in the wrong way.**' Or '**This clown comes out with a microphone.**'

It was common to refer to children as **a lass** or **a lad**. A man would address a boy he didn't know as **champ**, **sport**, **mate**, **pal**, **tiger** or even **Johnny**.

And if teachers couldn't pronounce a name, such as Surawski, like as not they would call you **Wheelbarrow**. 'Come up to the front, Megan Wheelbarrow.'

Similarly, there were words for objects you couldn't name. When a bloke asked you to pass him a spanner, and he couldn't quite think of the name, he would ask for the **thingummybob**, or the **thingummyjig**.

Parts for machinery were called a **doover**, a **dooverlackie**, a **whatsit**, **a gizmo**, or **a doodad**.

Places were given mysterious names:

Sticks — out in the sticks, the bush, the outback, **the mulga**.

Timbuktu — the furthest place anyone could imagine. It was beyond the **Black Stump**, **back of Bourke**, out in **Woop Woop**.

'**Come with me to the kasbah**,' Mum would say if she was asking you to come with her on a boring everyday trip, like to the shops or to hang out the washing.

Talking dirty

Sometimes dirty didn't mean a person hadn't bathed, didn't mean they were foul-mouthed, it was simply a word men used to exaggerate: this **dirty big bloke** arrived; a **dirty great ship** went by.

Or, you might be **dirty on** someone, meaning very, very annoyed with him.

Then you would likely call him **a dirty bastard**, or **a dirty mongrel**, because he had **done the dirty** on you.

Bastard could be affectionate. But mongrel could never be. It was as bitter as a man could get: a **bit of a mongrel**, a **bloody mongrel**, he comes from **a mongrel family**. But, conversely, an Australian sportsman having **some mongrel in him** was extremely admirable, meaning he was **as game as Ned Kelly** and wouldn't give in easily. This was the highest praise.

Someone could also be a **miserable mongrel**, which didn't mean the bloke was at all unhappy, it meant he didn't have a generous nature. He was miserly and **stingy. Living on the smell of an oily rag**.

Dirty could also be used in a jocular fashion: **you dirty stopout**, meaning you were very lucky because you were out having a good time while I was stuck at home.

Double talk

- **Argy-bargy** — when they were deciding who would be club president, there was a lot of argy-bargy down at the RSL.
- **Jiggery-pokery** — there was so much jiggery-pokery going on, the candidate who got the most votes didn't win.
- **Willy-nilly** — the committee made up new rules willy-nilly, without consulting anyone.
- **Hurdy-gurdy** — they had us on the hurdy-gurdy, running around in circles getting nowhere.
- **Hurly-burly** — they created such a hurly-burly we couldn't think for all the commotion.
- **Hocus-pocus** — then they went on with a lot of hocus-pocus to cover up the rort they were trying to pull.
- **Nitty-gritty** — at first it sounded alright, until you got down to the nitty-gritty, and then it looked like a con job.
- **Ridgy-didge** — then we all realised the election was not ridgy-didge, not **on the level**.

- **Holus-bolus** — so the members got together and threw out the whole committee holus-bolus, threw out the whole **kit and caboodle**.
- **Namby-pamby** — unfortunately the new president we've elected is a bit of a namby-pamby fusspot.
- **Fuddy-duddy** — he's such an old fuddy-duddy, he still stands up when a woman enters the room.
- **Higgledy-piggledy** — he wrote up the minutes, and his writing is all higgledy-piggledy up and down the page.
- **Odd bod** — in fact, he looks a bit of an odd bod in his funny hat.
- **Heebie-jeebies** — he's so creepy, he gives the ladies the heebie-jeebies when he comes around patting them on the shoulder.
- **Jimjams** — and he gives them the jimjams, the willies and the stirks.
- **Collywobbles** — so much so, one of the ladies now has the collywobbles and can't stop the shakes.
- **Hanky-panky** — but there's no hanky-panky going on.
- **Lousy-powsy** — it turns out his ideas are so lousy-powsy, no one can work out what he means.
- **Hoity-toity** — and the bloke is so hoity-toity he looks down his nose at everyone else.
- **Stingy-mingy** — one thing we do know, he is so stingy-mingy, he reuses the tea leaves.
- **Mingy-scringy** — but we can't complain, because he's also mingy-scringy with the club funds.
- **Shilly-shally** — when we asked him not to shilly-shally on the issue of new members, he said:
- '**Holy moly! Okey-doke**.'

Now we've got that sorted out, everything is **hunky-dory**!

ARPY DARPY

Arpre darpou garpodarping tarpo thdarpe sharpop — are you going to the shop?

So that adults could not understand them, many girls in the 1950s spoke their own language.

The language was called Arpy darpy because they would alternately say arp or darp before each vowel, or vowel sound-alike. Thus **'Who is he?'** became: **'Wharpo darpis harpe?'**

Unless you were skilled, it was impossible to understand because they could speak it faster than normal speech.

It had rules of grammar too. For example, if the vowel was silent, as in the 'e' in James, you only inserted 'arp' once: 'J-arp-ames'. Also, the 'p' must be pronounced all the time. Thus 'How are you?' became 'Harpow darpre yarpou?'

Nothing that didn't flow was allowed, so, if it were impossible to pronounce 'darp' you used 'arp'. In a word of three syllables like Anthony they said: 'Arpantharponarpy'.

My sister Gay always called her friend Pipsy O'Donovan 'Parpipsarpy'.

When the nuns heard them speaking this at the convent, they would say: 'How come you are so bad at Latin and French, and yet you can speak this unknown language?'

This sort of altered language was known as **Pig Latin**.

Dolls

- -

- A bird
- A chick
- A sort
- A good sort
- A real looker
- A young lass
- A floosie
- A dame
- The old girl
- Your old woman
- We were just bits of girls
- The girls

- A battleaxe
- A dragon
- An old boiler
- A bat
- An old bag
- The old duck
- The old dear
- The old biddie
- The missus
- The wife
- Duck
- Woman ('Don't harp, woman. Don't nag, woman.')
- Mother
- Snookums
- Snooks
- Dear heart (sarcastic)
- Some parents called each other 'Mum' and 'Dad'

Tickled pink

There were plenty of joyous things to say when things were **going along swimmingly**. Most joyful of all, perhaps, was **Whack oh the diddley-oh!** Followed closely by **everything is tickety-boo**, and **everything's hunky-dory**.

A boy would be described as **happy as a sand boy**, while a woman who was particularly happy was said to be **over the moon**, **walking on cloud nine**, **on top of the world**.

Men would describe something wonderful they received as **crackerjack**, saying: **It's a real doozey**. If his life was going particularly nicely, he would say he was **living the life of Riley**. If he or his family was praised up he might say he was **as proud as Punch**, or **as pleased as Punch**, or **no show without Punch**.

When a man was **tickled pink** at the sight of a woman he would report to his mates: '**My word she was a beaut**' or '**By crikey she was a good-looker**' or

'*My word she was good-oh.*'

On the other hand, if he was unimpressed, he would say: '***She was nothing to speak of.***'

Hooroo

Visitors would appear at the back door, look in at you, and say: **Anyone home**?

You would reply: **Come in if you're good-looking**.

And they would walk in, saying: **Greetings and salutations**.

Or, if they were worried about being in trouble for arriving disastrously late for dinner, they would say: **Will I throw my hat in first**? If they hadn't seen you **in donkey's ages** they'd say: **Long time no see!** If you were really glad to see them, you might add: **You're a sight for sore eyes**.

When a woman greeted her favourite niece, or a young girl she liked, she might say: **Hello petal**. If she had **her husband in tow**, it meant she had dragged her spouse out with her.

If a man let his wife walk in first he might joke: **Age before beauty** or **Lead on, McDuff**.

How are you doing?

I'm doing damn-fine-splendid.

Once a visitor was inside, the hostess might say: **Where are my manners? Please pull up a pew**, or even, **Pull up a perch**.

How are you battling?

Fair to middling, how's yourself?

What have you been doing?

I've been doing wonders eating cucumbers!

Where's Betty?

She went mad and they shot her.

What gives with Sheryl?

She gave me the cold shoulder (she had given him **short shrift**, or was unusually distant). **Not an edifying spectacle, I can tell you. Then blow me down if Sheryl didn't turn up just as I was leaving with Ned. I was lost for words I can tell you. Words failed me. Then she went on and on with this whole rigmarole about what had gone wrong. As sure as eggs are eggs she'll be back.**

Are you still in one piece, dearie?

I couldn't for the life of me think what to say. I could have stinking well fallen over.

When it was time to go you would thank your hostess for listening to your tale of woe. But she would **hear nothing of it**, saying, '**I knew you before you were nobody**.'

I'm gonna love you and leave you.

Give us a toot some time.

I'll pop in, in a couple of days' time, and say hooray.

Yes, if you're in the district just toot and come in. You know, the Egyptian Pharaoh.

To greet someone from a distance: **Yoo-hoo**! To grab someone up close for a conversation: **collar** or **buttonhole** them.

Ways of starting a conversation

- At any rate
- By the way
- By gee
- By jingo
- I'll tell you what
- I mean to say
- I had to laugh ...

Old Australian farewells

- Ta-ta
- Hooray (a Tasmanian man said that, when he was visiting friends in Queensland, they said '**hooray**' every time he left, and he thought they were all very glad he was going.)
- Have fun
- Ooroo
- Hooroo
- Tooraloo
- Toodle-loo
- Toodle pip
- Toodle off
- Cheerio
- Nice talking to you
- Talk to you later
- Bye for now
- We must get in touch down the track
- See you when the brumbies come to water — not for a long time.

Give us a hoy

- Yell out if you need me
- Give us a shout
- Give us a yell
- Just sing out
- Give us a hoy when you're finished
- Let's know when you're done
- I'd better make myself scarce
- Time I made a furrow
- I'm going to do a disappearing act
- I'd better skedaddle
- I'd better shoot through
- I'd better scoot
- I'd better make tracks
- I'd better ping off home
- I must be off
- Keep out of mischief
- Be good, and if you can't be good be careful. And if you can't be careful, don't name it after me. (In the days before reliable contraception.)
- Let's know when you're back in town

- Here's your hat, what's your hurry?
- He was off like a shot out of a gun
- I'm off. Like a bad smell
- I'm off. Like grandfather's pants
- I'm off. Like grandma's socks
- I'm off. Like a piece of cheese
- Yours to a cinder
- See you
- See you when I see you
- See you round like a record
- See you anon

- See you later
- See you in church
- Catch you later
- Back in a tick

Good night,
Sweet repose
Half the bed
But all the clothes.

RUDE SIGNS

Back in the 1950s you would stick your thumb up in the air to tell someone to **go to Hell**; it was definitely *not* a positive sign as it is today. Or you would **give them the forks**, showing them the back of your right hand with the forefinger and middle finger up. This was *not* a victory sign, *nor* a peace sign.

In Brisbane, the forks was called '**Two to the Valley**' because every tram in Brisbane went through Fortitude Valley, and you might put up two fingers when buying tickets from the conductor.

Now, as in the Hollywood pictures, most Australians use just the middle finger of either hand. In 2005 an Australian politician got mixed up between the old and the new in Federal Parliament when he gave the other side of the House 'the finger'. But he only showed his forefinger. Once upon a time this would not have caused any offence at all.

Jim's English lesson

Jim Egoroff, a Russian, arrived in Australia in 1950 aged nine and always spoke Russian at home. A few years ago, while overseas, Jim was asked to give an English lesson to a group of Russians who thought they knew English. Jim drew on his experience of learning to speak Australian English in the 1950s. He told them the following story and laughed uproariously because they couldn't understand a word of it.

His glad rags in a total shambles, his horse scratched, poorly shod Ted caught some dreaded lurgy in the clink and nearly snuffed it. He was real crook, so he asked to see a man of the cloth. Before he went downhill and gave up the ghost, he was a real spunk and could have parked his shoes under any girl's bed any day. And a half-decent wench could always afford to pay his parking fees. He could charm birds off trees, and he could tickle any lady's fancy — even if, occasionally, he might tickle the till in the café.

He said that before he was ready to kick the bucket, before he was dead to the world, he was going to try to extract some guts from the local pigs who framed him. 'They stitched me up good and proper,' Ted said. If he had his way, Ted would have them hung, drawn and quartered.

He said when the police caught him red-handed, 'My heart was in my mouth.' He swore black and blue that he didn't do it and told them they were talking a lot of bull, saying, 'Pull the other leg, it plays "Jingle Bells".'

Whilst Ted was out of circulation at Her Majesty's pleasure, his old lady dropped her bundle and hit the roof. She couldn't believe that after working around the clock, her niece — her own flesh and blood — could dob Ted in to the local constabulary and spill the beans about the hot gear stashed in Ted's pad.

In the district

'The district' was a bush term. You went **into town**, you never went **into the district**. You were **from the district**. All the towns or houses within easy travelling distance of your home were 'the district'. One of the most repeated phrases was: 'He went all round the district looking for ...' Whereas, in a city you would say you walked 'all over the suburb' or 'all over town' looking for …

District was a concept that was different for each speaker.

If it was a place that was especially cold in winter, you'd call it **Frog's Hollow**. You might say it was a **one-horse town** or a **two-pub town**. If you were talking about places nearby, you'd say they were in **this neck of the woods,** but you would say you hadn't seen Edith **around the traps** lately.

If someone moved into the district and joined the local clubs you'd say she **put down roots**. But if she used to live there years ago, she'd say she had come 'back to **my old stomping ground**' (or **stamping ground**).

If she had made a few mistakes in life, perhaps married the wrong man, or invested in the wrong deal, she'd say: 'I've been **up a few dry gullies** in my time.' Or, '**I've had as many ups and downs as a bride's nightie**.' But if she then announced she was leaving for some time, or to go a long way away, everyone would say: '**She's gonna go bush**.'

And if she left without telling anyone, they'd say: 'She just **up sticks** (or **up stumps**) and went.'

Chapter seven

MOTHER KNOWS BEST

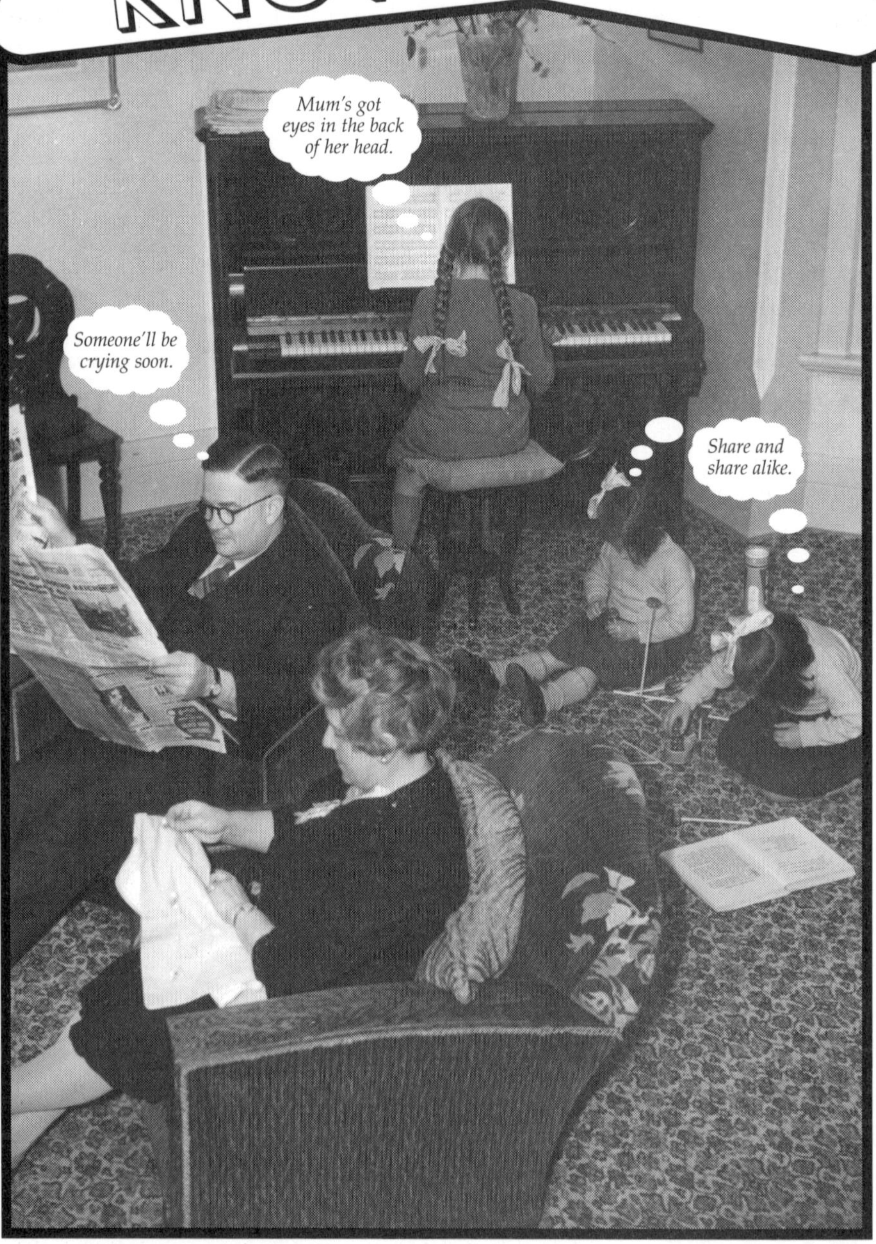

LOST FOR WORDS EPISODE 6:
Stop that Tomfoolery!

Parents didn't mince their words when it came to chastising their children. They meant business. They didn't want to be the child's best friend. They thought it was their duty to keep children in line, not to get down on the floor and play with them.

Lost for Words. The story of Bert and Grace and their trials and tribulations bringing up a young family after the War.

It was the weekend and the boys — Syd, Lex and Morris — had their cousins Ronnie and Reggie over to stay. While Grace was reading the newspaper in the dining room, the five boys were hanging about her chair, asking for treats.

'Boys,' Grace finally said. 'Will you stop buzzing around me like blowflies? You're making me dizzy. Reggie, you'll meet yourself coming back if you don't watch out. Have you got ants in your pants? Stop pestering! Why don't you go and play outside? Or, better still, go play down the creek and don't come back till after dark.'

But the kids had other ideas. They ran out into the yard. The games were getting rowdy, with the kids running up the front stairs, ringing the bell to be let in.

Bert and Grace would have none of this.

'Round the back!' yelled Bert without getting out of his chair next to the wireless. The back door was never locked.

So the kids began chasing each other up and down the back stairs, then running in through the back door, leaving it swinging open.

'Do you live in a tent?' yelled Grace from her chair. 'Shut the door! Put a bit of wood in the hole!'

Next thing the children had covered all the windows in the boys' bedroom to play Dark Room.

'Cut the cackle! Pipe down!' yelled Grace. But the kids' games were growing rougher and noisier. Now it was a pillow-fight.

'Someone will be crying soon!' warned Bert without looking up from his book. And he was always right.

Eventually, Ronnie ran bawling to his Aunty Grace, whingeing that he'd been poked in the eye.

'Oh, Ronnie, you're like a stuck record,' Grace said. 'Turn off the waterworks. I'll come in directly and sort it out. Just as soon as you stop snivelling and moaning.'

So she stormed into the bedroom.

'Stop that tomfoolery!' she shouted at the boys. 'Your father told you this would all end in tears, but you wouldn't listen, would you.'

The children were silenced.

'You've all been acting the goat, fighting like Kilkenny cats. Now you've been warned, no monkey business. Settle down. Show some couth, Syd, or you'll come to a sticky end. Remember, I've got eyes in the back of my head.'

Grace returned to the dining room, but soon the racket started again.

So Grace came back, folding the newspaper in her hands.

'It's bedlam in here!' she raged. 'I've told you till I'm blue in the face. If I've told you once, I've told you a thousand times. Stop mucking up! Stop those shenanigans!'

Morris, the oldest, spoke up: 'Sorry, Mum, it won't happen again.'

For a while the house was quiet, but soon a few giggles and pushes turned into a riot with five screaming boys fighting it out.

Now Grace was really on the warpath.

'Give you kids an inch and you'll take a mile,' she declared at the door. 'Who's making all the racket? Morris, you're carrying on like the wild man from Borneo; I expect better from you. Act your age.'

That shut Morris up.

'Lex, drop those bows and arrows. You'll put someone's eye out.'

'But, Mum, that's not fair ...'

'Neither is the inside of a Jersey cow. You sound like a fishwife.'

That shut Lex up, even though he had never seen a fishwife.

'Syd, put Reggie down, and give him back his tomahawk. Share and share alike. Do what you're told, when you're told.'

'But, Mum, Reggie cheated! He ...'

'Speak when you're spoken to. You're behaving just like your father.'

That shut Syd up.

'Good,' said Grace. 'Now, Ronnie and Reggie, one more word out of you and you'll be sent packing. And, kids, your father's ropeable. He's liable to fly off the handle, and you know when he does, he's a lot more dangerous than a tomahawk.'

But the dire warnings failed to work.

So finally Bert appeared at the doorway, with his reading glasses pushed up on his forehead, book in hand. That's when the kids knew they were dead meat, cactus.

'Are you kids looking for a hiding? Because you're going the right way about it.'

'But Morris had us in stitches, Uncle Bert,' said Ronnie. 'I cacked myself. I nearly died laughing!'

'Don't be cheeky.'

'Yes, Dad, we haven't broken anything,' added Morris.

'You're living on borrowed time.'

'Then how long have I got?'

'You're in for a rude awakening, m'boy,' said Bert.

'But, Dad, you said we shouldn't keep running up the front stairs,' said Lex.

'You're sailing close to the wind.'

'We were only doing what you told us to,' said Reggie.

'Don't give lip.'

'But Mum said we weren't allowed to play in the dining room, so we had to play in here,' said Syd.

'Don't answer back, you impudent pup, or I'll knock you into the middle of next week.'

> 'Good, then I won't have to go to school *this* week.'
>
> Bert shrugged his shoulders, and turned to Grace, laughing: 'I'm lost for words.'

Remedies

Mothers were home doctors with plenty of good advice.

Wear a **singlet** to prevent chest infections.

Always have an **ironed handkerchief** in your pocket.

Don't drink milk when you've got a cold, because it '**creates phlegm**'.

Better out than in — if a child was chesty and coughing up pleghm.

Bed rest is best.

Stay out of **the night air** or you'll get **chesty** and **catch your death**. Once the sun set, it was considered that the cold change was bad for you and could even set back **a recovering convalescent**. For some reason, you could be freezing cold in the middle of a winter's day and no one noticed, but if you went out after dark when it was even slightly chilly, everyone warned: 'You'd better **rug up**.' If you already had a sniffle, mothers would warn it would **freshen up your cold**.

ALL BETTER

Whenever Mother produced one of her remedies she would always give you confidence by saying: '**This will do you the world of good**.' Or, if it was something she couldn't fix, she'd say: '**You'll grow out of it**.' Or, '**You're not sick, you're only thirsty**.' Or, '**I'll have to jolly you along**.'

When you wouldn't take your medicine your mother would say, '**Don't be a sook**.'

When you were sick in bed, your mother would ask, rhetorically, '**What are we going to do with you, you silly sausage? Put you in a box, tie it with a ribbon, and throw it in the deep blue sea**?'

For some reason, this made you feel much better.

If you had **a buster** on your bike and you were about to burst into tears, your mother would grab your hands and lift you up briskly while saying, '**Upsadaisy! Whoopsydoo! I'll kiss it better**' in a cheerful no-nonsense manner, and it would, nine times out of ten, distract you long enough to halt the tears.

But the absolute best thing your mother could say when you were sick or crying was '**There, there**'. This was pre-antibiotic but it worked almost as well. Like when she put a bandage on and always said: '**All better**.'

HOME REMEDIES

Put a cut onion in the room where there's measles.

If you burnt your finger, Dr Mum told you to put your finger on your earlobe, to take the heat out of it. Or she put butter on the burn.

For sunburn: rub with a cut tomato, or dab with cold tea. No one had heard of the dangers of skin cancer, so kids would enjoy peeling off their dead brown skin (killed by the sun's UV rays), revealing the new pink skin underneath.

A sore throat? A drop of kerosene on a spoonful of sugar. **Open wide!**

To make clothes whiter, your mother would dip a **blue-bag** into the water. Such a bag was put on bee and wasp stings to give relief.

For **nits** (head lice) your mother would spread a sheet of white butcher's paper on the kitchen table. You leaned over this while she combed your hair with a double-sided fine-toothed comb to dislodge the nits which she would then crush with her fingers.

Cures for hiccups:

- Fill a glass with water. Bend upside down, then try to drink.
- Breathe into a paper bag with your head tilted down.
- Burst a paper bag behind the hiccuper's head to give them a fright.

When in doubt, apply a poultice. A **poultice** was a handful of mush, hot or cold, that mothers made up from kitchen ingredients and applied to your skin with a bandage.

Chest complaint or pleurisy? Apply a mustard poultice to the front of the chest and lie still.

An infected splinter in your hand? Apply a poultice made of steaming-hot bread onto the hand to draw the splinter out through your skin.

Splinters were serious.

If you had a splinter in your foot, your mother would order you to **go like a horse** and you would stand and bend your leg up backwards. Then she would inspect the sole of your foot, just the way a blacksmith would inspect the shoe on a horse. When she found the splinter, she sterilised a needle in the flame of a match and dug deep to get it out, always joking that she had 'a miner's licence'.

Mothers never minded causing pain if it made you better.

With splinters, Mum was always on the lookout for **a red streak**. A red streak meant danger. If the splinter became infected, a visible red streak would begin to head up your leg or arm. And it was always said that if it reached your heart you'd die.

Crushed brown sugar was applied for **proud flesh** (when a wound or ulcer developed a thick, bright red layer).

Metho was applied to a blister.

Nervous mothers were always on the lookout for something called **night starvation**. No one had ever heard of night starvation until someone invented a product to cure it. According to the wireless advertisments, it was a serious problem if you woke up hungry in bed. The only solution was to buy Horlicks powder, which you mixed into a drink. Cynical folk would say as a joke: 'I used to fear night starvation. But not anymore, now I take Horlicks!'

Brandy would give kids a good night's sleep at home.

Brown paper and vinegar on the forehead for headache.

If you had to have an aspirin Mum would crush it and mix in honey or sugar to make it more palatable. But usually only adults took headache powders. **Vegenan** was a strong one for adults.

For earache, a teaspoon of oil would be warmed with a match, and then a little poured soothingly into your sore ear. Or hydrogen peroxide would be dropped in, using a **rubber dropper**. It bubbled up and tickled, relieving the pain. But it had to be the correct strength.

Vegemite on dry toast for an upset tummy. (Vegemite in hot water made a cheap nourishing drink, similar to Bonox or Bovril.)

Grated apple for both constipation and the runs.

If you had just got home from hospital you would be put on **the invalid diet**, which seemed to consist only of hot clear soup and barley water.

Half the advertisements in magazines were for cures for constipation, which was considered to be a terrible affliction. To prevent it, some mothers encouraged their kids to pick the long black beans off the cascara tree. The children would then open up the beans and gladly eat the sweet, sticky black interior. If the cascara bean didn't work, there were two choices your mother offered, neither enticing: castor oil, or an **enema** on the kitchen table.

A dessertspoon of castor oil was so foul you couldn't swallow it without almost vomiting, so it was also used by mothers as a threat or punishment.

There were different recipes for **enemas** depending on whether it was for worms or for constipation: soap and water, olive oil, or a liquid made from pouring hot water on senna leaves. Nowadays the procedure is called colonic irrigation. At any hour of the night, your mother would appear with a torch to search your bum for worms. If you had any, she'd iron your pyjama pants to kill any eggs.

LIES YOUR MOTHER TOLD YOU

If you asked your mother what she'd been doing all day, she might reply: '**I've been to Timbuktu and back**.'

- The bogeyman will get you if you don't hop back into bed.
- Good things come to those who wait.
- Cheats never prosper.
- Crime doesn't pay.
- If glass isn't removed from a wound, it will travel to an artery and slice it in half.
- If you stand on a needle, it will travel to your heart and kill you.
- Let's see what I've got in my little bag of tricks, and we'll fix up your problem in a trice.
- If you don't eat your crusts, you won't get curly hair.

Chapter eight

DOMESTIC SCIENCE

LOST FOR WORDS EPISODE 7:
Sunday baked dinner

In past years when many people worked a half-day on Saturday, families got together for lunch on Sunday. There was a tradition of a hot baked meal, whatever the season. Perhaps the food cooked while everyone went off to church. But even so, in summer they returned to a very hot kitchen.

Lost for Words. **The story of Bert and Grace and their trials and tribulations bringing up a young family after the War.**

On this Sunday, Bert and Grace and their children were expecting Aunty Myrtle and Uncle Cyril at noon for Sunday baked dinner.
'You kids set the table, and don't forget the bread-and-butter plates,' said Grace. 'And don't go spilling any condiments on my best double damask.'

Just then, a blowfly came buzzing into the kitchen.

Grace, who had tied on an apron over her floral house dress, put down the junket tablets. 'I know what this means,' she said to nobody in particular. 'We're going to get an unexpected visitor. I wonder who it will be? That nice Mr Dawson, or maybe Kevin? It's always a treat when a *do-drop-in* drops in.'

The children — little Morris, little Syd, little Lex, little Delma and little Ima — were hanging about the kitchen table. Little Lex was shelling peas.

'Mum, can I lick the bowl?' asked little Morris.

'If I've told you once, I've told you a thousand times, Morris, it's *"may* I lick the bowl", and, no you may not. I must have the patience of Job. Now get out from under my feet. Run down and get me some mint from under the tap. And no dawdling.'

As he scooted out the back door, little Morris bumped into Uncle Cyril and Aunty Myrtle walking in.

'Anyone home?' said Cyril.

'Come in if you're good-looking,' Grace called back.

They exchanged greetings.

'I've brought you the honeymoon tart,' said Cyril, winking. He glanced about and spied the steaming hot chook covered with strips of fat bacon: 'Curl the mo! Look at the size of that chook. If that isn't the biggest chook I've ever seen, I'll give a sucking-pig to the Royal Hospital!'

'Yes,' said Grace. 'It's been fed on Farex. It's so big I had to break the breastbone to fit it into the oven. I've been basting it every eight minutes, like you told me, Myrtle.'

'It looks scrumptious,' said Myrtle. 'I've been feeling a bit peckish all morning. I've actually brought tapioca pudding.'

'Goody goody gumdrops,' said little Syd to his sister, little Delma, who replied 'Yummy, yummy, chookie's bummy.'

Grace frowned at her daughter, and turned to her sister-in-law. 'Please excuse pigs without tails, Myrtle,' she said. 'Tapioca! Thank you so much. That'll go down a treat. We're all set. I'm making junket, and there's flummery, and ice-cream.'

'Ice-cream?' yelled little Ima. 'You scream, I scream, we all scream for ice-cream!'

'Your nippers are in high spirits today,' said Cyril. 'They're up to a few high jinks, I'll be bound. They need to let off steam, have a bit of a lark.'

'And, Aunty Myrtle, Mum tried to make a blowaway sponge,' piped up little Delma.

'Thank you very much, balsam seed,' said Grace. 'Any other family secrets you need to get off your chest? Myrtle, it didn't rise, so it's not fit for General Exhibition.'

Grace's husband Bert walked in from the veranda.

'Pull up a pew, Cyril,' he said, 'and take the weight off your feet, Myrtle.'

'Where should I sit?' asked Myrtle.

'Wherever your bum will fit,' said Bert. 'Grace, the worms are biting. And I'm so parched I could drink through an Afghan's nightie.' Then he picked up little Ima in his arms. 'Now, what's eating you, princess?'

'I can't see what's for din-dins,' she replied.

Bert lifted her further up.

'Oh no! Not the chicken!' said little Ima.

Grace, still at the hot stove making the gravy in the baking dish, was not amused. 'And what would you prefer? Lark's tongues?'

'Yes please.'

'Don't be cheeky, Ima, or you'll taste my stick. We can only afford chicken twice a year, and I had to dress this one myself, so you'll consider yourself lucky.'

'Is it wearing a dress, Mum?' asked little Ima.

'No, I mean I had to kill and draw and pluck and truss and stuff this one myself. I've made a sauce from the giblets, Myrtle, using your recipe.'

'What are the giblets, Mum?' asked little Ima.

'That's the heart, the liver and the gizzard,' replied Grace. 'Now, Ima, wipe that look off your face or the wind will change and you'll be stuck with it. Get your clodhoppers off that chair, and give your aunty some room.'

Just then, Bert's old snooker mate, Kevin, came stomping up the back stairs carrying a small biscuit tin.

'Look who's just bobbed up! A blow-in!' exclaimed Grace, tucking her petticoat strap back under the sleeve of her dress.

'Shut the doors, they're coming in the windows!' said Myrtle.

'Shut the windows, they're coming in the doors!' added little Morris.

'Look what the cat dragged in!' said Bert. 'Kevin, I thought you were busy today with *a certain someone*. Come in, pull up a stump, but don't take it too far!'

'It's like old home week,' said Cyril.

'Ta muchly, Bert,' said Kevin. 'G'day, Cyril, Myrtle, champs. Nice to see you, Gracie. How are those lovely sisters of yours?'

'They're all fighting fit, thanks, Kevin. Nice of you to inquire.'

Kevin opened up the biscuit tin. 'Gracie, you wanted to see a picture of my family.'

All the kids gathered round.

'None of us are camera-shy,' said Kevin. 'That's me on the left.'

Little Morris said: 'Gee, Uncle Kevin, this is you? You look different.'

'This was taken when I was much older,' Kevin said, blushing.

'Would you like to join us for a bite?' Grace asked Kevin.

'Well, this is a surprise,' Kevin said, blushing again. 'I'm lost for words. Thanks, Gracie, I don't mean to intrude, I could use a feed but. My stomach feels like my throat's been cut. As I always say to my sister-in-law at home, "Call me anything, as long as it's not late for tea".'

'Ah! A man after my own heart,' said Grace. 'I like a man with a healthy appetite. Delma, set another place for Kevin, and remember, he's a mollydooker, so put his knife on the left. I'll dish up. Kevin is last in, so he's first served and you know what they say: *First in, best dressed*. Do you prefer breast, wing or thigh, Kevin?'

'Oh, Gracie,' said Kevin. 'I'll be happy with a drumstick. I'm so hungry I could eat a horse and chase the rider.'

'The nearer the bone, the sweeter the meat,' added Cyril.

'Mum, I want the pope's nose,' little Syd called out, from a stool at the end of the long table.

'In my family, we always call it the parson's nose,' said Kevin.

'I like that part the best,' said little Syd.

'Little Syd!' warned Grace. 'The rule is *FHB*. That means *Family Hold Back*. Now, we don't stand on ceremony around here, so if it can fly you're allowed to pick it up with your fingers. But first, will you say grace for us, Kevin?'

Kevin bowed his head, and all followed suit.

'Bless us, Oh Lord, and these, thy gifts, which of thy bounty we are about to receive, through Christ Our Lord. Amen.'

'Two four six eight, bog in, don't wait,' added Bert.

'Now, Myrtle,' said Grace, taking off her apron. 'I am sorry you've been served last.'

'I had to wait to be born,' replied Myrtle.

Sunday baked dinner got underway, everyone tucking in and talking at once.

'Ah!' said Grace, looking about. 'I love a full table.'

Little Ima couldn't get a word in edgewise, so she stood on her chair and yelled. Then one of her brothers, little Lex, stood on his chair and yelled over the top of everyone. 'Silence in the court, the monkey wants to talk!'

Little Ima piped up, 'I want to know ...'

But she was drowned out by the rest of the kids chanting, 'The first one to talk is a monkey!'

'I don't want to stifle social intercourse, but ...' said Kevin, and all the kids shouted, 'You're the monkey, Uncle Kevin!'

'Don't mind the peanut gallery, Kevin,' said Bert.

'Feet off the chairs, elbows off the table!' said Grace to the children.

🐾

'Anyone for seconds?' asked Grace. 'There's one potato going begging. Now don't be bashful, who wants to be the old maid? Kevin? I'm sure you won't be an old maid. Myrtle?'

'Not for me, Grace, thank you,' said Aunty Myrtle putting down her cloth napkin. 'I've had elegant sufficiency, as they say in the classics.'

'I've had my whack,' said Bert. 'Save it for Ron — later on.'

While little Syd started on his third helping, little Lex wouldn't eat his chokoes and white sauce, and little Ima wouldn't eat her cauliflower and white sauce. Grace tried to encourage them: 'Eat up, kids, look how the visitors are eating!' This comment stopped Kevin, with a fork of sweet potato midair.

'Come on, princess,' Bert said to little Ima. 'Think of the starving millions in China. Eat up your carrots, they're good for your eyesight. Have you ever seen a rabbit with glasses?' Bert took a dim view of his kids leaving food on their plates. 'The trouble with you animals is you're all too well fed. Your eyes are bigger than your bellies.'

'I'm full up to pussy's bow, Dad,' said little Ima, trying to get out from under.

'I'm chockers,' said little Lex.

'I've got a stomach on me like a poisoned pup,' said little Morris.

'I'll bust if I eat any more,' said little Delma.

'You mean burst, dear,' said Myrtle. 'A woman has a bust, but balloons burst.'

'Those kids are talking for the sake of talking,' said Grace.

Then little Syd leapt up and began pulling apart the two halves of the fresh loaf of bread, exposing the soft, moist heart.

Grace noticed. 'Ah, the kissing crust. That's one temptation I can't resist.'

Bert noticed. 'Syd, you'll eat us out of house and home one day. But while you're up, fetch another tumbler. Kevin looks like he needs a drink, he's red as a beetroot.'

Little Syd brought the glass to the table, then went back to his bread, sawing off an enormously thick slice.

This time little Morris noticed: 'Look at the garbage guts!' he yelled. 'Stop hoeing into it and leave some for us, you greedy pig! Dad, look at the doorstop Syd has cut for himself!'

Little Syd was now buttering it.

Myrtle had noticed too. 'That child must have worms.'

Bert didn't miss it either. 'Go easy on the butter, boy, it's two-and-six a pound.'

'But I'm still famished!' replied little Syd, licking his chops.

'Well don't guts yourself, son. You'll finish up with a guts-ache,' replied his father.

'But, Dad, Mum says you need three square meals a day to grow up big and strong: breakfast, dinner *and* tea.'

'Butter wouldn't melt in his mouth!' said Cyril. 'He must have a cast-iron stomach. I'd keep feeding that fang merchant until you bust the bugger.'

'Language, Cyril,' cautioned Myrtle. 'And it's burst, not bust.' Then Myrtle turned to Grace for sympathy, adding, 'Can't take him anywhere.'

Little Morris began giggling until Cyril said, 'You'd laugh if a pudding crawled.'

'The greedyguts,' said Bert. 'He's a good nosher, is Syd, he's good on the tooth. But one day he'll have to learn to do without.'

'Excuse me for speaking while you're interrupting,' said Cyril. 'But I'd rather keep little Syd for a week than a fortnight.'

Little Ima stood up on her chair yet again and, clasping her hands together in front, recited: 'Oh! what a bird is the peli*can*; his beak holds more than his belly can.'

Grace was happy that none of the adults had left a skerrick on their plates. 'Now, kids,' she announced, 'clear the table and I'll boil the billy. Who's going to be my washer-upper-er? Little Delma, that plate is a sunbeam, you can put it straight back in the sideboard.'

'I'm full as a goog,' said blow-in Kevin, rubbing his stomach guiltily with his right hand. 'By Jove, Bert, your Gracie certainly keeps a good table.' Then he stood up. 'I'll wash up for you, Gracie. Here I come.'

Making do

Compared with today, Australia was a very poor country after World War II — populated by a people who had lived through the horrors of the **Great Depression** or who were being raised by parents who had. Thus parents constantly warned their children: '**Be frugal. You never know where your next penny's coming from**.' So everyone was very careful with money as they struggled to **keep their head above water**. There was a tailor in Toowoomba who, during the Depression, said times were so tough, that 'even those who *don't* pay, don't buy suits any more'.

Australians became accustomed to **making do** with what they had, and **going without**. Parents would say to children who wanted something: '**You'll have to learn to do without**.' Or, if they left food on their plate: '**You're eyes are bigger than you're stomach**.'

Because people had to be frugal there were many recipes for imitation meals. Such food was prefaced with the word **mock**. There was:

- 🖝 **mock crab**: cheese, Worcestershire sauce, mustard and tomato sauce mixed into a sandwich paste;

- **mock chicken**: minced tripe (from the stomach of an ox) with herbs in a white sauce, popped into vol-au-vents;
- **mock duck**: rump or bladebone steak rolled in a mixture of breadcrumbs and butter, then baked;
- **mock goose**: alternate layers of lamb's fry and potato and onions, baked.

There were even **mock meal** recipes for the times when you couldn't afford the cheapest offal:

- **mock brains**: rissoles made from leftover porridge, beaten egg, and onion;
- **mock tripe**: onions and butter boiled in milk and thickened with flour.

Mock desserts included:

- **mock maple syrup**: honey, golden syrup, cinnamon, lemon essence;
- **mock cream**: milk, cornflour, butter, sugar;
- **mock ginger**: vegetable marrow, sugar, ginger powder, lemons;
- **mock raspberry jam**: tomatoes, sugar, raspberry essence, lemon juice, orris-root powder (from the root of an iris) and cochineal;
- **mock pears**: sweetened, boiled choko. Everybody grew a choko vine over the dunny or the back fence. It produced bountiful crops of pear-shaped chokoes, hence **chokoes and white sauce** and **mock pears with custard**. Chokoes were boiled whole, then split lengthwise, and the seeds removed. Your mother might say chokoes had a delicate flavour. They were almost tasteless, but not tasteless enough.

White sauce was invented to cover up the taste, appearance and name of affordable, vile foods. It was particularly useful if the cook wanted to offer up **tripe, sheep brains, choko** or **cauliflower**.

But there were some dishes that could not be disguised and just had to be suffered. For example:

- Lamb's tongue
- Lamb's fry: the liver of a one-year-old sheep
- Pressed tongue: a cold dish using a flap of mutton and six sheep tongues
- Sheep's heart
- Hogget: meat from a young sheep
- Mutton: meat from a mature sheep
- Mutton knuckles and neck chop pie
- Stewed knuckle of veal
- Mutton flap and kidney casserole
- Calf liver
- Kidneys: pig's, calf's or lamb's
- Ox tail, heart or cheek
- Rabbit
- Pig's head or trotters.

IT MIGHT COME IN HANDY

The general rule was that you didn't throw anything out. The rule was recycle, reuse and repair. As in Dickens's London, anything that was broken or worn out was still valued.

Because so many things around the house needed repair, fathers would say: '**The house owner's lot is not a happy one**.'

As an adult put an item aside, he or she invariably said: '**It might come in handy**.' And when they needed it years later they'd say: '**This is just the doll's eye!**' Or, '**That will fill the bill**.'

Bits and pieces were needed for when something went **on the blink** (which was anything that stopped working: car, stove, cistern).

Everything came in a **hessian bag**, a pine **crate** or **brown paper**. There was no K-Mart or Bunnings or Crazy Clarks or McDonald's. Austerity was the key, so there were several rules, called **economies**, which were basic habits, even among people who could afford waste.

1. Always switch off the light when you leave the room. (Houses were built with one ceiling light and one power point per room.)

2. Use a pressure cooker to save power. Pressure cookers were everywhere in the 1950s because food cooked much faster under pressure. There was a pressure valve on the top, which popped and rattled madly as steam poured out when the pressure was too great (preventing an explosion). Most recipes were designed to save money, so the less power you used, the better.

3. Turn the stove off before items are cooked, to use the residual heat.

4. Save all leftovers and fry them up for **bubble-and-squeak**.

Whenever you went to Grandad's place, he would say: 'You can have bread and butter, or bread and honey, but not all three.'

HELD TOGETHER BY A PIECE OF STRING

A hole in a sock was called a **spud**, perhaps because the knob of a heel poking out of the sock looked like a potato. You couldn't wear a sock with spuds, because the friction on the exposed skin would create a blister or callus. Men and women **darned** socks to fill in these holes, and it was a fine art not to create a hard lump of wool which would rub anyway.

To save money, nearly everybody resoled and reheeled their own shoes, or took them to the **bootmaker** in the local shopping strip. If hand-me-down school shoes were too big for a child, a mother would say, '**You'll grow into them**' and push in wads of paper to keep the toes from turning up. If the family was particularly poor, they would cut an outline of the shoe from cardboard and slot that into the shoe, replacing it every couple of days, to save the cost of a new sole, or, worse, the cost of new shoes. A reader of *Over the Top With Jim* wrote to tell me of the little boy in her class who came to school wearing, in place of shoelaces, the string from Sunday's roast.

Another would come to school with his **hand-me-down** shorts held up by a length of **string**. Cruel kids might nickname a boy '**patch pants**' if his mother made him wear repaired clothes to school. It happened to me.

Eat up

- -

The main meal at night, **tea**, was generally meat and three veg. Meat was usually: beef or pork sausages, lamb or pork chops, hogget, mutton, steak, or mince.

The meal in the middle of the day was **dinner**.

A Sunday roast or baked dinner could be a joint, a shoulder or leg of mutton accompanied by roasted potato, pumpkin, sweet potato and onion, and perhaps Yorkshire pudding. The vegetables would be baked with the joint in the baking dish, so they absorbed as much animal fat as possible. The roast would be basted in the fat every eight minutes. Next day you would have a cold joint.

Dripping was the fat left in the dish after cooking meat. You could buy anodised aluminium tins with a Bakelite handle and the word DRIPPING embossed on the side for storing this fat. People ate **bread and dripping** with salt and pepper as a tasty meal. Mothers also reused the dripping to fry the next meal, if they had run out of **Supafry**. The **veg** part of **meat and three veg** were any three of the following, boiled: beans, peas, cauliflower or cabbage; mashed potato or pumpkin. No one had heard of broccoli or aubergine.

Most home cooks in the 1950s had a strange set of aluminium cooking pots: three triangular pots with a catch on the outside where the handle should be, with triangular lids and little aluminium baskets fitted inside. Put together, they made a circle that fitted on top of the hotplate. The peas and beans might be boiled in one (with bicarb to make the peas a vivid green), potatoes in the second, and pumpkin in the third. Potato and pumpkin would be mashed with butter, milk and salt. The cook had a single handle which slotted into the side of each pot to move it on and off the stove.

It was one kid's job to pick the mint from under the tank stand tap. This went into the mashed potatoes and the peas. Kids were also given the job of **shelling the peas** because it was time-consuming but simple. Thus the saying: 'It's as easy as shelling peas.' Last year I took some fresh peas still in their pods to a fiftieth-birthday barbeque. When I put them on the table the two youths in their early twenties had no idea what they were. They hadn't realised that peas came in a pod, having only ever seen tinned or frozen peas.

A salad meant only one combination: lettuce, cucumber, tomato, tinned pineapple and tinned beetroot.

(Apart from coloured aluminium, kitchen canisters could be made of Haxbyware, a sort of hard plastic, often in cream with red lids. Tumblers might be Nallyware, precursor of Bakelite, and most people had a silver-like patterned tea tray of Ranleighware.)

Other meals were homemade meat pie with savoury dumplings, chow mein, spaghetti bolognaise or a tin of camp pie.

Hamburgers were rare. If you wanted a quick, cheap lunch you bought a **meat pie**, a **pasty** (like a pie with meat and vegetables), an **apple pie**, or a **custard pie** (called **dirt pies** because of the nutmeg sprinkled over the top).

Breakfast was toast and eggs, or a jaffle, or porridge, or packet cereal.

No one had ever heard of muesli.

Names for food were:

- **Tucker**
- **Chow** — a meal, or food from a cheap Chinese restaurant
- **Grub** — your lunch
- **Crib** — the lunch you took to work or school.

It was **pudding** after tea, not **dessert**. Favourites were tapioca pudding, sago pudding, bread and butter pudding, honeymoon tart and lemon delicious. The most common was **junket**, made from junket tablets — an ultra-smooth white delicious cold dish — and **jelly** made from Jellex jelly crystals. The most popular was red jelly, but I loved the rarer green.

There were also the milk desserts: **blancmange** which kids liked to call **blank-mange**, and the gelatine-based **flummery**. A favourite was **rice pudding with nutmeg** — the major reason for having rice in the pantry, as rice was rarely served with a main meal.

Meals were always followed by a cup of tea. Some people poured the tea into their saucer to cool it, and then drank from the saucer.

That wasn't a good cup of tea!

No, it wasn't a cup of tea's hind leg!

Free milk — all schoolchildren, at least in Queensland, were provided with a daily ration of a third of a pint of ***free milk*** to ensure they started the day right. Mothers taught their children: ***Milk is a food***.

CAKES

A ***cream bun*** was very much sought after by kids. The buns were cut across the top and filled with whipped cream, then covered in icing sugar with a dob of blood-red raspberry jam on top. If you were walking around eating one, an adult would be sure to say: '***Where did you get the sore hand***?'

Sponges were the most popular cake; mostly round, they also came in heart shapes. A sponge covered with passionfruit icing was best. Women loved to try to make a ***blowaway sponge*** because it was so light and fluffy.

Kids' birthdays always featured ***rainbow cake*** — three layers of chocolate, vanilla and strawberry, iced over with soft coconut icing.

Sand cakes were shaped like a child's sandcastle with a hole in the middle. Their very fine texture was covered with thin white icing, which cracked when cut.

Every school fete and cake shop sold **lamingtons**. Fetes also sold **chocolate crackles**, made with Copha, cocoa and Rice Bubbles.

Other popular cakes were **napoleons, meringues, custard slices, butterfly cakes, patty cakes, jam tarts, fruit mince tarts, chester cakes** and **rock cakes**. Many adults preferred to buy a pound of **fruit cake**: either **genoa** or **sultana**.

FAMILY LORE

- **A bought sponge is a successful sponge**. Buying a cake took the worry out of entertaining.
- **Neighbourly cake** — a woman who lived next to my friend Ken Fletcher's home at Annerley in Brisbane remembered her mum passing a cake through her lounge-room window into the Fletchers' lounge-room window next door, balanced on a straw broom.
- **On the nose** — if the leftover chicken has gone off, it is **a bit on the nose** or it **stinks to high heaven**. It **pongs**, it **honks**.
- The meat went **rank** and the butter went **rancid**.
- If someone is after **a double bunger** they have already eaten at home, and then they turn up at someone else's dinnertime, hoping to be invited to stay.
- **Swing the cat** — after rinsing the leaves, you wrap them in a fresh tea towel, and then swing it around to remove most of the water by centrifugal force.
- **Shanghai surprise** — every mother had a never-fail dish she could whip up on a lazy Sunday night. Thus, one mother's recipe for when she didn't feel up to cooking was 'Shanghai surprise' — fried-up leftovers with rice. The kids loved it so much that in later years, they would ask: 'Mum, can we have Shanghai surprise tonight?'
- **Asparagus mornay** — another Sunday-night triumph was a dish made up of tinned asparagus with slices of boiled egg, grated cheese and a white sauce made with the asparagus juice, all on a bed of white rice.

- **Beggar's Banquet** — whatever's left in the fridge.
- **Damper** — My grandpa Jack Duncan would make **damper** in the ashes of the fire in our garden. We smothered the hot crusty loaves with honey when they came out of the ashes.
- **Milk** in the 1950s came in a glass bottle with a cardboard lid, or, later, a foil lid. Every night, you put the empty milk bottles in a little wire or plastic basket out on the doorstep so the milkman could take them away and replace them with full bottles in the early hours of the morning. Back then, there was only one type of milk — full cream — so it always had a one-inch layer of cream at the top of the bottle, which kids fought over.
- **Bread —** shops and bakeries didn't sell or deliver sliced bread. You had to go to all the trouble of cutting it yourself, whether it was Promax, Vienna or ordinary bread, brown or white, half or full loaf. When sliced bread became available, it became a benchmark for every new product: **that's the best thing since sliced bread**.
- **This'll stick to your ribs** — a sustaining meal
- Put in **a shade more sugar**
- Add **just a dash more salt**
- **Hogged out** — ate too much
- **A little bit of what you fancy does you good** — it's healthy not to get too obsessive about eating

Bibs and bobs

- -

The home of the 1950s had a few items which just don't exist any more.

- **Soap-saver** — a little wire basket on a handle into which you placed a cake of soap. You swished this around in the kitchen sink and, depending on the softness of the water, it created soap bubbles in which the family could wash the dishes.
- **Flypaper** — a cardboard cylinder which your father uncurled and hung from the kitchen ceiling, right above the table. It looked wet and was always a yucky milky-brown colour. It was so incredibly sticky that a fly

would only have to touch it with a wing or a foot to be caught; hence, if you were in trouble with the law, you had **one foot on the flypaper**. The flies would gradually die of starvation, leaving a revolting display of dead, dying and decomposing flies hanging above you at teatime, like a ghastly Christmas decoration. When the flypaper was so full of flies that no other fly could find anywhere to land, you threw the lot in the bin and unfurled a fresh one.

- *Flyspray* — those who were too squeamish to use flypaper used a hand pump (like a bike pump) with a tin can attached underneath, which you filled with flyspray from a glass bottle. As you vigorously pulled and pushed the wooden pump handle, a fine mist of insect killer gradually spouted out the top of the can into the air. After you had pumped for a while, the spray continued to emit itself for some time as if by magic.

- *Tank key* — water was so valuable that you needed the steel tank key to turn on someone's rainwater tank. This prevented children from wasting water. In one family, instead of a key to the house, the children were given their own tank key upon turning twenty-one.

- *Hatpins* — every woman had at least one **hatbox** under the bed full of hats, and a selection of decorated **hatpins** on the duchess. They were like jewellery and part of being **all dressed up**. They also kept the hat on in a breeze.

- *Wristwatch* — people chose a wristwatch depending on how many **jewels** it had. Seventeen was considered about normal. The number of jewels might be written in gold on the face. But you never saw these jewels because they were inside the watch. Hopefully. The more jewels, the more expensive the watch.

An ordinary watch cost nearly the basic wage in the early 1950s, so they were very special and sought after. Fathers kept theirs on top of the lowboy. Kids loved to imagine they owned a watch, so if you asked a kid the time, she'd look at her wrist and say: '**Two hairs past a freckle**.'

You had to wind a wristwatch once or twice a day.

Then came the movement-powered, so-called self-winding watch. Then the battery watch. Then the battery digital watch.

In the pre-digital 1960s, the word 'analogue' was never used for a watchface. There was no need for a descriptive word because there was only one type of watchface. When digital clocks first arrived in Australia no one knew what to call them. At first, people called them **direct-reading clocks**.

Mattresses — came with various fillings, such as:

- **Coir** — the coarse, curled brown fibre from the outside of coconuts. The fibres gradually pushed their way out through the ticking and stuck into you all night. No matter how many you pulled out and threw away, more would appear just to annoy you.
- **Horsehair** — more comfortable, but more expensive.
- **Kapok** — a soft down that comes from trees, like cotton wool balls, but too soft for a good night's sleep. You sank right into it.

- **Ashtray** — lounge rooms always, *but always,* contained an ashtray because almost every man smoked a pipe, or **tailor-made cigarettes** ('Time for a Capstan: the dependable cigarette', Craven-A, Ardarth or Players) or Monopole cigars or **roll-your-owns** (Champion Ruby with Tally-ho papers). Very, very few women smoked.
- **Crazy tea set** — mothers would acquire more and more cups and saucers, each one of a different pattern, usually of flowers, for what was called a crazy tea set; crazy because none of the cups matched. That was perhaps the limit of zaniness in 1950s suburbia. The crazy tea set rested on an embroidered or crocheted **doily**, which was still a symbol of **good homemaking**.
- We aspired to an EPNS (electroplated nickel silver) knife and fork set with **faux mother-of-pearl** handles; and a teapot, creamer and sugar bowl in **britannia metal** (this was not silver, but an alloy of tin, copper, zinc and antimony which looked almost as good as silver).
- **Dressmaker's dummy** — some particularly clever women kept a sort of headless, armless, legless torso in a corner of the dining room, or on their side veranda, on which to fashion clothes and **run up a skirt**. It could be wound in or out to suit the size of the person for whom the woman was

making something. It was always rather scary for children. Often instead of a neck and head, there was a turned wooden spindle, and it always stood at adult height, which made it even more eerie.

- **Singer sewing machine** — sometimes women borrowed a neighbour's treadle machine, just as their husband might borrow a Qualcast push mower to do the lawn. This was called **a loaner** — meaning you understood that, no matter how many years you had it, the neighbour could turn up at any time and claim it back.

- **Rucksacks, duffle bags**, and **haversacks** (now called backpacks) — these bags would contain your cricketing gear, **field glasses** (now called binoculars) or your wooden tennis racquet which was held in a wooden frame with four **butterfly nuts** to stop it warping.

- **Dummy egg** — many people had a chook pen in the backyard, and roosters would be heard crowing before dawn all over the city. Householders collected the **cackleberries, googs** or **hen fruit**. If the chooks weren't laying, you placed a fake crockery egg (a dummy egg) in the pen. If a chook still didn't lay, you chopped off its head and had roast chicken for tea.

Chapter nine

SUNDAY

Sunday arvo

For most families Saturday morning was the big shopping event. Then Saturday afternoon was reserved for four hours at the **flicks** — the local **picture theatre** — to see two feature films, a couple of cartoons and shorts, several **trailers**, a newsreel and the latest episode of the 15-part serial.

So on Sunday after church the suburbs were full of **nippers** and **mutts**, as all the children poured out of their homes to enjoy their family's one full day off for the week. Children would shin up trees, yelling out to adults and toddlers below, '**I'm the king of the castle and you're the dirty rascal**!'

In trees, children created their own little world, as if they had evolved to survive there. They built **cubbyhouses** from old boards, fruit boxes and roofing iron, with lookout posts and cupboards for storing cool drinks. There was no need for a rope ladder because all children were skilled climbers from the age of six. They made their own telephone system: two empty jam tins connected by a length of taut string. Hello? Adults did not build cubbyhouses, and you certainly could not go to a shop and buy one.

Near the cubbyhouse, kids set **mantraps** in the paspalum. They would tie long bits of the grass together, so that anyone running through would be tripped up.

Kids defended their castles with **Bowie knives** and **tomahawks** and **gibbers** (large pebbles), and they made their own weapons: **nulla-nullas** (a stick dipped into wet, hot bitumen, with shards of broken glass pushed into the soft tar), **spears** (a stalk of tough grass with one end sharpened), **bows and arrows**, or **shanghais**, which were also called **gings**. The shanghai was made from the fork of a small, flexible tree branch with two strips of rubber from a bike tube tied to each end of the fork and joined with a leather patch. The patch held a stone or a ball bearing (depending on how vicious you were). You pulled back the leather patch as far as it would go, and then released it, so the missile was propelled between the forks.

Shanghais were much more dangerous than a **Daisy air rifle** or **slug gun**, which boys also owned. These fired little lead slugs. You might spend Sunday shooting **sprags** (sparrows) with the Daisy air rifle. Kids put the sparrow heads into a jar of methylated spirits, and took it into the local council where they were paid a penny for each head.

There was also the **spud gun** (the point was inserted into a potato and twisted to create a little potato pellet), the **blowgun** (which required a lot of puff as you blew split peas at people walking past your tree) and the **popgun** (which fired a cork).

Kids might take to wearing bottletop badges, to show they were part of the same tribe. They'd take the cork out of a tin bottle top, push the bottle top onto the outside of their shirt while pushing the cork back in behind the cloth. The bottle top itself was metal with a sharp serrated edge.

Bottle tops were saved up, especially to make sharp, miniature frisbees. Both boys and girls exchanged fire across the street, and also **pelted** stones at targets to show off their **dead eye**. Anyone who was an expert was called a **Dead-Eye Dick**.

Stone throwing was important because you could control an area around you of at least 50 yards … to chase off a dog or a horse or an enemy gang. Children would also throw stones to attract someone's attention, to hit a target like a street sign or a lamppost. And if they came across a body of water, **ten to one** they would all start picking up stones and throwing them. Then, **what's the bet**, the **smarties** would start **skimming flat pebbles** across the water, so that the pebbles bounced seven or eight times and appeared to dance on the water.

Young boys could be seen running along with their dog and an old car tyre next to them, patting the tyre forward with their hand or a stick — seeing how far they could get before it fell over. Such boys usually had a collection of tyres, with favourite ones. They might pile them on top of each other and hide inside with their dog.

Dogs were rarely kept behind fences or taken on leads. Dogs, like kids, roamed freely throughout the neighbourhood, running all day till they fell panting to the floor, **dog-tired**.

In every suburb, there would be three blokes leaning over the open bonnet of a car, either a Holden or a Ford, and there they would spend the whole weekend, **tinkering** and revving. Every bloke knew how to clean the spark plugs and tighten the fanbelt. If the leather fanbelt was broken they would replace it with a woman's stocking.

Every household had something in the backyard for burning rubbish in. Usually it was a **44-gallon drum** with no ends and four or five steel prongs (or perhaps a small panel of **K-wire** fencing) through the middle, so all the household and garden rubbish would sit in the drum burning, but the ash could fall to the ground. There were no plastic bags to make the incinerator noxious, but still the air would be filled with acrid smoke, particularly if the householder was fussy and liked burning the fresh grass clippings. But mostly the clippings were raked up in a remote corner of the yard, and all the neighbourhood kids would arrive and start gleefully jumping over and into the pile, until they were exhausted. Then it was time for an itchy walk home.

Most young children walked everywhere — even if it was a long, hot, barefoot walk in the afternoon sun to the corner store to buy lollies, trying to leap from grass to cement without stepping on the hot melting black bitumen or green bindi-eyes. Girls would stop to play hopscotch on the footpath and to carve their initials into a passionfruit.

Walking around the suburbs, you would hear some poor kid practising the piano, since, before TV, every second house had a piano for singsongs and entertainment. You would also hear other kids yelling out the refrain of most games: '**Eight nine ten, coming ready or not, no back answers!**' or '**I'm Bar!**' or '**I'm It!**' They'd be playing **What's the Time, Mr Wolf?** Or **Tiggy** or **Brandy** or **No Time for Standing** (where you had to knock everyone else off their feet).

If they weren't playing **cowboys and Indians** children might be testing their skills:

1. Balance a bottle on your elbow, then fling your arm forward. The bottle will fly in the air and you try to catch it.
2. Hold a pound note suspended above your opponents' fingers. You let it go and they have to catch it.
3. Would you like a game of ping-pong? **I ping and you pong.**
4. Crouch down and up again on one leg.

If you heard an **explosion** you'd know if it was just a car **backfiring** or someone shooting their rifle at a target. Either way, you just ignored it. It was all part of the music of suburban life.

If it was **bucketing down** or **teeming** or **pelting** rain, most kids would make little paper boats and put them in the flooded gutters. They'd run alongside watching their boat race the length of a street until, battered and overturned, it disappeared through the bars of a **monkey hole** (grate), never to be seen again. When playing **Hide-and-Seek** or **Beware-of-the-Bear** or **Hit-the-Tin**, children would lift this grate and make it their **hidey-hole**, not realising the danger if there was a sudden rush of water.

On steep streets there might be a group of boys test-driving their latest **billycart** — homemade from a fruit box, old pram wheels and a rope to steer her by. Or it might be called a **hill cart** or a **hill trolley**.

Boys heading for the creek would be carrying a **homemade canoe** tipped upside down over their heads — plugs of black bitumen visibly filling all the holes in the flattened-out corrugated roofing iron. The first time anyone got into a canoe he'd end up **in the drink** — the canoe would wobble so much that, until you learnt how to get your balance, you'd fall out.

Because of the weight of these canoes, boys only brought them home for repair and refit. Otherwise they sank them in the muddy creek water so other boys couldn't **souvenir** them.

Little boys could be seen riding **scooters**, with a sister perched on the platform between the wheels as the boys pushed along with one foot and coasted down hills. These were the precursors to skateboards, which, for some obscure reason, university students play on today.

Other boys zoomed around on their **three-quarter semi-racer** bikes. If you needed to transport an empty fruit box, you popped it on your head so the front edge rested on your forehead and the back edge on your back.

You'd hear squeals when someone had a **buster** on their bike. They'd end up with an **egg** (a large round bump on the head) plus **gravel rash** (not a rash at all, but what you got on your knees, where the skin was shaved off in bloody tracks, and you had to pick the little stones out of the wound). Or they'd **bark** their shins.

Usually kids would **double** (**dink** in some states) a brother or sister on the crossbar of their bike. Or girls might sit astride the book rack over the back wheel, with their feet stuck well out, for fear of their toes being caught in the spokes. If riding a girl's bike — which didn't have a crossbar and always had string on the back wheel to stop skirts becoming entangled — the boy stood up on the pedals and the sister sat on the seat behind and held on.

Bikes with gears were very rare. Every bike had a pump attached and a tool kit hanging down under the seat. This kit always contained a **vulcaniser set** for burning patches onto the tube when you got a puncture.

Most bikes had footbrakes, but these didn't work when the chain fell off, and this was the major cause of crashes. Few bikes had handbrakes on the handle. All had a bell to warn pedestrians and a flange for hooking a light on between the handlebars.

Boys tied a bit of leather over the cog of each wheel, so as they rode along it cleaned the silver cog. All bikes had oil points with tiny lids where you put oil in, to keep everything well tuned.

Having a bike enabled kids to cross suburbs quickly or to push deep into nearby bushland with a Daisy air rifle or .22 rifle (a **twenty-two** — called a **peashooter** by adults) for some target practice. Just when you thought you'd reached a spot where no one else had ever been before, you'd see a sign painted on a fallen tree: **TOM WALLACE CYCLES**. Or **FOO WAS HERE**, with a drawing of a little head with its nose peeking over a wall. Or an advertisement like: **WHY LIVE IN MISERY WHEN YOU CAN BE BURIED FOR THREE POUNDS TEN SHILLINGS?** Or **BILL POSTERS WILL BE PROSECUTED**, which made you feel sorry for Bill.

LOST FOR WORDS EPISODE 8:
Mowing the Lawn

Within the family circle Australians didn't have arguments, they **had word**s. And when they did, they gave the other person **an earful**.

Lost for Words. The story of Bert and Grace and their trials and tribulations bringing up a young family after the War.

It was a summer weekend when Grace discovered Bert lounging on the couch, listening to the races.

'This won't buy the child a frock!' Grace exclaimed. 'Get out and do the yard.'

'Heavens to Betsy, Grace, a man's got to have an interest, and the only interest I allow myself is the gee-gees,' he said. 'Anyway, I've got a constitutional objection to mowing the grass. So there.'

'You're always getting out from under, Bert', complained Grace. 'You never face up to your responsibility to keep the yard tidy. God knows what the neighbours think.'

'Well, if a thing is worth doing, it's worth doing well,' said Bert. 'Even laziness, to be effective, has to be carried out properly.'

'That's neither here nor there, Bert. I'm not just talking about today. You're always trying to skive off every weekend onto that couch. If you lie down any more you'll get bedsores.'

'I must be a terrible fella.'

'You don't have to gild the lily, Bert.'

'I can see intelligence is rife around here. Well, for your information it's stinking hot out there. And there's flies.'

'And? Who do you think you are? King Farouk?'

'That's correct-o-mundo.'

'I'll pay that one.'

'Is that a threat or a promise, Gracie?'

Bert called this sort of conversation 'getting the rounds of the kitchen'. And if it happened after work, he said he came home to 'a dinner of cold shoulder and hot tongue'.

As Bert reached out to turn his mantle radio off, he muttered: 'I'm going to kick up a stink.'

'Go for your life, sweetheart,' said Grace. 'But, tell me, Bert, why have you got this big bugbear about mowing the grass? Every man in the suburb does it and the exercise is good for your constitution.'

'Well, just for starters, the last time I mowed the grass I cut myself sharpening the blades.'

'Serves yourself right. I told you to stop fiddling with it and take it over to Cyril's. He knows all about mowers.'

'Small things amuse small minds.'

'For pity's sake! The cure is worse than the disease!'

'Grace, don't get all hot and bothered, love. Don't burst your boiler. I'll saddle up and box on after the next race at Flemington.'

'Well, Bert, you're getting on my works. I'll tell you what! What if I make your favourite for tea: roast beef and Yorkshire pudding?'

'You mean one hand washes the other.'

'That's the ticket, dear. Now you're cooking on gas.'

'My education has been sadly neglected. But what if I promise to do it next Saturday when I can get off to an early start?'

'Not on your nelly, Bert. It's got to be done today. No buts about it.'

Bert struggled up out of his low Genoa lounge chair, muttering: 'To keep the peace, I'll have to dig up the mower.'

Ten minutes later, Bert called from the shed: 'Grace! Where did you hide the lawnmower?'

Since she never mowed the grass, Grace yelled back: 'I wouldn't

> have the foggiest. It must be floating around there somewhere. You couldn't have lost it, Bert.'
>
> 'More's the pity,' Bert said. 'I'm lost for words.'

Sunday driving

Most men (and working women) worked Saturday mornings as well as Monday to Friday, so on Sunday — if you were lucky enough to own a car — Dad took the family, and maybe a relative, a friend or a neighbour, for a drive.

There was no **Sunday driving** until well after World War II because petrol then was rationed to two gallons a month — which would just get you from Brisbane to the Gold Coast, but not back.

But even when there was plenty of cheap petrol after the War, most cars were old and unreliable, so they were known as **rattletraps**, **bombs** or **crates**. A real crate would have its **dings** patched up with **bog**. If the car **conked out**, Dad would announce '**The donk's stuffed**' as he **tinkered** with the engine or operated the **crank handle** to try to turn the engine over.

Most cars had a **crank handle** on board. If the car wouldn't start, your father got this handle out of the boot and stuck it into the engine through the front of the car and swung it around vigorously until the engine coughed. Men said that you had to hold onto the handle tightly because the compression of the engine could kick back and break your arm.

Before cars became so reliable, and before it was the habit to give away 24-hour roadside insurance, it was common to see cars broken down.

Cars were so uncomplicated then, that when you lifted up the bonnet you could clearly see the bitumen road underneath. Many men knew how to fix engine problems. On the open road you often saw cars pulled off to the side with the bonnet up, and at least two blokes leaning over it scratching their chins. Inevitably, some **good Samaritan** had stopped to help. If nothing could be done he would tow the sick car to the next garage using a rope tied to his back steel bumper bar, and your front steel bumper bar.

Towing cars was an art. Because so many cars broke down, many motorists kept a **tow rope** in the boot of their car. The rope had to be just the right length: too long and the rear car would swing wide on curves; too short and it might run into the towing car. Going downhill, the bloke behind had to touch his brakes slightly so that he didn't ram the car in front, but not too much because he'd break the rope. Men always tied a red rag to the centre of the rope before setting off — so other drivers would see that the two were joined.

DRIVING YOUR PARENTS MAD

Motoring was relaxed because there were so few cars on the road, and this was reflected in the language of the time. No one had heard of 'tailbacks' or 'bumper-to-bumpers' or 'tailgating'. Instead, motorists **toodled** or **toddled** or **beetled along**, or (if going fast) **tooled along** at a fast lick, **showed some toe**, or **a lot of toe** ... eventually **lobbing** at their destination.

If you offered a friend a lift, they might accept gratefully, or they might answer: 'I'll get there **under my own steam, if it's all the same to you**.'

Official speed signs near schools said simply: **DEAD SLOW**.

Getting away from home was the only hard part, with everyone in the family needing to go back for something. So mothers could be heard calling out '**Huuurrry ... uuppp**' — said as slowly as possible. But when the family reached the beach, and everyone dropped everything to get to the water first, yelling '**Last one in is a rotten egg**', she would call out '**SLOW DOWN!**' — said as quickly as humanly possible.

What annoyed mothers was that they had to get everything ready for the trip. '**I packed like the Devil was after me**,' Mum would mutter. Meanwhile, Dad would tell the youngest kid to '**Sit in the back, that way you'll get a longer drive**'.

Before setting off, Dad would check the **petrol roster** in **the paper** so you could buy fuel on the way. Only a few **garages** opened on weekends because it seemed such an imposition to ask them to **serve petrol** on a Sunday. So the garages took it in turns. By the time garages had become 'service stations' in the late 1960s they automatically dispensed petrol in exchange for 20-cent coins fed into a slot in the wall.

Dad would also want some **FREE AIR** (a sign outside nearly every garage), meaning you could pump up your tyres for nix.

On the way through the city the kids would warn Dad of any upcoming **dumb or silent coppers** — a helmet-sized lump built into the middle of major intersections. Before traffic lights, a policeman stood in the middle of busy intersections directing traffic around them. The law required that these **silent coppers** were to be driven around as if they were traffic policemen.

'**That's a piece of cake**,' Dad would say, before driving up a **dead end** (streets that led nowhere were dead ends, not cul-de-sacs). An angry uncle would say, 'Your father has **driven up a dead duck's arse**.'

If another motorist dared to **toot** the family out of the way with the car horn, shouting, '**You couldn't drive a nail in a wall**', the girls would surely yell back, '**What else did you get for Christmas?**'

Before DVDs and mobile phones and computer games in cars, all you had was **I Spy** plus a prize for the first person to see the ocean (if you were heading for the beach), or to see a koala (if you were **going bush**), or to see an **aeroplane** (if you were going for a drive to the **aerodrome**, which was once a favourite pastime). 'I Spy with my little eye something beginning with … K!' would echo through the car for the whole journey. To give people a clue as to how they were going you said, 'You're getting cold, warm, warmer, hotter …' as they got closer to the answer.

The older kids always won.

If you got lost, which was easy because signs were few, you asked a local who always ended his instructions with '… **and you can't miss it!**' This proved a foolishly optimistic appraisal, since you had already proved you could.

If Mother thought Dad went around a bend **flat chat**, she would warn 'That was a **COD corner**'. COD stood for 'Come Over, Darling' because, before safety belts and with **bench seats**, the girl on the passenger side could be deliberately propelled towards the driver. On country roads, Dad always tried to avoid any **whoa boys**. These were dirt humps built into a steep track to channel water away in a downpour. It was a sensible design and kept the track in good nick, and safe from erosion.

When Dad started **scooting** along the **open road** he might urge the kids to '**keep an eye out** for any policemen. We don't want to get **pinged**.' If there were police on the road, Dad would say: '**They're having a field day**, **it's open slather**.'

Then Mother would say: 'Don't be **a hoon**. You're going **like the wind**. We don't want to **skittle** some poor pedestrian. Easy on the **lead foot**, dear, there are children on board. We don't want a **hairy ride**.'

But the boys would urge their father to go faster, saying, 'Dad, pass that **slowcoach** in the **tilly**' (a ute). Sons loved cars that looked and went fast, and called them a **betsy**, a **chariot**, a **jalopy** or a **heap**.

When passed by a **spiffy** new, model car with a **big donk** that was **hairing along flat strap** with its **souped-up** motor, going **like the clappers**, the boys would say: 'Give this **buggy a kick in the guts. Hoot along**.' But usually Dad would say he was already **herbing along** nicely and didn't want to have **a prang**.

He had to be **careful of the duco** because he didn't want to end up with a ding in the **family automobile**.

'**Gun it**, Pop,' the boys would say. '**Pull a ton**, Dad.' (Do 100 miles per hour — impossible in family sedans then. Now so-called 'family' sedans can do twice that speed.)

And the father would reply: '**Relax. Dad's the engineer**.'

When it was time to go home, your mother would say, as a pleasant joke to the driver while the whole family piled in: '**Home, James, and don't spare the horses**.'

THE MOTOR CAR

When you bought a brand-new Ford Zephyr or a Holden Special, it came with **everything that opens and shuts**, plus a **90-day warranty**, compared with three to five years now.

You were required to drive these cars under 30 miles per hour for the first 1000 miles to **run them in**. Since this meant you would be holding up the traffic on the narrow roads, everyone with a brand-new motor car would write a sign on cardboard and stick it in the back window saying: **RUNNING IN**. This was to explain to motorists behind why they were being held up.

People with a pair of tight new shoes also said they were 'running them in'.

Before airconditioning became standard, in hotter parts of Australia most cars had a metal sun visor that stuck out over the windscreen to keep the sun off the front seats. Most cars had **quarter vents**, triangular windows you pushed out, which directed a constant cool breeze into the car as you drove along. The 1936 Hillman had steel wings that pushed out from under the dashboard to direct cool air in at seat level.

Most cars had a heart-shaped red or green **insect deflector** sitting on the front of the bonnet to deflect air and insects away from the split-screen windscreen.

There was usually a strip of rubber hanging down from the back of the car trailing on the bitumen. It was said to stop passengers getting **carsick**, by eliminating static electricity.

Few cars had reflectors built into the tail-lights until it became compulsory in 1956, so an Australian invented a stick-on red reflective tape, which in the mid-50s almost everyone cut up and stuck in stripes across the chrome rear bumper bar. It worked brilliantly. As a joke, a garage might send the apprentice out on a wild errand, to the grocer's for '**Some red kerosene for the tail-lamps**'.

People and governments saw private cars — not public transport — as the future. Eagers Motors in Brisbane ran an ad with a drawing of a tram. The caption read: '**Get off that tram, you'll never own it.**'

The power of car engines was measured in **horsepower**, which was more commonly reduced to '**horses**'. '**The Ford Zephyr has more horses than the Holden.**'

Most roads were narrow with dirt and stones at the edge, so, while passing cars going the other way, drivers would reach out and push the back of their hand against the inside of the windscreen. This was to help lessen the impact of any stone that was tossed up and hit it.

Because of weak headlights and poor wipers, many motorists would rub a cut potato over the windscreen to make rain run off more quickly.

In Queensland before 1950, Sid Ash would ride his motorbike from Toowoomba to the Gold Coast; it took ten hours. 'If it was holiday time you could be delayed at the Coomera ferry for a couple of hours,' he said. 'This often meant a game of cricket on the flat near the ferry. The bat and ball was always there, no one would think of taking it: and no one would **jump your claim** if you were a bit late moving forward as the line of waiting vehicles was reduced.'

When you took your car to the **petrol bowser** at the garage for some **go juice**, the attendant had to physically pump the petrol himself. There was a handle three feet long on the bowser which pumped the petrol high up into a glass cylinder on the top. The attendant pumped the required amount then released it down through the hose into your car. At least you **saw for yourself** how much petrol you were getting.

Petrol stations on the road out of town would put out a sign: **LAST CHANCE AT CITY PRICES**, to catch motorists.

HAND SIGNALS

Drivers hated **hood huggers**.

Before airconditioned cars, everybody had their right elbow out the window in summer, to channel cool air under their arm and into their shirt. Some drivers would rest their elbow on the windowsill and hook their fingers in the little gutter that channelled the rain off the roof. These drivers were disliked because they gave the impression they were about to give a **hand signal** and change direction.

Hand signals were necessary because few cars had indicators. Thus, if turning right, the motorist put his hand straight out the window parallel to the ground as far as he could. If about to stop, the arm went out, forearm bent straight up, hand in the air. To **turn left**, he put two fingers of his right hand across his face, under his nose. A little bit of elbow thus stuck out the window. But because most drivers believed others couldn't see this, they would put their arm out the window and point repeatedly over the roof of the car to the left with their index finger.

Before executing a U-turn, the right arm was held out the window with the forefinger pointing down. The finger was then swung around in large circles.

The slowing-down signal was called **pat the dog**. The driver put his arm out (palm facing down) and waved it slowly up and down.

Because bus drivers couldn't get their arm far enough out the window, they had a lever in the cabin which operated a small yellow metal hand on the outside of the bus. By moving the lever, the driver could extend the hand out into the traffic and move it.

In the 1950s, Volkswagens and Morris Minors had an indicator that was a light on the end of a little arm on the sides of the car. It actually lifted up and stuck out to indicate turning right or left.

Chapter ten

BUSHY-TAILED

Physical jerks

- -

Before modern medical advances, your state of health centred on what everyone called your 'constitution'. You either had a **good constitution** ('I'm **as fit as a mallee bull, and twice as dangerous**') or **a bad constitution.** Or you might have **a poor constitution** or **a weak constitution**.

A son with constitution problems was always called **a sickly child.**

People would tell you that this product, or that mattress, or barley water was **good for your constitution**. A man might say he was taking his **morning constitutional**, meaning a morning walk. If it was cold or hot he returned with red cheeks, which was excellent because **rosy cheeks** meant good health.

In the 1950s a morning walk was considered to be enough exercise for everyone except Olympic athletes. No one ever imagined that getting puffed would improve your health. No one had heard of personal trainers, or stretching. Sport was usually played in **sandshoes**. All footy boots were leather ankle boots with miles of lacing.

Before jogging was invented, if a man did **train up** for a football match (usually the day before) he was said to do **physical jerks**. This was done on the patio or veranda.

It probably involved squeezing a spring in one hand, stretching a rubber sling in both hands, lots of jumping, plus throwing and catching a **medicine ball** full of horsehair, which was as heavy as lead. He might even squat down and get up again on one leg. Most people could at least get down on their haunches, because most jobs involved physical labour. Mothers got down on their hands and knees to wash and polish the floor. No one would ever think to pay someone to do their garden.

After an afternoon of slashing and burning in the backyard, a man would boast he was a **he-man** who had **animal magnetism**. He actually meant that he could attract girls, not animals.

If you asked afterwards '**How did you pull up**?' or, '**How are you holding up**?' he would answer: 'You don't have to worry about me; I've always been a healthy **bod**. **Never better**. I'm **sparking on all fours, sparking on all cylinders,**

bright-eyed and bushy-tailed. I've got the **constitution of an ox**. I **sleep like a top**. I'm in **fair nick**. What am I saying? I'm in **good nick**. I'm **fit enough to burst a grape**. I'm **as fit as a fiddle; if I was any fitter I'd be dangerous**. I'm **fighting fit**. Why, I'm **a ball of muscle**. And everything's going well **downstairs** [meaning **the waterworks, the plumbing**]. I can **pee like a brewer's horse**. I'm **in the pink**.'

When the doctor was about to give him a needle, or lance a boil (cut it open), or pull off plaster bandages, this fellow would say: '**Do your worst**.' He would be a non-smoker, and if introduced to a smoker was sure to recite: '**It's not the coughin' that carries you off, it's the coffin they carry you off in**.'

He would be a good eater, a **good fang merchant**, or have, as he put it, **a healthy appetite**. To a nation that had lived through the Depression, a couple of World Wars, rationing, coupons, suspender belts and, later, beehive hairdos, health had a different connotation. Healthy was eating well, eating a lot, and enjoying your food.

Peter's ice-cream called itself the '**Health Food of a Nation**' because ice-cream was made from milk and cream, both highly recommended foods. Cadbury's chocolate promoted itself as containing 'a glass and a half of fresh full-cream milk'.

If a chap considered himself to be quite tough and able to go **a round or two for a pound or two** with anyone, he was said to be **a bit of a pug**.

He was the sort of bloke who never got sick, but all his family did.

- How's your uncle?
- **He's under the doctor.**
- How's your brother?
- **He's sick in bed with a nurse, and sitting up taking a little nourishment.**
- How's your aunty?
- **She kicked the bucket.**
- What did she die of?
- **She died of a Friday.**
- How's your mother?

- *She's taken to her bed and now she's on an invalid diet.*
- How's your father?
- *He's up and down like a yoyo.* (This could mean happy, then not happy; well, then not well; healthy, then not healthy; or it could just be that he keeps jumping out of bed.)
- But how is he in himself? (This was the nearest anyone got to indulging in a bit of counselling. It meant, how's his equilibrium? His mental state? Is he cheerful?)
- *He's suffering from low spirits. He's looking a bit pale around the gills. I had the Devil's own job to get him off to work today. I told him he's got to crack hardy.*

Men never said they were sick — because they didn't trust doctors and only saw them if rushed to hospital by ambulance. They didn't want to be labelled an **old crock**. Thus men had lots of stock answers if asked how they were. Perhaps the all-time favourite, if a bloke was feeling **really lousy**, was the reply: **Not too clever**. Or he might say he was:

- Only fair to middling
- Not real flash
- Not too crash hot
- Pretty ordinary
- Only so-so
- A bit crook.

All of these really meant he was **as sick as a dog** and was **coming down with something**.

However, men were happy to admit that physical labour had worn them out. If he said he'd had **the Royal Order**, it meant he was **rooted, knackered, bushwhacked, stuffed, buggered, jiggered, knocked-up,** or **bushed**. (**I'm bushed** also meant you were lost.)

A wife knew her husband was ill if he said he was **crook as a chook** or **crook as Rookwood**, which meant he was a **cot case.** (Rookwood is a Sydney cemetery that is so big you can't see across it.)

If he said he thought he'd **got a bait** (must have eaten something bad) she knew he was really ill. And it was definitely time to ring the ambulance if her husband said, using cricket terminology, 'I'll tell you what, dear, I **won't be opening for Australia**.'

When a mother was sick she'd say, 'I've lost my **get-up-and-go**.' Or, '**I feel like death warmed up**.' Or, '**I look like death warmed up**.' Or, '**I look as pale as a ghost**.' Or, 'I'm feeling a bit **old and mouldy**.' Or, '**I think I've picked up a wog**.'

Then she'd be **in a bit of a state**. Or she'd end up **laid up**, meaning 'I've been in **my sickbed** so you haven't seen me around lately.'

Often mothers blamed the weather for any pain: 'This weather **plays merry hell** with my **lumbago**.' Or your mother would stand up and stretch her back painfully and say, '**Every picture tells a story**'. People used to scratch their backs on doorjambs and say, '**Ahhh, the Duke of Argyle**'. But if someone kept whingeing about how sick they were, you'd say: '**The creaking hinge creaks the longest**', meaning 'She'll outlive us all.'

If her children were sick, a mother would say they were **a bit off-colour**, which meant she didn't yet know what was wrong. If it turned out to be the **dreaded lurgy** (the flu) she'd say: 'He's been **barking all night**', meaning coughing. If the cough kept up during the day she'd say you had **a bad bark**. Once you were getting better you were **on the mend**. Then, when you were **all better**, you were said to be **right as rain**.

When her son broke a bone fighting or playing football a mother would not blame the other boys. She would instead say: 'He must have **chalk bones**.'

Self-diagnosis

- He had **a bit of a turn** — no one had any idea what had gone wrong, or you were being deliberately vague.
- **The collywobbles** — worried, or sick with a sore belly.
- Dusty — he's feeling **a bit dusty**.
- A man might be **black and blue** after falling down the front stairs.
- A **dicky knee** — always said to be **playing up**, causing pain, **causing gip**.
- A **dicky heart** — when there wasn't much anyone could do for a diseased heart.
- A **basket case** — really ill.
- **Dog's disease** — very sick, usually in bed with a bad cold.
- You might get sympathy for a bad cold, but if you were blowing your nose too noisily, someone in the family would be sure to yell out: '**Can you play "Annie Laurie"?**'
- **Having a bad trot** — probably needs **a tonic**. People would go to a chemist and ask for a **pick-me-up** and the chemist would mix up his own formula, usually a pink liquid, which you drank standing at the counter. It was called **a draught**. A woman might ask the chemist for a **nerve tonic**, because she felt just **too awful for words**, she was feeling so **skittish**, just **a bundle of nerves** these days.

UNUSUAL AILMENTS AND INJURIES

Explorers were forever getting **sandy blight**. You learnt about this in **Social Studies** at school. It sounded gruesome, but was actually an inflammation of the eyelids.

If you coughed a lot, someone would ask: 'Have you got **galloping consumption**?' But if your mother thought you were putting on a cough to get out of going to school, she'd say: 'I think you must have **galloping con-something**.'

People 'caught' **urti** (actually an acronym for upper respiratory tract infection) but they were always 'coming out in' **hives**. Kids were 'infested' with **nits** (head lice), but 'got' **boils**. Really big boils were called **carbuncles**. You 'suffered from' **prickly heat**, and after a **guts-ache** you'd get the **runs** or the **scours** (diarrhoea). This meant you could be **caught short** if there was no lavatory around.

Smokers often complained of **catarrh**, so switched to menthol cigarettes.

If more than a couple of people in a town or a household got the same illness, or started acting strangely, or perhaps became unusually generous, some wag would say: '**It must be something in the water.**'

There was a whole lexicon for vomiting
- **Calling for Herb, George and Archie.**
- Ladies would say they were **feeling bilious**.
- Men would say they **spewed their heart out**. Or **hurled**, or had a **chunder**.

Hasten, Jason, fetch the basin.
Oh, too late, bring the mop.

Under your skin

The human body was the source of much colourful language.

If a person annoyed you but you couldn't tell them so, they **got under your skin**. Even more infuriating, they would then ask: '**What's eating you**?'

If they had many faults but were compassionate, you said: '**But his heart's in the right place.**' Whereas if your **heart was in your mouth**, you were frightened.

If someone was generous with their help they were **bending over backwards**, which sounds uncomfortable.

However, if they weren't, they might be told: '**Put your nose to the grindstone, your shoulder to the wheel, head down, and your best foot forward. Then see how impossible it is to do anything in that position!**'

If someone was a coward he was **lily-livered**.

A man who could eat anything without getting an **upset tummy** had a **cast-iron stomach**. Whereas, a man who whinged a lot was said to be **bellyaching**.

Someone who frequently had to go for a **widdle** or a **piddle** was said to have *a Woolworths bladder.*

Derrière was a polite way of saying **backside**, which was a polite way of saying **bottom**, which was a polite way of saying **bum**.

TEETH, TONGUE AND MOUTH

Your teeth were your **toothypegs** or your **pearly-whites**, even if they weren't.

If you had started something early in life you always said you **cut your teeth** on it. '**I cut my teeth on** Dickens' meant that you started reading him from an early age, when your teeth first emerged. You were always allowed to exaggerate.

We fought **tooth and nail** for that bonus.

If you'd **had a gutful** of something or of someone, you were said to be **fed up to the back teeth**. Or, **I've had him up to my back teeth** meant you'd had **quite enough**.

If a project would really challenge or absorb you it was **something to get your teeth into**. And if you refused to give up a job or task, you'd be **hanging on by the skin of your teeth**.

Teeth were seen as very valuable. 'There are lots of women who would **give their eyeteeth** to go out with him.'

How old are you? **I'm the same age as my tongue, and a little older than my teeth.**

How old is she? She's **getting a bit long in the tooth**. (A little kid is all gums with tiny baby teeth poking out. But as you get older your gums recede and you end up showing just teeth — a mouth of all teeth!)

She's sorry, **from the teeth out!**

- He gave me **a real tongue-lashing** — he **went crook**.
- **You'll feel the edge of my tongue** — a threat.
- A **silver-tongued** salesman — his words slipped out easily. Persuasive and a little bit risqué. Grandma would comment: 'He must have been to **Charm School**.'

- **It's on the tip of my tongue** — I can almost remember it!
- If you didn't want to have to **eat your words** you were advised to **hold your tongue** or **button your lip** — shut up!
- **Bite your tongue** — you shouldn't have said that, and don't say it again.
- **Have you lost your tongue?** Say something!

Your mouth could be called your **gob** or your **trap**, and the general area was known as your **chops**.

- **Keep your trap shut** — don't go round telling anyone about this.
- He always had **a smile on his chops**.
- **Shut your gob**. (A large lolly that overfilled your mouth was a **gobstopper**.)
- Stop **giving lip** — stop being cheeky by giving **back answers** to your elders.
- Kids who were always fighting were said to be **at each other's throats**.
- **Pucker up** — what blokes said to girls before they kissed them.

FACE, NOSE AND HEAD

- Why the **long face**? When you're sad, you actually do get a long face, because you drop your mouth and chin.
- A smile on his **dial**.
- He got hit **in the moosh** — punched in the face.
- You **paid through the nose**.
- It's **no skin off my nose** — I don't care if you do that.
- **Looking down your nose** at someone; or **turning up your nose**.
- He's **on the nose** — it means no one wants to know him because of something he's done; they're giving him the **cold shoulder**.
- **Follow your nose** — do what you think you should.
- He **gets up my nose** — annoys me.
- He's always **poking his nose in** (where it's not wanted).
- His nose was **out of joint** — he was envious or offended.
- **Up your nose with a rubber hose!**
- It's **on the snoz** — it stinks.

- *Keep your nose to yourself.*
- It's as plain as the **nose on your face**.
- No use **cutting off your nose to spite your face** — you are going to hurt yourself more than the other person.

The head had various names: **scone, melon, loaf, noggin, nut**. Thus a redhead was a **bloodnut**.

- *Use your pumpkin*
- *Use your noodle*
- *Use your nous*
- *Laugh your head off*
- *Keep your hair on*
- *Pull your head in* and *don't stick your neck out*
- *You can't put an old head on young shoulders* — everyone has to make their own mistakes.
- Don't **chew my head off** — don't give me a hard time.
- He was **snoring his head off**.
- I need that **like a hole in the head**.
- *You need your head read* — you're stupid if you continue like that. (In Victorian times, people believed you could judge a person's character by the shape and bumps on the head. So you would have your head read.)
- *You need your head examined.*
- *Have you got your head on straight*? Meaning, do you know what you're doing?
- *Are your ears on straight?* What adults said to kids, meaning: are you listening to me or not?
- *I'm all ears* — I'm sorry I've not been attentive, but I am now.
- *Coming out of my ears* — if you had too much of something, whether pies, mangoes or work.
- He could do that **on his ear** with one hand tied behind his back, and blind-folded.
- He's still **wet behind the ears** — inexperienced.

● *I use my head to save my legs* — if you load up you only have to make one trip.

🐾

Mum always said she had **eyes in the back of her head**.

'Mum! I can't find it!'

'**You'd lose your head if it wasn't screwed on. Use your eyes instead of your mouth. Use big eyes**!'

A bloke who tried to pinch your girl from you was trying to **get under your neck**.

BRAINS TRUST

I've got **a brain like a sieve**. Or, I've got **a mind like a steel trap** but she's got **a memory like a sieve**.

If you had a great memory it was **like an elephant**; if not, it was **the memory of a goldfish**.

I haven't got a memory, I've got a forgettory.

If you said **touch wood** for luck, you would pat your own head, or someone else's.

If congratulated on being smart you might point to your temples and say '**kidneys**'.

Here's an idea **off the top of my head**.

It came out of the back of my brain — it leapt into my head from nowhere.

I've had **a brainwave** — a brilliant idea.

The best brains in the country.

Brainy — she **twigged**, she **got my drift**, she was **awake up** (a **cluey lady**). A brainy boy would be **the full bottle** on trains, insurance, gardening, dinosaurs. He would be said to **know his onions**. He'd be described as **a mine of information**. Whereas young Billy was **behind the door when the brains were handed out**; ditto when the looks were handed out.

If his brains were dynamite they wouldn't blow his hat off.

She **brained him** with a lump of wood — she hit him on the head.

HANDS AND FEET

He grabbed it **in his mitt**. Get **your mitts** off me.

We won **hands down** — easily. A boxer left his **dukes** down because he was so much better than his opponent.

Ham fisted — physically clumsy or clumsy in love. Not subtle.

Left-handers — teachers didn't like them and tried to make them write with their right hand. Most wrote with their wrist above the line instead of below. Also called:

- Mollydooker
- Cack-handed
- Kak-handed
- Cacky-handed
- Southpaw
- Sinister-handed

When you went without shoes you were said to **wear bare feet**. 'I've got my bare feet on,' was a common saying in Queensland.

- Big **mundoeys**
- **Clodhoppers**
- He's getting **a bit toey** — wants to get going. Or, feeling **a bit toey** — looking for an argument.
- He may also be **cooling his heels** — waiting for someone, kicking the ground.
- Show **a clean pair of heels** — get going.
- He's got **a lot of toe** — a fast runner.
- He's showing **plenty of toe** — he's very quick.
- **Hit the toe** — get out of here.
- She **stuck out like a sore toe** — because she was the only one all **dolled up, done up like a sore thumb, done up like a sore toe, dressed to the nines**.
- **Toe jam** — the dirt which collected between the toes of little boys.
- She said she arrived **on tippy toes** last night (without her shoes on), but I still heard her.

- I can't dance, I've got **two left feet**.
- **Shanks's pony** — by foot.
- Put your **best foot** forward.

ARMS AND LEGS

If something was sold too cheaply it was **sold for an arm and a leg**. When a man made too many excuses he was said to have **a list of excuses as long as his arm**.

The point of your elbow was said to be your **funny bone**, because when you got hit there it made your arm go numb with pins and needles. It was peculiar, but certainly not funny.

Getting the elbow wasn't funny either; in sport it meant becoming too nervous to play properly.

I don't need glasses, I just need longer arms.

Legs were usually called **pins**.
- She's **on her last legs** — can't last much longer.
- Are you **pulling my leg? Pull the other one, it's got bells on.**
- **Shake a leg** — get a move on.
- **Bandy** — your legs bowed so much your mother would say: '**You wouldn't stop a greasy pig!**' Or, '**You're as bandy as a boundary rider.**'

The dentist

You went to the dentist to see if you had any holes in your **fangs**. No one went to the dentist unless they had a toothache. No one went for a check-up. No one went to have anything else done except drill, fill or remove a tooth; or to get false teeth.

There were no crowns. No fluoride scrubs. No cleaning with the dentist's drill. No whitening or polishing. No gap filling. No titanium plugs or veneers to cover up past indiscretions.

Thus most adults had false teeth, which were kept in half a glass of water beside the bed to be inserted first thing in the morning.

Getting a needle

Antibiotics came in after World War II, but there were no antibiotics in tablet form until the 1960s. Before that, a dose of antibiotic invariably meant an injection of penicillin.

Penicillin was a thick white liquid, therefore the needle had to be the size of the lead in a lead pencil. So it hurt. Needles were reused over and over and over again, becoming blunter and blunter, just as hospital bandages were washed and used again. (Patients in the waiting room at hospitals would be gainfully employed rolling up washed bandages.)

Penicillin needles had to be forced through the skin into the arm, leg or buttock. After four penicillin injections a day in your thighs, for a few days your legs wouldn't work.

Childhood diseases

Childhood before the 1960s was, as a doctor friend said to me recently, 'a pretty horrific experience'. You needed luck and a good immune system just to survive. This was because there were so many infectious diseases that could kill, before mass vaccinations for most childhood illnesses became common. Thus children were not allowed to visit sisters or brothers or friends in the children's hospital because of the danger of contracting these deadly diseases. As my doctor friend said: 'The only method of combating infectious diseases before immunisation was to put a fence around the children who were sick.'

At Catholic schools in the 1940s and 50s we always seemed to be praying for very sick schoolmates in hospital.

DIPHTHERIA

This was the most spectacularly awful, devastating and common of all child-hood diseases: a sticky mucus blocked the airway and caused the child to choke to death.

Until the miracle of immunisation by the 1950s, whole wards were set aside for children with diphtheria. It was so contagious that other children were not allowed near such patients. Scattered around each ward were special trolleys on which sat the **emergency tracheotomy set**. If a child's throat suddenly blocked with mucus and they couldn't breathe, the nearest nurse would grab the **diphtheria bell** and ring it furiously. Everyone within earshot then knew that there was some poor child suffocating to death, and they would wheel the **tracheotomy trolley** quickly towards the sound of the bell. The doctor would immediately cut a hole in the child's neck through the windpipe so the child could breathe through the hole. There was just no time to lose.

Pre-World War II, children were especially prey to diphtheria. About 30 per cent of children with the disease died. Mothers were terrified. I heard of one who dipped a chook feather in kerosene and painted her child's throat with it, hoping to stop the disease.

In a family I know, one of the eleven children, Bruce, was called **a carrier**, so nurses would squirt yellow liquid up his nostrils, and he would scream. His youngest sister, Norma, age four, was put into the hospital's diphtheria ward in the mid-1920s. The disease was so contagious that none of her brothers and sisters, nor her mother, were permitted to visit.

Children would only be able to wave to their family through a window. Little Norma was kept warm by pink wool wrapped around her neck and chest.

Any clothes the family brought in, even delicate woollen jumpers and cardigans, would be boiled in the hospital laundry to reduce the risk of infection. A friend of the family, feeling sorry for Norma, bought a celluloid doll and stitched a beautiful pink dress for it. Norma thought it was exquisite; she called it Amy, and slept with it in her hospital bed. Being one of so many children in a far less prosperous Australia, Norma had few toys, so she really

loved Amy. But when the time came to go home, the hospital said she was not allowed to take Amy with her, in case the doll was infected.

Norma still recalls today how she howled when she left Amy behind in the diphtheria ward.

POLIO

This was the most feared childhood disease. In almost every school in the early 1950s, a child was crippled with twisted legs or arms as a result of the poliomyelitis virus. The disease was most common in children, and led to deformity and wasting away of muscles.

The prettiest girl in my class at Mary Immaculate Convent, Annerley, Maureen Meggitt had been crippled by the virus in 1951 when she was 11. She and her eldest sister, Shirley, 13, were transferred to an isolation ward where they were kept for 22 months.

'We went in as children and came out adults,' Maureen told me. 'Our lives changed forever because we had seen, and heard, our friends dying beside us.

Zeeta Cramb, a girl from my class at St Finbarr's (Ashgrove, Brisbane) — there were four of us from there in with polio — died in the Iron Lung.' Maureen had been a very fast runner. 'Since then I only run in my dreams. Sometimes I dream of climbing the big mango tree I had last climbed.'

Maureen said she had been standing, looking at her blue satin ball gown hanging on the wardrobe ready for the upcoming school ball, 'when my hands slid down the wardrobe as my legs folded under me. My mum found me in a heap and she screamed.'

She knew.

There was no protection from the polio virus except avoiding contact with it. Thus picture theatres and swimming pools would simply be shut by the government during a wave of polio. Mothers could be seen crocheting little bags to hold slabs of camphor. They would hang the camphor on a cord around their children's necks, in the vain hope that the resultant vapours would rise up, ward off the disease and save their child.

It didn't.

Polio was only stopped in its tracks following compulsory immunisation of all children in 1956 after the discovery of the Salk vaccine. This was considered a miracle at the time.

TUBERCULOSIS

Whole hospitals were set aside in Australian cities to keep tuberculosis, or TB, patients in isolation for up to a year, so as not to spread the disease. The condition was chronic and very difficult to cure. Thus chest X-rays became compulsory for every Australian, and for anyone migrating here. Huge silver X-ray caravans were parked in main streets with queues of people outside waiting their turn.

Tuberculosis struck adults and children willy-nilly and could kill anyone, rich or poor, old or young, happy or sad, living alone or in a family. The nearest thing in modern society to TB, scientists say, is death by car accident, because of the random nature of the deaths.

RHEUMATIC FEVER

With this disease the body's immune system fails to distinguish between the attacking bacteria and the child's own protein, so it attacks the connective tissue in the joints, the child's heart valve or, less likely, the kidneys. Many children were left with weak hearts.

So little could be done for rheumatic fever that theories developed stating no exercise, no salt, and no pillow could help the child. They didn't. My brother Jack spent ten months in hospital with rheumatic fever, and no pillow or salt. Patients would lie in bed with a cradle holding the weight of the sheets off their legs, so painful were the joints.

Luckily, Jack ignored the ban on exercise (once out of Mum's sight) and recovered with no lasting damage.

TETANUS

This was quite rare, but it is worth remembering that before vaccination almost 100 per cent of children who got tetanus died. It was also called **lockjaw** because a symptom was a child could not open the mouth because all the muscles went into spasm.

WHOOPING COUGH AND OTHER AFFLICTIONS

Whooping cough was rarely deadly, but when it was the child would die a terrible death from coughing night and day, and from the complications that followed. Children could also die of complications from **measles**, **mumps** and **chickenpox**, which were dangerous. As was **scarlet fever** which could affect the kidneys. **Mumps** caused the glands underneath your ears to swell and become very tender and sore. Rarely, it could go to a boy's testicles. My mother Olive warned that if it did they would swell up like footballs. So when I had mumps I stayed dutifully in bed like never before.

Children died from all of the above if their fever became too high. 'Parents

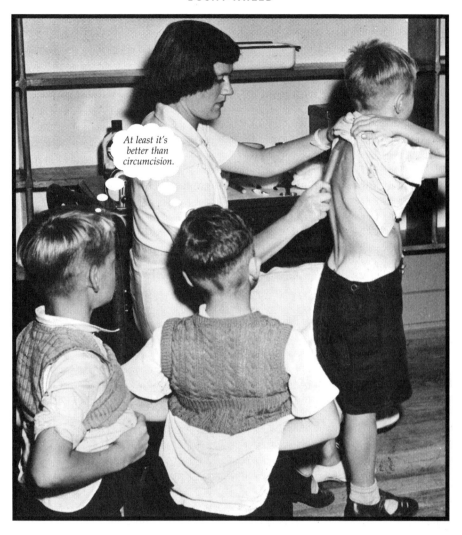

and doctors back then were used to seeing children have fits and convulsions from high temperatures,' my doctor friend said.

Most people have forgotten all of this now, or are too young to know, and have become complacent about immunisation. In the 1950s, immunisation was considered a miracle cure because health professionals saw these horrible diseases and their deadly consequences in action every day. Now some doctors never see them in their lifetime.

'They think these diseases are from Roman times,' my doctor friend said. 'In our era people accepted compulsory immunisation programmes despite the very rare fatal outcomes. But not now. Many people have become anti-immunisation, not realising the pain, lifelong torment and devastation these diseases caused so many, many children in the past.'

The doctor said the problem is that if Australia now has a pool of people who are not immunised against, say, polio, and they go on holidays to, say, India and bring it back, they can infect the young. 'What those against immunisation fail to realise is that, with 100 per cent vaccination, the organism dies out. But if only 10 per cent refuse, it lives on and is a danger to all children in the future. Those who don't get vaccinated are an ever-present danger to society. Make no mistake, there will be **a dreadful reckoning** at some time in the future.'

Children also had to negotiate many other terrible medical events when I was a child.

Most children had operations to have their tonsils and adenoids removed

'in most horrific circumstances,' my doctor friend said. Nowadays the medical profession realises that when the tonsils and adenoids become swollen and infected, this builds up the immune response and resistance to the many organisms a new child breathes in — and that these appendages become quite small naturally by ten years of age. Such operations are now considered unnecessary in most cases. Operations before the 1950s were an appalling event, partly because the anaesthetic used was chloroform or ether. As I went under I felt I was suffocating to death and tried to fight for life. When I said this to an anaesthetist recently, he replied: 'You felt like you were suffocating, because you were! That's how it worked!'

Almost all boys in Australia also had to survive another unnecessary operation: **circumcision** — having the foreskin cut off their penis and thrown away. This was always performed without anaesthetic because, as a doctor who had done these operations, explained: 'That's how it was done.'

And there was no counselling afterwards.

Pushing up daisies

- I'm still on the right side of the grass
- Still in the land of the living
- Still alive and kicking
- He's kicked the bucket
- Swallowed his birth certificate
- Bought the farm
- Dropped off the twig
- Dropped off the stem
- Dropped off the perch
- Carked it
- Croaked
- Turned up his toes
- Dead as a doornail
- Where's the cemetery? The dead centre of town.

- She's pushing up daisies
- No longer with us
- On the wrong side of the grass
- My grandfather would turn over in his grave if he knew what was going on.

A quick way to the grave was said to be to go up in an **aeroplane**: **Flying is like taking poison, one drop and you're dead.**

Bag of bones

People who lived through the Depression, or food rationing, believed that undereating was a health problem.

- She's as thin as a rake.
- She's so thin she needs a good drink of muddy water.
- She would have to stand up twice to cast a shadow.
- She has to jump around in the shower to get wet.
- She's as skinny as a ninepenny rabbit.
- She's fading away to a shadow.
- If she swallowed a green pea she'd look pregnant.
- She's as thin as a yard of pump water.

- He's built like a chewed-up piece of string.
- He's got muscles like a chicken's instep.
- He looks like a match with the wood scraped off.
- He's a long streak.
- He's a long streak of misery.
- He's all wire and whipcord.

Women would say:

- What you need is *a decent feed*.
- If you don't eat you'll end up *a bag of bones*.
- I'm not going to worry and *get skinny legs*.

If a dog was too thin, men would say: '*That dog has seen more dinnertimes than dinners*.'

An overweight man would be called *tub guts* or *lardarse*. A strong but short man was *nuggetty*.

- He's fading away to a monument.
- He's got a fair sort of awning over the toolshed.
- He's been grazing in the best paddocks.
- They'll have to cut off his corn supply.
- He's got a face like a cabbie's arse: fat, round and shiny.
- He's been living on *stodge*.

Men might say of a plump woman:

- She's got a bit too much pudding on her hips.
- She's carrying a bit too much gloobly-glub.
- She's a bit beefy.
- She's a bit hefty.
- Once round her is twice round the gasworks.
- She's two axe handles across the backside.

Whereas a woman might say to an overweight woman: 'You're looking very well!'

Chapter eleven

THE WAY WE WERE

Job for life

In the 1940s and 50s people got a job and stayed forever. Many of these jobs no longer exist. Instead of asking, 'What do you do?' people back then asked, 'What game are you in?'

And the answer came expected: 'I'm in the stationery game'; or 'I'm in the fruit game'; or 'I'm in the trucking game.'

Some such jobs were:

- **Traveller** — a bloke who went around with samples to shops and took orders, delivered them, and put them on the shelves. Usually referred to as **silver-tongued**.
- **Quiz kid** — a detective
- **Newspaperman**
- **Touch typist, stenographer, shorthand typist**
- **Clerk/typist** — most of the Positions Vacant in the newspaper classifieds seemed to be for a clerk/typist.
- **Telephonist** — ran the switchboard, switching phone calls through to the correct person; answered queries from the public; put through **trunk calls** and **long-distance calls** for staff.
- **Bank jockey** — a teller
- **Deliverymen: bread man, milkman, dunny man, pig man, clothes prop man, iceman.**

Before refrigerators, a man delivered blocks of ice for people's ice chests every couple of days. He carried steel tongs with sharp hooks that stuck into the ice block. Clothes lines were made of propeller wire, held above the ground by thin saplings with a fork on the end. It was an art to hang the wet washing on the line, then lift the stick to prop it up. The clothes prop man went into the bush and selected thin, forked saplings or limbs and cut them to the best length. He would trawl up and down every street on his horse and cart, yelling out: 'Clothes props, clothes props' until some housewife would realise she needed a new prop and would run out into the street yelling.

The **postman** would cycle by and blow his whistle as he left a letter. There were no angle-grinders, concrete pumps and tile saws to drown out the sound of the whistle. He delivered Monday to Saturday. The **PMG** was in charge of the mail and the telephone system in Australia. The initials stood for **Post Master General**, but everyone called them the **Public Money Grabbers** or **Punch Me Gently**.

The **Rawleigh's man** would come up the back stairs with a large port full of goods from shampoo to '**a salve for man and beast**'.

Shop assistants didn't say 'Are you having a good day?' when you walked in, nor 'Have a nice day' as you left. They would simply say 'Yes please?' and 'Thank you.' The golden rule was: **The customer is always right**.

Headline news

The hottest news in the 1950s was **communism**. Most stories from overseas in the newspapers had '**reds**' in the headline.

Everyone was extremely worried about **red aggression** and falling under **the iron heel of communism**. People were always talking about **communist fronts**, and '**self-confessed communists**'. It was said that there was **no place to hide** from communism. But anyone who became alarmed, rather than just alert, was said to be looking for **reds under the beds**.

This was after World War II in which we fought with England against Germany and with the USA against Japan. During that war, people kept their hopes up by saying:

England was England
When Germany was a pup;
And England will be England
When Germany's buggered up.

After World War II was over we got involved in the **Cold War** between us in the West and communist countries like Russia and **Red China** (the common name for the People's Republic of China). War was so much on everyone's mind that toy shops sold little yellow plastic Russian MIG jets and our RAAF Sabres side by side. Little kids like me could recognise the MIG's high tail *from a mile off*.

The big joke then was: Surgeons in Russia remove tonsils via a patient's bum — because Russians have to keep their mouths shut.

Red China represented what was known as *the yellow peril* — the threat of invasion from Asia. At that time, the Australian government had an official policy to keep Australia a land of white people. It was called the **White Australia Policy**. Given that the original inhabitants were Aborigines, it seemed to be a ludicrous name. But in the 1950s no one seemed to notice the irony. Though many Australians would always declare loudly: **'I don't care if he's black, white or brindle.'**

'New Australian' was the official government term for any **foreigner** who moved here. The name was supposed to make them more acceptable to **'us fair dinkum Australians'**. Almost all immigrants at that time came from Europe. To become Australian they swore their allegiance with their hands on the Bible.

Pro-Labor Party people always referred to newspapers as **the Tory press**. **'The Tory press force-feeds us with tripe every day,'** my Uncle Cyril used to say.

Boys with guns

Because of the perceived threats to our country, defence was taken seriously. So seriously that 13-year-old boys were required to join school defence force cadet units. Either the army, the air force or the sea cadets.

Cadets were issued with full summer and winter uniforms, which they wore to school once a week (the day they stayed behind for two hours of marching and rifle drill). Plus cadets did one or two week-long camps with the armed services each year until the end of grade 12.

In the case of army cadets, you were issued with a .303 rifle and got to fire it on the range and in mock battles. You knew that the cry of **'Limber Up!'** meant to throw yourself forward onto the ground and prepare to open fire, by releasing the safety catch and taking **first pressure** on the trigger, which was then to be squeezed slowly, not tugged. After firing, you knew to **re-line, re-load and relax**. We also got to fire Bren guns, Vickers machine guns, and mortar bombs.

Learning to shoot a .303 back then was called **musketry**.

Leaving school did not mean the end of army life. Throughout the 1950s anyone who turned 18 in Australia became a **Nasho** — a national serviceman. These youths did six months full-time as soldiers and then were in the army reserve for five years.

Fighting words

In the 1950s, a mother might give her first grandchild a pair of boxing gloves as a birthday gift.

Fighting in the boxing ring, and with your fists on the street or in the schoolyard, was once so much a part of life that it was built into the language. But using knives, machetes, baseball bats or guns was considered too cowardly to contemplate.

If a boy smashed his nose or cut his face, his mother would offer consolation by comparing him to a boxer: 'It just makes you look like a pug.' On the other hand, if her son wouldn't stick up for himself, she would say: 'You're a bit of a **Palooka**': a boxer who couldn't fight.

Fathers would teach their sons how to stand in a **stoush**, with their **dukes up**, and they would describe people who got around together, or who worked together for years, as **old sparring partners**. You might say: 'My brother and I were **having a spar**' and it meant you were having a box, not sitting in a bubbly bath together.

If someone surrendered, or gave up on a project or exam, they were said to **throw in the towel** — which is what a boxer's trainer did if he wanted to **call it quits** because his man was no longer capable of defending himself in a bout.

On the other hand, if someone refused to be intimidated, or to give up on a project, you would say: '**He doesn't know when he's licked.**' Or, '**He's dead but he won't lie down.**'

When someone put themselves forward for a position at the local cricket club they were always said to **throw their hat into the ring**.

If a job was going badly, or a relationship needed mending, a man would say to his mate: '**We'll have to box clever.**'

Major boxing title fights were always preceded by several preliminary bouts. So when a boy missed out on a prize at school his father would console him by saying: 'Never mind, champ, it was only a **preliminary bout**.'

Every Friday night the fights were broadcast on the wireless and most fathers and sons listened together at the kitchen table:

The stadium is so full they're hanging from the rafters ... the red corner, the blue corner ... a left rip to the body, a right to the head ... they're going toe to toe ... an uppercut to the chin and his legs are wobbly ... a right cross to the jaw ... his face a mask of blood ... he's gone down for the count ... one, two, three, four ... he's up and the referee is wiping his gloves — in the neutral corner ...

When a man wanted to know the weight of a boy for a football team he would always ask: 'What's your **fighting weight**?' This was because boxers always knew their best weight for the ring: not too light to lose strength, not too heavy or they wouldn't **go the distance**.

Boxers also always fought someone of similar size and weight, so it was considered unsporting in Australia to fight someone much smaller than yourself. Thus a favourite saying during arguments was: **'Pick on someone your own size.'**

It's difficult to understand now, but boxing was seen not as fighting but as an art: **the art of pugilism**. By the time he was ten, my brother had an instruction book called *The Gentle Art of Boxing*. The most popular comic in the local rag was usually **Joe Palooka**. Joe, a champion, was always losing till the last round, when his girlfriend, who had been kidnapped or ill, would arrive and he would revive and deliver his famous knockout punch.

Thus it was that everyone knew a lot about boxing ... except perhaps why a roped-off square was called a ring!

Everyone knew the boxer's stance: feet apart, one in front of the other, one hand extended and the other covering one side of the face and ready to launch a **haymaker** to the **moosh** at any time; and the characteristic touching of the nose with the thumb as he danced around and let out 'sisssss', 'sisssss' as he tensed his stomach muscles.

People followed boxing so closely they wanted to know which hand a boxer led with. Most led with the left, but a boxer who led with his right hand was called a **southpaw**.

Men knew the weight of individual boxers in stones, pounds and ounces and thus which division they fought in: **flyweight, featherweight, welterweight** etc. They knew if a boxer had a good **straight left**, a good **uppercut** or a **glass jaw**.

Back in the 1950s, athletes didn't do weight-lifting, so if some bloke did, he would be described as being **muscle-bound**.

FISTICUFFS

Most boxing matches were between two males — either boys or men — with no gloves at all. The fight would always be preceded by insults.

- *I'll knock you rotten!*
- I'll do you like a dinner!
- *You couldn't beat time with a stick!*
- I'll give you a lift under the lug!
- *You couldn't fight your way out of a paper bag* or *a brown paper bag* or *a wet paper bag!*
- I'll drop you!
- *I'll deck you!*
- I'll shake up your liver bile!
- *I'll give you the raspberry!*
- I'll clock you!
- *I'll give you a fat lip!*

The pair would eventually **resort to fisticuffs**. This happened when they both **got their ginger up** and **did their nana**. Then they'd **bung on a blue**, **go the knuckle**, **go to town**. There would be a **big barney** as each endeavoured to give the other a **Vegemite sandwich** (also known as a **knuckle sandwich**).

As in boxing, **kidney punches** were never used. They were considered unfair because you can't protect your kidneys in a fight.

If a woman happened onto this scene she would say: '**Don't disturb the peace**.' But once the fight started she might call out: '**Put some starch into him**.'

If a punch really hurt, the opponent would say that it **tickled**, but spectators would know it gave him **a bit of a hurry-up**. The injured bloke would **smile.** The worse it hurt, the more he smiled.

Eventually one of them would be **licked** and **give the other best**.

Spectators would say he was **done like a dinner**, but, even so, he was **as game as Ned Kelly**.

Imperfect contrition

GOOD CATHOLICS AND BAD CATHOLICS

There were many different types of Catholics in Australia in the 1950s.

Lapsed Catholics were those who didn't practise their religion. The very word **lapsed** implied what everyone knew: there was no such thing as an ex-Catholic, only those who had been temporarily distracted.

Catholics who went to Mass every Sunday and obeyed God's Commandments and the Commandments of the Church, and who practised 'fortitude, piety and fear of the Lord', were said to be **good Catholics**.

Protestants invariably referred to such people as **strong Catholics**.

There was also a type of man known by Catholics as a **bad Catholic** — you rarely saw him at Mass on Sunday and he complained loudly about the Church. Yet he would still say: 'I used to worship at St Mary's Church.'

If things went wrong, the **bad Catholic** was the sort of man who might exclaim: **'I think God's a Protestant!'** He was a very different fellow from the **lapsed Catholic**, who had fallen by the wayside but no doubt would soon be back at Mass, Confession and Holy Communion ... once he stopped going out with the **Proddo sheila** he met at the **Blind Institute** dance.

Bad Catholics were the sort of blokes who were said to interpret **Propagation of the Faith** as taking out Protestant women.

THE WORDS CATHOLICS USED

In the 1950s, Protestants were curious about what went on over the convent wall, but even for Catholics it took decades to learn all the words and understand all the little things that went on.

Even if there was no Mass, Catholics were still expected to pop into a church and kneel to say a prayer. This was known as **paying a visit**, that is, to visit the Lord thy God. As the Catholic **catechism** said: **When should we pray? Every morning and every night and frequently during the day**.

Thus Catholics were encouraged to say small prayers quietly to themselves — on the tram, at work, at the races. These were called '**aspirations**' or '**pious ejaculations**'.

The Church taught: **the family that prays together stays together**. Thus many Catholic families **said the Rosary** (which took about 20 minutes and involved more than 50 prayers, a prayer for each bead on the chain) together every night. Saying the Rosary was reputed to be wonderful for **the destruction of sin**.

A Catholic woman would have to cover her head when she walked into a church. She would bless herself with a drop of holy water from a font at the doorway, then perhaps reach up to touch the toes of the statue of a saint she relied on, while saying a prayer to that saint. So much so, that the toes of statues in Catholic churches were always worn smooth. During Lent, all statues and crucifixes were covered with purple cloths.

Before sitting down, a Catholic woman would **genuflect** before the gold

tabernacle in the centre of the altar. She might have dropped in to **confess her sins** to the priest and be given a **penance** to perform as punishment. This could vary from **three Hail Marys** (reciting the Hail Mary prayer three times), to a **Rosary**, to several extra Masses — depending on how bad her sins were.

Some Catholics went to confession more than once a week, though you were only required by Church commandment to attend 'at least once a year'. Catholics were always worrying that they weren't being good enough. This was called **wrestling with your conscience**.

SINS AND CONFESSION

A sin was 'any thought, word, deed or omission against the law of God'. There were two classes of sin and it was vital you knew the difference. Your whole afterlife depended on it.

1. **Venial sins** — if you died without confessing these small sins (such as impure thoughts) and receiving **absolution** (forgiveness), you'd go to **Purgatory** where you could sizzle for a few months or years until being allowed to ascend into Heaven. There were two ways to get out early: (a) you had earned **indulgences** during your life through prayer and attending Mass and Communion often or (b) once you died, others could **offer up** prayers or suffering to get you out early. So, if someone stubbed their toe, instead of swearing, they could **offer it up for the Holy Souls in Purgatory**. Another, unofficial, way was for Catholics to be happy and laugh; it was said that every time you laughed, you got a **Holy Soul out of Purgatory**. **Purgatory** had nothing to do with **Limbo** — the desolate nowhere-land for the souls of people who hadn't been christened.

2. **Mortal sins** — having even just one of these left on your slate at death meant damnation in **Hell** forevermore: *Depart from me, ye cursed, into the everlasting fires of Hell which were prepared for You, the Devil, and his Angels.* This was why it was vital to confess all **mortal sins** to a priest before you died and receive the **Sacrament of Absolution**. Catholics prayed that they would die in the presence of a Catholic priest. A mortal sin might be an **impure action** or the breaking of a Commandment.

The worst sins were said to be **calumny and detraction**: telling terrible untrue stories about someone, ruining a person's reputation. It was said to be like loosing an arrow from the top of the church tower: you could never get it back.

These were called **sins of doubt and presumption**. But if you were the subject of the gossip you were urged to just pray:

Do good to them that hurt you.
Love them that hate you.
And pray for them that persecute and calumniate you.

Then there were the **sins of commission** and **omission**.

Protestants laughed at the idea of **confession** and used to sing a little ditty at parties to the tune of 'I do like to live beside the seaside':

Oh I would like to be a Roman Catholic.
Oh I would like to join the Church of Rome.
You can do what you like in the pale moonlight
And confess it all in the morning ...
If you like.

But it wasn't that simple. When you went to confession you had to have a **firm desire of amendment** or your sins would not be forgiven. In other words, you had to be genuinely sorry and promise, and believe, that you would not sin again — which was said in the **Act of Contrition** prayer.

It was still more complex.

Catholics were taught that there were two types of contrition: **perfect contrition** and **imperfect contrition**. Imperfect contrition was being sorry in order to avoid being punished in the afterlife; perfect contrition was being sorry because you had offended God.

The Catholic Church in the 1950s seemed to be mainly worried about **impure thoughts** and **impure actions**. The Church felt the best basis on which to proceed through life was not to simply **resist temptation**, but to *avoid* it. Thus we were constantly warned to avoid **occasions of sin**; **evil company**; and **dangerous occasions**.

Protestants found all of this mysterious. But the Holy Catholic Church had its own **mysteries of religion**. Catholics were supposed to **meditate upon these mysteries**, which were divided up into the Joyful mysteries, the Sorrowful mysteries and the Glorious mysteries.

There were important days called **Feast Days**, which had nothing to do with eating. They were days to commemorate a saint, such as St Patrick or St Joseph. Not the birthday, strangely enough, but their death day. It was sort of to remind you that saints (as *you* should be) were more interested in the here-after than the here and now, which is not surprising, since a lot of them died in terrible ways after much persecution.

Feast Days were usually a holiday at Catholic schools. Some were **holy**

days of obligation, which meant you were obliged to attend Mass **on pain of mortal sin**.

There were five such days a year:

Christmas Day

New Year's Day

The Assumption

All Saints' Day

Ascension Thursday

Being a Catholic schoolkid meant knowing lots of unusual words like **relics, contrition, iniquities, unction, dolours, scapulars** and **miraculous medals**. (Some Catholic mothers would sew a miraculous medal into the hem of their sons' footy shorts to protect them in the scrum when playing Protestant schools.) Plus phrases like **fruit of thy womb, Immaculate Conception**, and **the infallibility of the Pope**.

Catholics were sensitive to the fact that Protestants laughed at the Catholic belief in **infallibility**. Thus it was emphasised in Catholic schools that the Pope was infallible *only under three strict conditions*: 'When speaking as head of the Church, and binding all the faithful, he defines doctrines of faith or morals.'

In those days, the Holy Spirit was called the **Holy Ghost**. And by the time we were seven we knew the **Seven Gifts of the Holy Ghost** off by heart:

1. Wisdom
2. Understanding
3. Counsel
4. Knowledge
5. Fortitude
6. Piety
7. Fear of the Lord.

Plus we had learned by heart **the seven sacraments**. A Catholic priest was the only person who could receive all seven sacraments (if he was married and widowed before he became a priest):

1. Baptism
2. Absolution
3. Confirmation
4. Blessed Eucharist
5. Matrimony
6. Holy Orders
7. Extreme Unction.

Grace was my favourite word as a child.

Hail Mary full of grace … was the start of the prayer said most often in the Catholic religion. These words meant that Jesus loved his mother Mary, so she was full of God's love. An Archbishop is always **His Grace**, and we said **grace before meals**: 'Bless us, Oh Lord, and these, thy gifts, which of thy bounty we are about to receive, through Jesus Christ Our Lord. Amen.'

Grace also means beauty of form or motion. You could only enter the **Kingdom of Heaven** if you were in a **state of grace**.

Chapter twelve

OLD-TIMERS

LOST FOR WORDS EPISODE 9:
Visiting Grandma

Lost for Words. **The story of Bert and Grace and their trials and tribulations bringing up a young family after the War.**

'That's a fine how d'y'do!' said Grandma to Doris. 'That's a nice state of affairs! What possessed you? What were you thinking of, you saucy minx, agreeing to go to the dance with two different fellows? That's beyond the pale.'

'But, Grandma, they both asked me and I couldn't say no. I can't choose which I like best. It all happened accidentally,' said Doris.

'Accidentally on purpose, I'd say. Do you think there's safety in numbers? You must have had a deprived childhood! I never thought Cyril and Myrtle would breed such a flighty flibbertigibbet. Were you brought up or dragged up? What do you do at that school of yours? Spend all day reading the penny dreadfuls? You brazen hussy. You giddy young thing. Don't you know one at a time is good fishing? Blind Freddy could see that it would all end in tears. Don't keep me in suspenders, who are these poor boys?'

'Arnold Jones and … '

'Arnold Jones! With all the best will in the world I couldn't recommend him! He's a loaded gun! He's the greatest villain unhung. He couldn't lie straight in bed. He's a lazy good-for-nothing. He's a rotter and a stinker. I tell you, he's on the nose around here after he blotted his copybook. That man has no couth, no shame, he's a right heathen. If he shows his face around here, everyone will give him the cold shoulder. And you too. And I'll tell you another thing, my girl, if you start walking out with Arnold Jones, no other boy will want to marry you. You'll be shopsoiled. Now who is the other lad?'

'Sandy Strong.'

'Sandy! Well at least he's got a head on his shoulders. But when he was doing my yard the other week, do you know, he took his shirt off and was working in just his dungarees. And if there's one thing I can't abide, it's a naked man. But, give him his due, full credit to him, Sandy has a mind like a steel trap. He's no fool. He's as smart as paint. He's a real live-wire.'

'I didn't mean to say yes to both, Grandma. I told a lie and then it just grew like Topsy. Sandy was so bashful about asking me, and when I said yes, he was that chuffed. He was so thrilled, his shirt nearly ran up his back. He was beside himself.'

'I'd take that with a grain of salt.'

'And then Arnold asked me, and it all just happened so suddenly. I meant to say no to Arnold, but ...'

'The road to Hell is paved with good intentions, Doris.'

'What will I do? It's all a mess.'

'Oh what a tangled web we weave when first we practise to deceive. You've made your bed, Doris, now you've got to lie in it. You'll just have to tell one of them that you're going to the dance with the other.'

'If I had my druthers I'd like to go with Sandy. But how can I go back to Arnold and say I'm going to the dance with Sandy? He'll never speak to me again.'

'Good riddance to bad rubbish I say. In fact, this will bring him down a peg or two. He's got so many tickets on himself, one day the wind will blow and all those tickets will blow away.'

'But, Grandma, couldn't I tell both of them I'm sick, so I'm not going to the dance at all, and then at the last minute I get miraculously better and turn up all by myself? Then I can dance with both of them and they'll never know.'

'My girl, I'm lost for words. You take the cake. You're the dizzy limit. It's no use hiding, because it will all come out in the wash. You're a beggar for punishment. You've called it all down on yourself. You'll get your comeuppance, never you mind. You've surpassed yourself in your audacity ... And they hanged Ned Kelly!'

What Grandma said

- **Obedience** — this was a quality that your grandmother put much store by. It was very real. If she said a little girl was 'very obedient', this was something to be admired. **Not to be sneezed at**.

- **Behave** — Your grandmother simply had to say 'Behave!' and you knew exactly what she meant. You were in trouble. You had to make changes. You had to stop looking around, shut your mouth, slow down, speak more quietly, stop hitting, nudging and pulling. It would be preferable if you didn't move at all. And, even better, not speak at all.

  If you didn't change, Grandma would say: 'Stop chiacking. Stop skylarking. Stop carrying on like the wild man of Borneo. You're just pixilated. I haven't seen such behaviour in all my born days.'

  When you refused to behave, Grandma was quick with the stick, her Golden Rule being: **spare the rod and spoil the child**. As she would often say: 'God may forgive you, but I can still use the wooden spoon!' If you were really very naughty Grandma might warn: 'I'll have your guts for garters.' What came next was: 'I'll belt you till your shirt runs up and down your back like a roller blind.'

- **Lazybones** — Grandma was always on the lookout for a **lazybones**, which, in children, was as bad as giving cheek. 'Stop that lolling, moping, loaaaaafing, slouching, lounging, shirking, mooching, and lying about the house like a slovenly sloth.'

- **Stop bunging it on** — if you fell over and hurt yourself and she thought you were crying too much, Grandma would say to your mother: 'That child is just bunging on a turn. Don't mollycoddle the boy, you'll spoil him.'

- **Using language** — say you told a dirty joke by accident and Grandma heard, she would then accuse you of 'lewd behaviour' and say you were 'using language'. She didn't need to say it was bad language or foul language — you knew what she meant. Then she would add: 'If I've told you once, I've told you twice, don't be vulgar. Don't be common.' Then Grandma would either demand you 'wash your mouth out' or she would threaten: 'I'll wash your mouth out with a bar of soap.'

If you could stay out of her reach, she'd say 'you should be hung, drawn and quartered.' Since you never knew what this actually meant, it wasn't much of a threat. You could be sure she had given up the chase when she said with a laugh: 'They couldn't hang you for the dirt around your neck!'

- **Due respect** — Grandmas demanded that children 'respect their elders' and 'never be cheeky to grown-ups'. Cheekiness was **answering back**. Adults commanded this **due respect**. **Being disrespectful** was a cardinal sin, as was **giving cheek.** If Grandma was shocked by what a child said she would exclaim: **The cheek!** Or, **What a cheek!** When you were game enough, or silly enough, to answer back she'd say: '**Don't you get uppity with me, miss**.' Or, when she was going to tell you in detail all your recent sins she'd say: '**I'll give you chapter and verse**.'

'You're **just a spring chicken**,' Grandma said if you were disagreeing and she thought you should show more deference.

If you tried to get back in her good books by saying, 'Oh Grandma, your pie is so nice, Grandma, it really is, Grandma,' she'd retort: 'Another *Grandma* and you'll taste my stick.' She knew you were using her name to get at her, and she wanted to let you know she was **awake up**.

GRANDMA'S WISDOM

Grandmas knew everything, but the trouble was they were always dispensing advice — and children soon got sick of all their old sayings.

Convince a woman against her will,
She'll hold the same opinion still.

- You can't make strawberry jam out of manure.
- Least said, soonest mended. Instead of going on and on and on, making excuses, just say you're sorry, and leave it at that. Otherwise you are only digging yourself a hole, making matters worse, gilding the lily.
- Fool me once, shame on you. Fool me twice, shame on me.

- Remember, all the saints are Catholics, but not all the Catholics are saints.
- Whatever is on a drunken man's lips is in a sober man's mind.
- You never miss the water till the well runs dry.
- Water finds its own level. (If someone is a ne'er-do-well, he can put on the dog all he likes and pretend to be reformed, but he'll soon give the game away by mixing with the wrong crowd again.)
- Waste not, want not. (Grandma's favourite.)
- Never take a generality as the truth, not even this one.
- You'll get nothing for nothing, and very little for sixpence.
- Don't marry for silver, but don't marry where it's not.
- It's as easy to marry a rich man as a poor man, but harder to find.
- Keep hair, keep care — don't keep a lock of anyone's hair; it's bad luck.
- Don't cut off your nose to spite your face. (When you get on your high horse, and refuse to back down, you might as well cut your own nose off, because you are the only one who will suffer.)
- Don't blow your own trumpet. (Because no one will take any notice.)
- Give credit where credit's due. (Another Grandma all-time favourite.)
- Never do things by halves.
- Good things come in small packages, like poison.
- Idle hands make mischief, and the Devil makes work for idle hands.
- Men are queer cattle.
- If you wear a hat you'll go bald.

When Grandma was advising you to put in a small amount of work now, or you'll have a big job to do later, she would say:

- Don't spoil the ship for a ha'penny of tar, or
- All for the want of a horseshoe nail, or
- A stitch in time saves nine.

When Grandma was **forecasting doom** she'd say:

- It'll nae (not) leave him till he dies. (He's got a fault, and he'll never change. You won't change him even though you think you can.)
- He'll never make old bones. (He's so foolhardy he'll do himself in at a young age.)
- I can feel it in my bones.
- I can feel it in my water.
- With the best will in the world, you cannot undo what is done.

GRANDMA ON ROTTERS

- They've always been **a stuffy lot** — meaning they are **up themselves**, and think they're better than Grandma.
- **If they don't come, they won't be counted** — they've accepted the invitation, but if they don't have the courtesy to turn up, we don't want them. **It's their miss out**.
- Give him **a long enough rope and he'll hang himself** — he'll condemn himself by his own mouth if you get him relaxed.
- He's **a bit much**.
- He's **all over the shop, he doesn't know whether he's Arthur or Martha** — he doesn't know what he's doing.
- Some people are just **cheap and nasty**.
- It was **a black act** when they took the will to the lawyers without telling him.
- She **blows hot and cold** — one day she wants to be your best friend, the next she wouldn't even cross the road to say hello.
- Oh that one, he's still **uhmming and ahhing** — he can't make up his mind.
- He's **a nasty piece of work** and she's **an odious creature**.
- **You couldn't kill him with an axe**.
- **I've never read about her on jam tins** — she thinks she's important but I'm not impressed.
- **He's a big man, but a wee coat fits him** — he's not as important as he thinks he is.
- **She's a gimme** — gimme this, gimme that.

NO NONSENSE

- I've got **a bone to pick** with you — I've been awaiting an opportunity to complain to you, and now it's arrived.
- Now that's a **half-baked** excuse!
- That's **all very well**. (Grandma is not convinced or impressed.)
- When she saw two young sweethearts canoodling: **Nothing makes me sick**.
- Mark my words, that boy will **never amount to anything**.
- Young man, I can see you're getting **too big for your boots**.
- **Small things amuse small minds.**
- When Dad was driving Grandma home she would say: '**I'd like to get there in one piece, if it's all the same to you.**'
- I've a good mind to go and **give him a piece of my mind**.
- No one got up at church and said any words about the anniversary. I think it was **very poor**.
- This dress will see me out.
- Just bury me in the backyard.

GRANDMA'S PROBLEMS

- **And with my own flesh and blood!** — when there'd been a family argument.
- It's all gone **out the window**.
- The cake collapsed in the middle, and then the scones were burnt **to boot**. Whenever there was an extra problem, Grandma always added 'to boot'.
- This was **sewn with a hot needle** and **a burning thread** — when Grandma bought clothes and the button came off immediately, or the seams came apart.
- In the days when people rode horses and bicycles everywhere, if the scissors were blunt, Grandma would say: '**You could ride to Sydney and back on these.**'
- **Some ungodly hour** — early morning or very early morning.
- **Where the devil** did they get that old thing from?
- Don't **tromp** around in the wet.

- I'm at **sixes and sevens** — don't know what to decide.
- I'm a bit **miffed** — put out, slightly insulted, feel slighted.
- We've had a bit of a **tiff** — a spat, a little fight that could escalate but might just peter out.

LOST FOR WORDS EPISODE 10:
Visiting Grandad

Lost for Words. **The story of Bert and Grace and their trials and tribulations bringing up a young family after the War.**

Horace and Sandy arrived to visit their grandfather.

'By Jove, things are looking up,' Grandad said, delighted. 'I've been sitting here all by myself like a mopoke all day. I've been feeling niggardly. The four walls don't come to conversation.'

'We thought we'd just pop in to see how you were,' said Horace.

'Well, if I'd known you were coming I'd have sent the welcome wagon round. And if your grandmother knew you were coming, she would have stayed home and baked a cake. Instead, she's on the rantan visiting Bert and Grace. How's tricks?'

'I went for my job interview yesterday,' said Horace. 'I tried to arrive early because I wanted to be the first cab off the rank. But there were seventy other bods all going for the same position! You wouldn't think so many fellas would want to be a counter-jumper. It's a bit of a sissy's game.'

'Did you see anybody you liked better than yourself?' asked Grandad.

'No, they were all very snooty. They didn't like me walking in without a tie on.'

'The apparel proclaims the man,' said Grandad. 'You know I've always told you, Horace, if you can't be a good cricketer, at least dress like one. The same goes at work. First impressions count. Clothes maketh the man.'

'Yeah, but, Grandad, it was only the interview for the job, not the job. How was I to know it was supposed to be formal? And anyway, why should a shop assistant have to wear a tie? The pay isn't too crash hot.'

'Cut your cloth according to your purse. You should always dress as well as you can afford; no more, but especially no less. Let your apparel be as costly as your purse will allow. So, Horace, did they ask you difficult questions?'

'The first thing the boss says is, "What are ya?" So I told him I wasn't a Catholic, if that's what he was getting at. So he seemed satisfied with that. Then he wanted to know if I had any vices. I didn't know what he meant, so I said I smoked roll-your-owns.'

'Better to smoke a little here and now, than a lot hereafter. Smoking may be a vice, but it keeps you away from all the other vices, the ones that will send you to the fires of Hell.'

'Anyhow, he asked if there was anyone who could give me a character, so I named you. Then he wanted to know what I thought of the firm. I should have said what I thought of him.'

'Horace, if you don't have anything nice to say about someone, then don't say anything at all.'

'He asked if I had any comments to make and I said "No".'

'Be thankful for small mercies. That's the ticket. Better be silent and regarded as a fool rather than speak and leave no doubt.'

'It's galling to see the way that fellow struts around like the king pea. He's only the floor creeper anyhow. All he does is wear a flower in his coat button and wring his hands and bow to all the ladies as they walk in the store. I don't even know if I want to work for him.'

'Beggars can't be choosers.'

'But perhaps I should try for an apprenticeship, or go to night school.'

'Horace, I've told you before, one at a time's good fishing. You can only have one experience at one time. It's better to stick at one task and know it well, than spread yourself too thin. What's your strong suit?'

'I didn't want to tell him I'm thinking about becoming a reporter. Reporters get to sleep in, and they get free passes to all the shows and all the footy matches.'

'Horace, you're a mine of information.'

'It seemed silly for me to be wasting my time when I've got bigger fish to fry.'

'But haven't I always told you, little fish are sweetest.'

'So in the end, I told him I didn't want his stupid job if I had to wear a stupid tie to get it. I told him he should give it to one of the other no-hopers.'

'It would make a grown man cry,' said Grandad, shaking his head. 'I'm lost for words. I suppose you can't put an old head on young shoulders. Well, Horace, you'll be a great help to your parents, if you ever grow up. You've got to always act square. Did you manage to part on cordial terms?'

'I guess so. Although, I did tell the boss he was an old fuddy-duddy stick-in-the-mud.'

'Didn't your father ever teach you to respect your elders? And your betters?'

'Don't jump up and down on your hat, Grandad. Don't get your dander up. Don't get off your bike, I'll pick up your pump. There's plenty more jobs. I might even become an actor or a traveller like Sandy. Or a pilot. I reckon I'd waltz it in.'

'That's just campfire talk.'

'No, Grandad, I know what I'm doing. I've had lots of experience.'

'Experience makes wise men fools. Where ignorance is bliss, 'tis folly to be wise, Horace.'

'What?'

'Clean the spuds out of your ears. It means: if you think you know everything, you're sure to find out later that you don't.'

'But, Grandad, all the rules have changed. In modern business today, the golden rule is you have to do it to them before they do it to you.'

'Fools make rules, and bigger fools obey them.'

'What?'

'Rules are made for the obedience of fools and the guidance of wise men. Haven't I always told you, get a job in the public service. Or in petrol or food.'

Grandad gave up on Horace and turned his attention to Sandy. 'Now, Sandy, you're a cocky young lad, what are *you* up to nowadays?'

'I've got a beautiful sweetheart called Doris. She's a fashion plate. I'm taking her to a dance next Saturday night.'

'And what are you doing for a crust?'

'On the weekends I'm mowing yards for people, but during the week I'm in the stationery game,' said Sandy.

'And how are you faring?'

'Well, I was going great guns, but now I'm having kittens over the fancy paper orders. I can never remember what you told me. Measure once, cut twice?'

'By jingo, are you two both tarred with the same brush?' said Grandad. 'Sandy, you're way off the beam. You're fighting above your weight, you big Palooka. It's measure twice, cut once. Do it right, do it once. If you do the job carefully and correctly, you'll only have to do it that one time. But if you are slapdash, you'll be wasting time in the end, because you'll have to start from the beginning and do it all over again.'

'I'll try to remember.'

'At my time of life it's often more difficult to forget than to remember. My life's not all beer and skittles, these days. I'm on my last legs. Shinbones should be behind us, boys, and then we wouldn't keep barking them on the sheets in bed. Now come and look at the chair I've been making for your mother in the shed.'

❧

'Gee, Grandad, will you teach me how to do it?' asked Horace.

'I'll tell you the do's and don'ts, show you the ropes, so you don't go off half-cocked,' said Grandad.

'Can I have a crack at it too?' asked Sandy.

'Go for your life. Now, this is a trap for young players. You've got to hold your tongue right. It's all in the wrist.'

Grandad demonstrated how to plane the wood, and then Sandy tried it with Grandad encouraging: 'That's the idea, that's the shot. Good man. You're a quick study, Sandy. See, it's as easy as taking wheat from a blind chook. C'mon, tiger, good on you, go at it hammer and tongs, you're as right as rain, and then Bob's your uncle. Don't give up the ghost yet, this will be another string to your bow. It's a cinch!'

Sandy produced the turned leg of the chair.

'My boy,' said Grandad, 'go to the top of the class. Any better wouldn't do. You're worth your weight in horse manure.'

What Grandad said

- If that's not your Aunt Ethel on that tram, **I'll go he** — meaning I'll **eat my hat**, I'll be **a monkey's uncle**.
- He **cried off** — he wouldn't wait.
- Don't **put all your eggs in one basket** ... unless you want scrambled eggs.
- **Fair-weather friend** — Grandad would warn you about these people; they were great company but would not support you when you needed help.
- **It's a great life if you don't weaken**.
- **A sugarbag** — a bee's nest with honey.
- If you have **bush instinct** you'll never get lost in the bush.
- **Widowmaker** — a giant tree limb that has broken off but is caught up in the lower branches and hangs like the Sword of Damocles, ready to fall, without warning, on those underneath. Hence, **always sit outside the drip-line** of a tree. And **look up**, **not down** when stopping in the bush.
- My father **took this country up**.
- They're **putting up** flats.
- **When you sell the back paddock, that's the end of you**.

To begin a conversation Grandad would say:

- At any rate …
- Early in the piece …
- Late in the piece …
- Now, I want to pick your brain …
- Now, we'd better have **a pow-wow**, you and me …
- Things are looking up …
- What's the bet …
- Like as not (a sure thing) …
- In this day and age …
- Still and all

Old-timers

- -

There were many expressions for anything that was old — people, objects, ways of saying and doing things.

- You kids think I'm as old as Methuselah
- I'm in my dotage
- She's a silly old duck
- She's out of the Ark
- He's a fair age
- He's as old as the hills
- He's an old fogey
- He's set in his ways
- You're never old till your fingers start patting the sheets
- You're never old until your shinbones cut the blanket
- You're never too old to learn
- I'm rattling at the hinges
- I don't do the baking any more
- My forgettory is better than my memory
- Age and want are an ill-matched pair

- How old are you? I can no longer climb trees and run up stairs two at a time. But my mind still takes the stairs two at a time.
- She's forty if she's a day
- She's still very spritely
- I'd rather be a has-been than a never-was
- My old man — strangely, a woman would say that about her husband, and a man about his father
- Grandma would refer to herself as the old girl
- That's so old it's got whiskers
- That's old hat
- They've been saying that since Moses was a boy
- That's been around since Adam wore short pants. Or, since Adam played full-back for Jerusalem.

Old chestnuts

When you talk about the Australian language, most people immediately think of these old words and phrases:

- Stone the crows
- ... and starve the lizards
- It's only two miles as the crow flies
- Give him a fair go
- Bonzer (Danny Kaye sang a song back in the 1950s: 'I think you're so bonzer, dinki-di I do.')
- Aussie cobber, digger, mate
- Spun me a yarn
- Fair dinkum
- Crikey
- A yarn spinner
- Come in, spinner
- Gone bush

- Gone walkabout — Europeans did not know what ceremonies or duties Aborigines had to perform as part of their culture. So when Aborigines would simply leave an area, perhaps leaving their place of work, Europeans put it down to a nomadic nature.
- I hope all your chooks turn into emus and kick your dunny down (Or, your fowl house)
- Shoot through like a Bondi tram
- Stir the possum — go in and start arguments just for the fun of sitting back and watching the others fight
- Don't come the raw prawn with me
- In like Flynn — like Errol Flynn, the swashbuckler
- It's better than a poke in the eye with a burnt stick.

Chapter thirteen

SCALLYWAGS

Children should be seen and not heard

It was said that if Mum and Dad wanted the kids **out of their hair** for an hour or so, they would spill a packet of **hundreds and thousands** in the woodpile.

Kids roamed neighbourhoods, looking for someone to talk to or play with. If anyone had a litter of puppies or kittens, there would be hordes of children visiting the animals every afternoon after school. Ditto anyone with a mango tree.

- In semi-tropical Brisbane, a backyard could have:
- A **mango tree**. It might be bullock's heart (huge mangoes with a strong taste), turpentine (stringy but nectar of the gods) or strawberry (a red tinge on the skin, no strings). The best and biggest mangoes were always on the outer edges of the tree. They were ripe if you gave them a very slight twist and they detached in your hand. Mangoes are surprisingly heavy when still green. Most people in Brisbane had a mango tree and some ordinary suburban blocks had six in their yard. No one bought mangoes in a shop; they were too plentiful.
- A **Queensland nut tree**. Although Queensland nut trees are native to Queensland, originating near the town of Bauple, they were taken to the USA where the delicious round brown Queensland nuts were renamed 'macadamia nuts'. Almost all Australians now call them macadamias — perhaps a metaphor for what has happened to our entire language. (I recently went into a fruit shop in the tiny town of Boonah and asked the young man for some Queensland nuts still in their shell. He offered me a bag of peanuts.)
- **A mulberry tree**
- **A passionfruit vine**
- **A honeysuckle vine** — you bit off the end of the flower and sucked the honey out.
- **A monstera deliciosa** — a special place for kids to hide because the giant

elephant-ear leaves had eye-sized holes you could peep through to keep a lookout, while eating the fruit. This fruit was conical-shaped, a foot long and green with tough dinosaur skin. When opened, the fruit offered hundreds of creamy seed segments. However, there was a sting: they contained tiny black specks that were like peppery barbs.

- **A persimmon tree** — yum yum!
- **A cascara tree** — with long black beans full of a molasses-type sugary substance that was delicious, but gave you **the runs**.
- **A loquat tree** — delish!
- **A guava** with sweet pink centres. Children made pretend pipes from guava fruit, using the hard hollow part of long grass for a stem.
- **Lady's finger bananas**
- **Cape gooseberries**
- **A custard apple tree**
- **A Brazilian cherry hedge**

If any of these trees were in season, the householder could expect lots of little visitors.

Adults were often also visited by bored children, but the grown-ups refused to put themselves out for children who couldn't **amuse themselves**. It was also an era when adults kept children, anyone's children, **in line**. If the grown-ups wanted some privacy they would soon tell the youngsters to **get going** and find themselves something to do:

Go and tell your mother she wants you.

What are you doing here, **me noble shaver**? Or, get out of here, you **snotty little grubber**.

Go away and chase yourself.

Another beauty was: **Why don't you go and play trains**? (The grown-up would have no idea whether the child had a train set or not, but few kids did.)

Adults might call a neighbour's kid: **the little girl at the back of the tribe, a little charmer, a shrimp, tiger, little rascal, whippersnapper**, or **scallywag** (a high-spirited kid who may be mischievous, but never malicious).

If a boy hung around anyway, because boys found adults interesting, a man might say: **Get on yer bike, sonny, get your skates on, buzz off, go fly a kite, scram, put on your running shoes, make yourself scarce, take a long walk off a short pier**.

If the adult was in **a real temper** he might say: **bugger off** or **ping off**.

But the best retorts were: **Make yourself scarce!** or **Go take a running jump at yourself**, which confused young children no end. Boys got to know this phrase so well that at school they used it on other boys in a shortened form: **Go take a running jump**.

If a child was making a lot of noise, yelling, or bouncing a ball for hours, parents invariably complained: **Children should be seen and not heard**. If the kids continued to argue or run through the house, the mother would say: '**You'll be the death of me!**' Whereas irate neighbours or relatives would lean out of the window and yell: '**Put a sock in it, Billy!**' Or, '**Cheese it, Billy, cheese it!**'

BACK ANSWERS

Adults infuriated kids with their ready, enigmatic **back answers**:

How long will you be gone, Mum?
I'll tell you when I get back.

I'm bored, Mum, what can I do?
Eat plum pudding as well as you.

I'm bored, Mum.
You don't look like a piece of wood.

I'm bored, I've got nothing to do.
Well, pee in your shoe.

I'm hot.

Hello, pleased to meet you, Hot.

What's for dinner, Mum?
Bread and duck under the table.

Where are we going to go tonight, Dad?
I know, let's go to ... Blanket Bay.

Mum, are we going out tonight?
Yes, you're going to ... the Blanket Show in Sheet Street.

There's no doubt about you: what an adult would say if you fell over or spilt something. **You're an innocent bugger**: what a man would say to a boy who claimed to have done nothing wrong.

ARGUING WITH ADULTS

Children were forbidden to quarrel with adults. Any child who attempted to win a dispute, even with the **old codger** down the road, would be told: '**Don't argue with your elders**' or, '**Don't argue with your betters**,' or, '**Bite your tongue!**'

If the child said something out of place to a relative, Mum would be certain to say: '**Show some couth, child!**' Or, '**Speak when you're spoken to!**'

If you tried to give your mother advice, she would laugh and say: '**Who's robbing this bank**?' or '**Who's robbing this coach**?' Or '**Who's chopping this chook**?' Then she'd say: '**Are you trying to teach your grandmother how to suck eggs**?' Or, '**Go teach your grandmother how to suck eggs!**' Or '**Alright, Know-All-Not, let's see you do it**.'

If a boy successfully pointed out a mistake his father had made when repairing a wooden toy, the father would remain unfazed, saying merely: '**My mistake, but you're wrong**.'

When a parent warned a child not to do something, such as lick a knife or drink from the milk bottle, and the child retorted cheekily 'But you do it', the

parent would say: '**Do as I say, not as I do**.' And if a child said, 'But Daddy swears' the reply came back: '**But he's a returned soldier.**'

Other retorts:

If I get up early ...

If is a very small word with a great big meaning.

I promise ...

Promises are like piecrusts, very easily broken.

But *I truly-ruly* promise I'll do it tomorrow …
Anyone who leans on you is leaning on a dead stick.

'But I can't … '
I can't is a mean little coward.
A boy that is half a man.
Set on him a wee little doggy.
For the world knows,
And honours,
I can.

I wish we …
Wish in one hand, spit in the other, and see which fills up first.

But I thought …
Thought only thought he thought, then thought was hung.

Why?
Y is a crooked letter and Zed is no better.

Hey!
Hay makes the bull fat. Straw makes it skinny.

What?
Watt made a steam engine.

And when your parents wanted to be contrary:
'Hey?'
'Don't say hey, say what.'
'What?'
'Don't say what, say pardon.'

Sprogs

A favourite uncle or aunty might recite a ditty while marking off the features of a baby or toddler's face.

Brow branty
Eye winky
Nose Nancy
Cheek cherry
Mouth merry
Chin chopper
and
Tickly-bones

There were various words for kids, none of them very complimentary:

- Our brood
- The hounds
- The animals
- Rascals
- Ragamuffin
- Rapscallion
- Scamps
- Tykes
- Brats
- Nippers
- Youngsters
- Littlies
- You ungrateful pups
- Jasper
- Pinhead
- A little shaver
- Guttersnipe

- Squirt
- Buggerlugs
- Sprog — a baby
- A tacker — a little boy about five years old
- Some snotty-nosed youngster.

Proddos and Micks

In the 1950s, everyone in Australia was considered to have a body and a soul; the soul lived on after the body died. Almost every Australian was brought up as a Christian at that time; so much so that if something was considered extremely rare it would be said to be **the only one in Christendom**. But that didn't mean that Christian didn't hate Christian.

There was an ugly social schism in Australia between Catholics and the numerous other Christian denominations, known collectively (by Catholics anyway) as **non-Catholics** or **Callithumpians** — people of vague religious beliefs.

Because Catholics insisted on having their own schools in every district while boasting that they were 'the one true Church', they lived an almost ghetto existence — preaching, for example, that it was a sin, punishable in the afterlife, to enter a non-Catholic church.

The Catholic Church 'abhorred' a **mixed marriage** — a Catholic marrying a Protestant. Catholics had to get special dispensation for the marriage, the Protestant had to promise to bring up the children Catholic, and the marriage ceremony had to take place at a side altar.

Catholic school kids wrote **AMDG** (all my work is done for God) on top of every page of their school **exercise pad**. Irreverent boys said AMDG stood for **Aunt Mary's dead goat**. Or they might write **JMJ** (Jesus Mary Joseph) or **VJM** (Viva Jesus and Mary) on top of every page. But Catholic teachers warned never to put these letters at the top of a page in a public examination, because it would reveal you were Catholic, and you might be failed by a bigoted Protestant examiner. And we believed them.

Many Protestants weren't allowed to go to Catholic school fetes because there was gambling. Anyway, most truly believed that only the Catholics were allowed to win.

Catholics boasted that only Catholics could work miracles, which created a lot of antipathy. This was most obvious in firms hiring either Catholics or Protestants, but not both; state police forces being firmly divided along Catholic/Mason lines; and daily fights between Catholic kids and Protestant kids around the country.

You knew when you were in a Catholic home, because there was sure to be a picture of the Sacred Heart of Jesus on the wall. Or, you'd soon know, depending on what grace was said before meals, or when the hostess was carving the chook and asked who wanted the **parson's nose** or the **pope's nose**.

But the great divide existed in many other subtle ways.

Many Catholic nuns, brothers and priests came from Ireland. The war there between Catholics and Protestants made it harder for Australians of Irish Catholic descent to fit into a country ruled by the King or, later, the Queen of England, who was also the head of the Anglican Church. All Catholic school-children in Australia sang rebel Irish hymns at school. One hymn longed for the day we 'may breathe free air again'. Another said there was 'a bloody law agin the wearing of the green.' One hymn I found particularly frightening, as I sang along loudly at Mary Immaculate Convent, said that all of us kids were also prepared to die for our Catholic faith:

Our fathers chained in prisons dark
Were still in heart and conscience free.
How sweet would be their children's fate,
If they, like them, could die for Thee.

The refrain was, *We will be true to Thee till death*, which was frightening enough, but I particularly didn't like the line *In spite of dungeon, fire and sword*.

Catholics were so different that they were given lots of uncomplimentary nick-names by others. Calling a Catholic an **RC** or a **Roman Catholic** would be taken as an insult by Irish Catholics who preferred to see their religion as Irish, or at least reflecting the meaning of the word catholic ('universal'). Other names were:

- Rock choppers
- Left-footers
- Cattle ticks
- Lick-the-cats
- Connie whackers
- Tykes — 'Tykes always get the best spots (real estate).'
- Romans
- Papists
- Micks.

Being of mainly Irish background, Australian Catholics particularly disliked fundamentalist Christian religions that were against drinking and gambling. Catholics called these people **wowsers**.

Schools provided by the government were called public schools in New South Wales, and state schools in Queensland. Thus, in Queensland, the pupils of government schools run by the state were known by Catholic school kids as **the State School Kids**. The most dangerous time of day for a schoolkid in the 1940s and 50s was walking to and from school. Not because of strangers or motor cars, but because that was when Catholics and State School Kids — both immediately recognisable by their clothes, their feet, their scapulars and their silver holy medals — ran into each other. Then all the old enmities from Britain and Ireland came out. They were like two ancient, foreign tribes suddenly coming across each other in the jungle.

Apart from throwing stones and firing homemade bows and arrows, kids came up with things to yell out to infuriate their enemy. This was called **slanging off**. Oddly, no swearwords were used. The common references were to snakes and frogs. But you'd **come a gutser** if you were slanging off at a lone

State School Kid, and then you discovered that he had six mates on the branches of the mango tree above. Then you **did a bolt**.

Proddy dogs
Sit like frogs
And eat meat on Fridays.

Catholic dogs
Live on frogs
And don't eat meat on Friday.

Catholics, Catholics
Sit like frogs
In your holy water.

Catholic dogs
Stink like frogs
Dipped in holy water.

Staties are taties.

Catholics, Catholics
Sit on logs
Eating the bellies (or maggots)
Out of frogs.

Catholics, Catholics
Ring the bell
While you State School Kids
Go to hell.

Or

Protestant, Protestant
March to Hell,
While the Catholics
Ring the bell.

Connie whackers
Stick like crackers
On a Sunday morning.

State school wowsers
We wear trousers
On a Sunday morning.

States, States
Sitting on gates
Eating the bellies out of snakes.

State, State,
Full of hate ...

Connie wowsers
Stink like trousers
Over logs and into bogs.

Catholics and Proddos would trade insults for a while, and then it would be **on for young and old**. Punches, headlocks, full nelsons, half-nelsons, straight lefts, uppercuts.

Near every school in Queensland was a sign: RACQ — SCHOOL. We all believed it stood for: **Race Around the Corner Quickly — School**, a warning to get out of there. In fact, it was a sign for motorists, put up by the Royal Automobile Club of Queensland.

Chapter fourteen
On the BIG BOYS' PLAYGROUND

The rules

The big boys' playground had its own rules and language.

You had a favourite **possie**. **I bags this**. Or, **This is bar!** Then no one could accuse you of **hogging** it. Possession was important. It was like dogs marking their territory. **Once you give a thing, you can't take it back.** If you demanded it back, you were an **Indian giver**. (This was an Orwellian term, as it was the whites who kept promising land to the American Indians but kept taking it off them.) If you lost it, **finders keepers, losers weepers**, unless it was something your mother was going to notice missing, like clothing or books. In a game, a tree or a person might be **Bar** or **It** or **He**. If you had a fight, being **bashed up** actually meant being forced to give in, or forced to the ground.

If a boy wore glasses or was known to have 'chalk bones', no one **picked him** (meaning 'picked a fight with him', as well as picked him on their team). It wasn't considered fair.

THE GOOD

It's
- a ripper
- a corker
- a beauty
- a cracker
- a pearler
- a bottler
- a real bobbydazzler
- a humdinger
- a ripsnorter

It's
- crackerjack
- superdooper

THE BAD

It's
- scabby
- mangy
- mingy
- mingy-scringy
- arse about
- hairy
- got me licked

- I'm boggled
- I can't fathom it
- I'm stonkered

THE GOODY-GOODY

An unpopular boy was
- a goody-goody
- a goody two shoes
- a conch
- a sissy
- a pimp
- a tell-tail-tit — *your monkey's in the pit*
- a piker
- a crowing winner
- a fibber
- a dobber
- a chicken
- a squib

ROUGH TALK

I gave him a Chinese burn.

Bully for you.

Then I put him in a half-nelson.

What do you want? A medal?

Then I practised jujitsu on him.

What do you want? A Davy Crockett hat?

This is honestly, honestly true. He put me in a headlock.

Stiff luck. Hard cheese. Tough cheddar. Tough titty.

So, as he pulled me down, I put my knee into the side of his upper leg and gave him a cork thigh.

No fooling?

Next time I'm going to put him in a full nelson.

Fat chance.

I'll put my arms under his arms from behind, grab my hands together behind his head, and push his head forward till he gives in.

He might know how to escape from a full nelson. He'll throw his arms suddenly into the air until they are dead straight, and at the same time, drop suddenly with all his weight. You won't be able to hold him.

Well then, next time I'll give him a rabbit-killer. I'll chop his neck with the side of my hand, across the Adam's apple. I've been practising on a full can of IXL jam.

Big talk, no action.

Dead set. Then I'll give him the knuckle punch. I'll punch the middle knuckle of my right hand into his forearm.

That's baby talk. I know something better than a knuckle punch. You grab the muscle just where the neck meets the shoulders and squeeze. It paralyses them.

If he comes at me with a knife, I'll disarm him.

With brass knobs on.

Honest Injun, if he comes at me with the knife up, I'll push my left elbow up and at right angles into his forearm, then I'll reach up with my other hand behind his upper arm, grab my own wrist, and bend his knife arm over backwards until he drops the knife. If he comes at me with the knife low, ready to thrust upwards, I'll reach out with my arms crossed at the wrist and block his forearm and push hard. Then, in one continuous movement, I'll push the knife arm around behind his back and upwards until the pain will force him to drop the knife.

Fiddlesticks.

I took a pot shot at that lamp-post with my shanghai and got it first go.

Big deal.

I took a shy at the stumps and got them first go too.

Three times proves it.

A cat was running past so I pegged a gibber at it and hit it.

Eeh-oore, eeh-oore, eeh-oore.

The cat was going like the clappers, it had a lot of toe, it was pelting along flat strap.

How many times does nine go into sixty-three?

I don't know. I can't do goes-intos. I've got a Phantom skull ring.

Goody goody gumdrops.

I sent away for it. When you punch someone, it leaves a skull mark on their jaw. But I never have the ink pad with me, so I haven't punched anyone yet. I'll let you wear it for a while.

That's real curly of you. That's real big of you.

Who gave you that black eye?

Nobody gave it to me, I had to fight for it. I fought Reggie Kelly.

Did not.

Did so too.

Honest Injun? Cross your heart and hope to die?

Your mother said you weren't fit to live in a pigsty, but I stuck up for you, and said you were.

Hardy har har har har. Do you wanta fight me, mate?

Alright.

Well, here comes me mate. You can fight him.

ROUSING THE TROOPS

- I'll give him a gobful
- Give us the gen, all the gen, the info, the dope, the news, the drum, the lowdown, the good oil, the intelligence, the general information
- We'll beat them like a dozen eggs
- We'll get him good and proper
- They'll be done like a dinner
- We'll knock the spots off them

THE STAND-OFF AND THE TAUNTS

- Pull your head in
- Shut your neck
- Shut your gob
- Get lost
- Get nicked
- Nick off
- Rack off
- Bugger off
- Buzz off
- Ping off
- Hop it
- Go to billy-oh
- Go jump in the lake
- Up your nose with a rubber hose

- You and what army?
- Stop throwing off at me
- Don't rubbish me, you low-down dirty dingo dog
- I'm gonna come around and rock your roof (throw stones on your roof)
- I can lick you any day of the week

- I'll smash you to smithereens
- I'll pelt you with stones
- I'll fix your wagon
- I'll drop you
- I'll make you eat your words
- I'll knock you rotten
- I'm gonna wipe you like a dirty slate
- You are cactus, finished, had it, kaput!
- You're for the high jump, mate
- You couldn't beat time with a stick
- You're as lucky as billy-oh, but you'll get yours

COWARDS ALL

- I was shitting bricks/packing death
- We'd better POQ
- He was off like a shot out of a gun
- He was scrubbed out
- He got clobbered
- He dingoed on us
- He's always pinging off just when he's wanted
- He's done a double bunk
- He bolted
- We'd better skedaddle/hightail it out of here/scoot/scram/shoot through/ run like billy-oh/make ourselves scarce
- I thought I was a goner
- How tinny was that?
- How arsy was that?
- We had Buckley's chance
- We didn't get the rub of the green
- If it rained pea soup, I'd only have a fork

Emu parade

Catholic boys in Brisbane wore shoes and socks to school, except on wet days when they might be allowed to take them off.

Whereas state school boys usually **wore bare feet** all summer. This was described as 'having bare feet on'. Thus they developed **state school heel** — cracked and bloodied heels from walking around on hard ground with no shoes on.

In bare feet everything is hot in summer in most parts of Australia. You would leap from concrete to concrete, because it was much cooler than bitumen, which got **as hot as billy-oh**. Nobody drank water from a vessel: boys gulped water directly from the tap into their mouth, while girls lapped water up from their hand held under the tap.

Before a footy match on the **big boys' playground**, all the kids would be lined up for an **emu parade**. In some schools this meant picking up rubbish, but in other schools it meant picking up bits of broken glass, sticks, **gibbers** and the larger stones, called **goolies**. A **goolie** or a **golly** was also a spit. If a boy **hawked up** a golly and spat it out on the ground in front of another boy, he would say: '**Pick the bones out of that.**'

The field was often referred to as **the paddock**, for good reason.

Because the playgrounds were dirt, a **willy-willy** or **whirly-whirly** (a spiralling wind) would swirl through, creating a funnel of dirt and paper.

Primary school boys played cricket with no helmet, no pads, no cricketer's box, no forearm protectors, no rib protectors, no batting gloves. And they played football in bare feet with no headgear, shoulder pads or mouthguards. Very few football grounds were grassed. Thus boys were used to **stone bruises** — an invisible bruise on the sole or heel of your foot. You can't see it but it **hurts like billy-oh**.

If you took the ball **up the guts of the field**, you'd **go for the doctor,** run **flat out, flat strap, pelting along full coit**. Then **ten to one**, if you didn't fall over your own feet and **go for a Burton**, you'd hear the cry, '**tackle low!**', and soon you'd **come a gutser, go for a row, go for a sixer, have a buster, come a**

cropper, fall head over turkey, go down like a pack of cards, be knocked flying, get donged on the noggin and be **knocked silly**. And after you were **skittled,** you might come up with a **blood nose** or a **blood blister** (a red blister full of bloody fluid trapped beneath the skin). If you were lucky, you'd have a **black eye** or a **shiner** to show off.

Footy matches were followed inevitably by **scabs** on knees and elbows. They took weeks to pick off slowly until the scab flapped around in the breeze. Some kids believed in the **scab fairy**, and when the scab finally came off, they kept it under their pillow, hoping the scab fairy was related to the **tooth fairy** and would leave them sixpence.

PRIMARY SCHOOL RHYMES

Glory, glory, Hallelujah,
Teacher hit me with a ruler.
I met her at the door
With a loaded .44
And she ain't gonna hit no more.

Copy cat,
Dirty rat,
Sitting on a butcher's mat.

Scaredy-cat, dirty rat,
Sitting on the butcher's mat/doormat.

Captain Cook swallowed a hook,
His sister swallowed a nail;
His father swallowed a kangaroo,
But couldn't swallow his tail.

Captain Chook chased his cook,
All around Australia.
He lost his pants in the middle of France,
And found them in Tasmania.

The boy stood on the burning deck
His pocket full of crackers.
All of a sudden his pants caught fire
And blew off both his ...

The standing playground joke was:
Q. *How many ears did Davy Crockett have?*
A. Three. The left ear, the right ear, and the Wild Front-Ear.

It's raining, it's pouring,
The old witch is snoring.
She went to bed and bumped her head,
And couldn't get up in the morning.

I can think up a rhyme,
Any old time;
I'm a poet,
And I know it,
Blow it.

Bread and butter and marmalade jam,
That's the name of my old man.
He combed his hair with the leg of a chair
And told his mum he didn't care.

Sam, Sam, the dunny man,
Washed his face in the frying pan.
Combed his hair with the leg of a chair ...

What's your name?

Billy Mclean.

Where do you live?

Down the lane.

What street?

Dog's meat.

What number?

Cucumber.

Sticks and stones

May break my bones

But names will never hurt me.

When I'm dead

And in my grave,

You'll think of the names you called me.

You're the sort of smarty

That breaks up every party.

Stickybeak, chocolate nose, lolly legs and peanut toes.

Holy Moses, King of the Jews,

Sold his wife for a pair of shoes.

When the shoes began to wear

Holy Moses began to swear.

When the swear began to stop

Holy Moses bought a shop.

When the shop began to sell

Holy Moses went to Hell.

When boys were caught out doing something silly or embarrassing, they retorted:

I made you look,
I made you stare,
I made the barber cut your hair.

Whereas girls would say:
Stare, stare like a bear.
You don't have any
underwear.

When swearing won't do

Swearing by children was rare, because punishment was swift. There were definitely never any four-letter words. So a lot of replacement words and phrases were invented.

- Jumping jewfish!
- Holy moly!
- Holy mackerel!
- Holy cow!
- Holy smoke!
- Whoops-a-daisy!
- Struth!
- Blow me down!
- Blow it!
- Darn it!
- Dash it!
- Shivers!
- Sssssssshhhhhh-ugar!
- Crumbs, crumpets and potato crisps!
- Cripes!
- Jeepers!

- Golly!
- Oh jingo!
- Oh jings!
- By gosh!
- By jove!
- By jingoes!
- Gee whiz!
- Gee whillakers!
- You rotten b-b-b-b-barmaid (instead of bastard)
- Up your arrrrrrrmpit!

Sitting on your port

The first time I realised that the word 'port' was basically only used in the north-eastern part of Australia was at Adelaide Airport in the 1970s.

After seven years working as a journalist overseas, I had returned to my home town of Brisbane and was working as a journalist on the *Australian* in its Brisbane bureau. I was on the last flight into Adelaide and so it was late at night by the time everyone had collected their luggage from the carousel.

Except me.

Finally, I went to the Inquiries Desk and said angrily: 'I can't find my port. I'm a journalist. I need my port tonight or I can't operate.'

The man behind the counter looked at me strangely.

'My port,' I said. 'It never arrived on the plane from Brisbane. You've lost my port.'

He picked up the phone, and shortly two security men arrived: 'This gentleman's looking for some port. He reckons he had some, but someone drank it. He's a journalist, and so can't write without some.'

It was a case of: be arrested for creating a disturbance, or explain that to a person from north of Newcastle a port was not an alcoholic drink, but the thing you carried your baggage in. A suitcase.

They wanted to know where we got such a word.

That was like asking where the word 'butter' came from. Though when I got home I made inquiries and was told it was short for portmanteau. A very upper crust word indeed. In fact, it's a wonder they didn't accuse me of putting on airs, because portmanteau is from the French word for a 'cloak-carrier'. In France it means a leather case which divides into two halves.

But to me, and anyone else in Queensland and the northern half of NSW, a port is, and hopefully will always be, just a bag you carried things in, whether on your back or by your side. Just like in Queensland a duchess is a dressing table with a mirror.

Every schoolchild in Queensland carried a port to school. At primary school in Queensland, boys wore their port on their back, just like a modern backpack. At secondary school we all wore long pants and carried Globite ports, full of books, in one hand, with football or cricket boots tied to the handle and hanging down the outside.

Such a port was very useful.

If you wanted to get the attention of the whole class when you arrived, you dropped your port on the floor and everyone looked up. At bus or tram stops all the schoolboys sat on their ports with one leg on either side.

Scouts

Every boy wanted a Scout belt, even if they didn't want to be in the Scouts. The Scout belt clicked together at the front with one piece of metal fitting into the other. One side of the buckle could be used to open soft drink bottles. You needed a bottle opener like this to open a soft drink down at the creek or in the movies, because there were no ring-pulls or screw-top lids back then.

Many boys joined the Scouts because they were allowed to wear a knife on their hip.

If a boy wanted to show he was telling the truth, even if he wasn't a scout, he would say **Scout's honour** and hold up two fingers together.

Chapter fifteen

VULGAR FRACTIONS

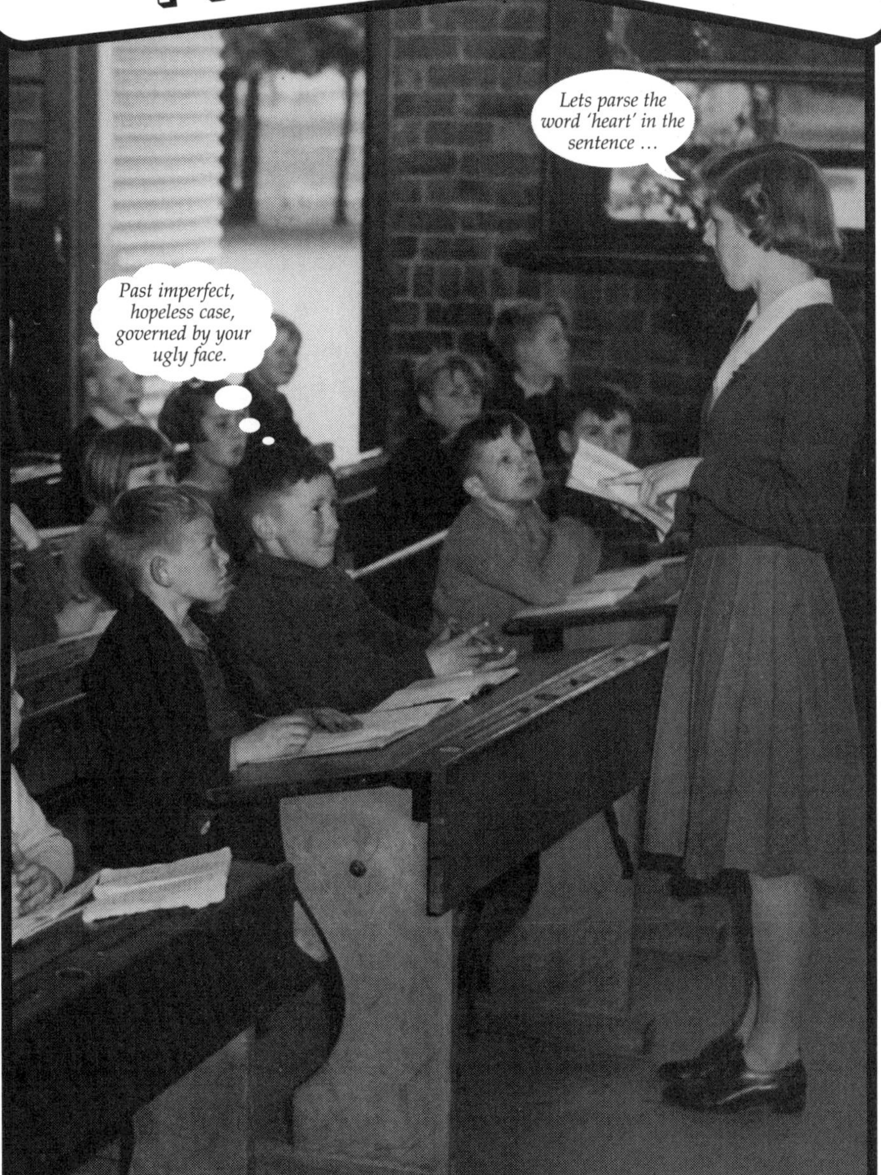

Rote learning

At primary school you learnt spelling, sums, poems and rules **by rote**, so you could repeat them **off pat**. Then you would proudly say: 'I know this **off by heart**' or '**I'm word perfect**.'

You learnt the alphabet and what each letter looked like off by heart: *a is like an apple on a twig, a says ah; b is like a bat and ball, b says buh; f is like a feather; i is like a boy with his hat in the air* … Good girls could even recite the alphabet backwards.

For English grammar you learnt rules such as: ***The verb*** *to be* **has the same case after it as before it. First person is the person speaking; second person is the person spoken to; third person is the person spoken about. When 'as' follows 'such' or 'same', the 'as' clause is always adjectival. Prepositions govern nouns or pronouns in the objective case. Place, where, time, and when clauses are always adjectival.**

Transitive verbs were regular. **Intransitive verbs** were irregular — that is, they changed the spelling with the tense. The transitive verb 'lie' in **to tell a lie**, goes: lie, lied, lied. Whereas the intransitive verb 'lie' in **to lie down**, goes: lie, lay, lain. These rules were needed to **analyse sentences** and **parse words**. Thus you needed to know an adjective from a pronoun, a verb from an adverb, and nominative case from objective. For example, parse the word 'heart' in the sentence: 'The song filled my heart with joy.' 'Heart' is a noun, third person, singular, objective case, governed by the verb 'filled'. 'The song' is the subject of the sentence and 'filled my heart with joy' is the predicate. If 'heart' were in the subject, it would be nominative case, instead of objective.

Kids hated this so much that they would parse their schoolyard enemy: *Past imperfect hopeless case, governed by your ugly face.*

You were expected to be able to recite poetry to entertain visitors to your home, or to impress relatives. Thus every child had to have a favourite piece of recitation. This was my classmate Jim Egoroff's:

Oh for the pirate Don Dirk of Dowdee
He was as wicked as wicked can be
But, oh, he was perfectly gorgeous to see
The pirate Don Dirk of Dowdee.

A friend of mine, Denise McLennan, says she recited *If Only:*

If only I'd some money
I'd buy a jolly boat
And get a pair of sea boots
And a furry sort of coat.
I'd sail away to the North Pole
And I'd sail away to the South Pole
Whichever I thought was best ...

I learnt *Hopkins:*

Hopkins is a warrior brave
He's made of special tin.
He has a sword, he has a gun,
In case the war begins ...
He keeps his war paint bright
He does his best to live at peace
He doesn't want to fight.

My cousin Johnny Duncan recited *The Inchcape Rock:*

Down sank the bell
With a gurgling sound.
The bubbles rose
And burst around ...

A classmate, Sam Aherne, specialised in *Hist! Hark!*

> *Hist! Hark! The night is very dark*
> *And we've to go a mile or so*
> *Across the possum park.*
> *Step ... light,*
> *Keeping to the right;*
> *If we delay, and lose our way,*
> *We'll be out half the night.*
> *Mopoke! Mopoke!*
> *Who was that that spoke?!*
> *This is not a fitting time to play a silly joke ...*

A poem kids were told not to recite:

> *Potatoes when I'm hungry,*
> *Whisky when I'm dry.*
> *Peggy when I'm lonely,*
> *Heaven when I die.*

And another:

> *Latin is a dead language*
> *As dead as dead can be.*
> *It killed off all the Romans,*
> *And now it's killing me.*

Children learnt **recitation, verse speaking, the art of speech, elocution** and **enunciation**. Teachers examined them on **expression, feeling** and **emphasis**. To improve enunciation various complex word combinations had to be learnt by heart and said quickly:

My brother Bob owes your brother Bob a bob. And if my brother Bob doesn't pay your brother Bob that bob that my brother Bob owes your brother Bob, then your brother Bob will give my brother Bob a bob in the eye.

Or: *A noisy noise annoys a noisy oyster.*

Or: *The hot-headed Highlander*
Hit the hard-headed Hollander
On the head with a heavy hammer ...

Like school choirs, there were also verse-speaking choirs and inter-school competitions. My choir recited *Raynard the Fox*:

> *The fox was strong, he was full of running;*
> *He could run for an hour and still be cunning.*
> *But the cries behind him made him shrill*
> *They were nearer now,*
> *And they meant to kill ...*

Mental arithmetic

Before calculators, primary school students learnt the **times tables** by heart so that they instantly knew the answers to all multiplications of simple numbers: 'Seven nines are 63; eleven twelves are 132; six nines are 54 ... ' If you knew these you could not only do your sums in a hurry, but you would do well at **mental arithmetic** — where you would be required to stand up in class and do **sums** in your head.

One important subject was called **mensuration**. This was measuring length, area and volume, which, under the imperial system of weights and measures, was complicated. You had to understand the system of **roods, perches and rods**:

4 roods one acre

40 perches one rood

160 perches in an acre

640 acres in a square mile.

In cities and towns, house blocks were divided up into perches: 16, 24, 32 or 40 perches. You also had to know there were 1760 yards and 5280 feet in a mile, and 22 yards in a chain (the length of a cricket pitch).

You did **long division** by age nine and knew what a **common denominator** was. You knew **vulgar fractions** had a **numerator** on top and a **denominator** on the bottom. Pre-metric fractions were a large part of school arithmetic: you had to work out $^7/_8$ (seven-eighths) or $^3/_{16}$ (three-sixteenths) of something, without a calculator.

You knew how to measure in **troy weight** and **avoirdupois**. There were 16 ounces in a pound, and 16 drams in an ounce.

School Inspectors were sent to schools to check up on students and teachers. They would ask the perennial question: '**What is heavier?** **One ton of feathers or one ton of lead**?' Or: '**If someone who lives in Rome is called a Roman, what do you call someone who lives in Naples**?'

You lost marks for answering 'Napoleon'.

If the inspector wanted to confuse you he might ask: '**If it takes a week to walk a fortnight, how many bananas in a bunch of grapes**?'

Now, children, let's multiply one pound, 13 shillings and 11 pence halfpenny by nine. Now, nine halfpennies are four and one half pence ... write that in the pence column. And nine elevens are 99 ... so that is 103 and a half pence in all. Divide that by 12 and we get eight shillings and seven pence halfpenny left. Put the eight shillings in the shillings column — see how simple it is ... and multiply the 13 shillings by nine ... and we get 117 shillings plus the eight from the pence column: 125 shillings in all. Now divide that by 20 to get the pounds, which gives us six pounds, with five shillings left. Nine ones are nine plus the six pounds from the shillings column and we have the answer: 15 pounds, five shillings and seven pence halfpenny.

Hands up all those who got the answer?

Getting the cuts

Unlike today, schools were much more formal places in the 1950s.

If the headmaster entered a classroom at a state primary school, everybody stood up. When reading out their marks, each pupil was required to say the teacher's name: 'Six out of ten, Mr Mayes.' At Catholic schools, when any teacher entered the room, everybody stood and said: 'Good morning [or afternoon] Sister [or Brother] and God bless you.'

Students were not allowed to talk at all in the classroom, unless they were answering a question from the teacher. And even then, the student had to raise one hand to ask permission to speak. If desperate, students would wave their hand and click their fingers and half stand up (because they weren't allowed to stand without permission). Girls who knew the answers to **arithmetic sums** would do this a lot, because their aim was to impress the teacher. If the teacher wanted the class to cease all talk and activity she would simply shout: '**Pencils down**, **hands on heads**.' And everyone would **jump to**.

Except for meal breaks, kids spent all day inside the classroom; very few activities were held outside. Children obeyed the teacher because the teacher could inflict **corporal punishment** with a cane or a strap. In fact, kids could be punished by just about any adult. And usually your parents backed up the adult.

Teachers, headmasters, parents and older relatives could all give a kid **a belting**; the bloke next door might even give a boy a **cuff over the ear** if he caught you pinching his mangoes. You wouldn't bother complaining to your mother because she would say '**Serves you right**'.

Until the 1960s, children — in Queensland at least — had to pass supervised state-wide public examinations if they were going to get a secondary education. The exams were so tough that children failed almost as often as they passed. In Queensland, at age 13, everyone did '**State Scholarship**', to see if the state thought they could succeed at secondary school and thus help pay for them to continue. In the 1950s, up to 40 per cent of children who did the State Scholarship (English, Arithmetic, History and Geography) were failed. Then, two years later, those who were still at school did the **Junior Public Examination** to see if they could continue on to Grade 12. If so, they did the **Senior University Entrance** public examination to try to get into the *only* university in Queensland: the University of Queensland. Less than five per cent of people made it all the way through to uni in the 1950s.

If you failed, you left school. There was no taking textbooks into the exam room either. Most exams for individual subjects involved two three-hour written examinations. Sometimes you handwrote public examinations every day for two weeks. In English I at Queensland University in 1960 the exam was three three-hour written papers with no notes available at all. Nowadays, some Australian universities offer subjects which can be completed in a long weekend.

Teachers didn't feel it was their job to be nice to students, or to cosset them. Their job was to try to drag the kids **kicking and screaming** through the difficult trail of public exams that lay in wait like booby-traps to stop them getting a full education. Thus teachers emphasised: **Hard work never killed anybody**. Students who hadn't done all their homework (which usually included learning something **off by heart**) were admonished for being **bone lazy**. If you answered a question wrongly, the teacher definitely wouldn't say '**Never mind, you did your best**'. They'd probably say '**Wake up, Australia!**' And all the other kids would laugh.

Most boys didn't want to be seen to be currying favour with the teacher and so they played up. Thus some teachers had a lexicon of words for such boys: **twerp**, **squirt**, **skunko**, **blithering idiot**, **pipsqueak**, **germ**, **specimen**, **squib**, **grizzler**, **clown**. A boy who failed to perform on the sports oval could be called a **sheila**, a **sissy** or a **girl**.

Teachers were always **rousing on** you and, at least at Catholic schools, boys **sweated buckets** expecting to soon get hit with the strap or the cane. Teachers called this **corporal punishment**, but kids called it **the cuts**. **Getting the cuts** involved the teacher producing his or her personal cane or strap and whacking you across the palm of the hand.

This could reduce 15-year-old tough guys to cooperative civility — for a few hours at least. Though the rule with boys was that you weren't supposed to cry. If a boy did cry after the cuts the teacher would say: '**Stop that snivelling!**'

A good belting was seen as character-building for kids and was administered by parents and teachers. In state schools you might be sent to the headmaster who would administer the cuts: a cane for the boys and a ruler for the girls. But at Catholic schools the nuns each had their own cane and the Brothers all carried with them a handmade, layered, stitched, stained leather strap.

Punishment was immediate.

The cuts were, for some strange reason, always given in even numbers — usually on the palm of an outstretched hand: two for a minor misdemeanour; four for failing to learn what you were told, and **six of the best** for being cheeky.

Nuns sometimes hit girls across the back of the legs.

If you were about to get the cuts, you warmed your hands up first, and blew on them afterwards, amazed to see the imprint of the stitches in your skin. If there was an opportunity, boys would rub rosin (the stuff rubbed on violin strings) on their hands, or peppercorns, or a leaf from the soap tree. Some desperate boys ran their hands through their hair first, **swearing blind** that Spruso hair oil helped.

But most boys just **took their medicine like a man**.

When a teacher was angry and getting ready to give the cuts he might say: **'Come out here, I've got a present for you, duckie.'** But if a teacher was really nice, they might say — before hitting you — **'This hurts me more than it hurts you.'**

A very few outstanding teachers didn't give the cuts: they didn't have to and ruled by teaching ability and force of personality.

The Brothers went to saddlery shops to get their straps custom made: several pieces of leather stitched together, anything from an inch to two inches wide, a quarter inch to half an inch thick. Bamboo canes were preferred by the nuns. One of my nun teachers had a cane that was so long it reached the ceiling when it was stood up in the corner of the classroom.

Because they dressed in black, students called Brothers 'the crows'. Many Brothers would throw chalk, or the duster that cleaned the chalk off the blackboard, at boys down the back who weren't paying attention. Class sizes were comparatively huge then, up to 120 at some Catholic schools, and this was one way of keeping control. Beaudesert Mayor Ron Munn told me that a Christian Brother who taught him in Toowoomba had a dog called Rex. When the Brother threw the duster at someone down the back, Rex would hop over all the desks, pick up the duster and take it back to the Brother to re-arm him.

One Brother didn't have to move from the front of the classroom. If he wanted to **go crook** at a boy down the back, he would simply grab the ear of a boy in the front row and twist and lift it until the boy at the back came up with the correct answer.

At primary school convents, where sexes were mixed, one punishment for a boy would be to sit him next to a girl.

LOST FOR WORDS EPISODE 11:
An idiot, Sir

Lost for Words. **The story of Bert and Grace and their trials and tribulations bringing up a young family after the War.**

🌻

The new teacher is walking around the classroom asking students their names.

'Algernon,' says a boy at the back.

'Did you just come out of the mulga?'

'No, Sir.'

'Where did you get that name from then? Off a jam tin?'

'No, Sir.'

'You're right: I've never seen Algernon on a jam tin. Who gave you such an unusual moniker?'

'My mother, Sir.'

'You poor benighted fool.'

By now the other children are laughing. The teacher swings around.

'You lot will be laughing on the other side of your face when I've finished with you … Reggie Kelly, stop smirking. Face the front. Stop acting like a lout!'

'But, Sir, I'm not acting.'

'That will cost you six of the best, son. Hold out your right hand. Now I want you to know, Master Kelly, that there is a fool at the end of this strap.'

'Which end, Sir?'

'Whadda you know; we have a comedian in the class! A cheeky Devil! Wipe that smile off your dial, Kelly, before I do it for you.'

Whack, whack, whack, whack, whack, whack.

'You'll have to mend your ways. Now sit down, son, you're making the place look untidy. And let that be a lesson to you!'

A few weeks later Reggie Kelly is five minutes late for school. He says there was an accident in the rain on the slippery road, and the bus was caught in heavy traffic so it was late and he missed his connection. He couldn't walk because he didn't bring his raincoat.

'Master Kelly, what's wrong with you, boy? Are you diseased? Are you a sugarbaby? Do you think you'll melt if you go out in the rain? You've got a list of excuses as long as your arm. Punctuality is the courtesy of kings. You're an idiot, son, what are you?'

'An idiot, Sir.'

Later, the teacher catches Kelly's mate Tommy Donovan — who hasn't done his homework — daydreaming. The teacher knocks on his head with a knuckle and says: 'Hello. Hello. Anyone there?'

This makes all the other kids laugh.

'You'll never amount to anything, Donovan. You're an also-ran. Your intellectual facilities are not sufficiently expanded to meet your fundamental requirements.'

Tommy Donovan starts to whimper.

'A crybaby! Don't be so thin-skinned, Donovan. I only called you a *lazybones*. You are laziness personified. Stop blubbering. What are you, a sook? A sooky-bear? You're acting like a sheila. We should put you in a glass case and throw sugar at you. We'll have to put you in cotton wool. Stop bunging it on, Donovan. You're just looking for notice.'

'Sorry, Sir.'

'That's alright, son, I don't bear a grudge once I've blown you up. Now, first things first, where's his nibs? Ahhh, Master Kelly: now you two palled up, you're as thick as thieves. By a freak chance of nature, did you do *your* homework last night, Kelly?'

'Yes, Sir.'

'Well, this is your chance to wipe the slate clean, son. Is your homework up to scratch? If it isn't, you'll have to do it again. So when was the Battle of Hastings?'

'You've got me stumped there, Sir. Gee, I'm stonkered! I did do the homework, but I just can't remember the precise details at this particular point in time.'

'Own up to yourself, Kelly. Tell the truth and shame the Devil. You're a tiger for punishment, because I'm awake up to you.'

'But, Sir, I thought ...'

'When did you start to think, Kelly, you scoundrel? You'll rue the day you tried to fool me, m'boy. I didn't come down in the last shower. You boys are going to have to realise that learning is all a case of *mind over matter*.'

'You're the mind and we're the matter, Sir.'

'You need your head read, Kelly. You're suffering from LMF — Lack of Moral Fibre. Now, since you did your homework last night, what's the last line of Alfred Lord Tennyson's *Ulysses*?'

'*The End*, Sir?'

'I'm lost for words! You're a dunce, Master Kelly. What are you?'

'A dunce, Sir.'

'The trouble with a specimen like you is that everything I say goes in one ear and out the other. You've got a mind like a sieve. You're skating on thin ice, m'boy. You'll have to turn over a new leaf. You're getting so big-headed you'll have to get a bigger hat.'

'Yes, Sir.'

'Now, everyone, I want you to put your thinking caps on. You're like rows of little cabbages, sitting there vegetating. Now, what was the last line of *Ulysses*? Don't look at me, the answer isn't on my face.'

A lone voice piped up from down the back: '*To strive, to seek, to find, and not to yield*.'

'Well done, Master Wright. You *have* been a busy little bee. What Tennyson wrote is a good lesson for all of you ... *to strive, to seek, to find, and not to yield*. That's what you're going to have to do if you're ever going to get to look through the paling fence at the university. Well done, Master Wright, you're a real bookworm. Give yourself a big tick. You've got a mind like a steel trap.'

'Up here for thinking, Sir, down there for dancing.'

'That's right, too many of you boys are thinking with your feet. And, Wright, the Battle of Hastings?'

'Was 1066, Sir.'

'Yes, as easy as falling off a log. As easy as shelling peas, if you do your homework.'

Implements of learning

In the first few years at school, to save on paper, children wrote on slates: a square of dark grey stone in a wooden frame. They wrote on this with a **slate pencil** which was like chalk but very hard, very grey, very thin, thinner than a pencil; sometimes it was wrapped in blue or red checked paper. It broke easily. Sometimes it came in a metal sleeve to give it strength. Every kid had a sponge and a little container of water so that when they'd filled their slate with writing they could then wash it off and start again, like a blackboard.

Children then graduated to pencils, called lead pencils, even though the writing point was actually graphite. Some had a rubber (eraser) on one end. Some needed a pencil sharpener, but with others the wrapper could be peeled off the pencil. If a pencil got too short it was put in a **pencil lengthener**, a special tin frame that extended it (like an artificial limb) so the pencil could be used right down to the end, and not wasted. (**Waste not, want not**.) There was also an **indelible pencil**, which, like ink, was almost impossible to rub out.

Some rubbers were half white, half grey; one end rubbed out pencil and the other rubbed out ink, but the ink part never really worked properly and just left a grubby blue smudge.

Some wealthy students had **propelling pencils**. These were metal pencils loaded with needle-thin graphite pieces. When clicked the end, it pushed the next bit down. Of course, every student and every teacher had a thick **red pencil** for marking work with.

To carry this equipment, kids bought a double-decker wooden pencil case, which doubled as a nulla-nulla in a fight.

Later, children graduated to **inkwells** and **nibs**. Desks had a groove for laying a pen, and a hole for the inkwell. The nib was the metal bit dipped in the inkwell. A child could write about three letters before the ink was spent, and they had to dip it in again. So there was ample opportunity for ink to smudge. Thus you had to have a **blotter**, a piece of very absorbent white paper, which was pressed onto whatever was just written. Some boys loved to throw the pen — nib first — into the desk, where it would quiver like a shot arrow, which is why ink blobs tended to fall off the end.

Every student was given a little grey book with perfect handwriting examples in it, which had to be copied. The teachers sat up the front correcting work, licking their forefinger each time before they turned over a page. Boys always ended up dropping a blob of ink on their **copybook**, which meant they got a very low mark, and the teacher would say: 'Your work looks as though the chooks have walked across it.' To the girls, they'd say: 'That's as neat as a pin.'

Thus, **'I've blotted my copybook.'** became one of the major phrases men said when they made a mistake in life. It all harked back to learning to write.

Then children graduated to fountain pens which had an internal bladder filled with ink, so they didn't have to keep dipping the nib in a pot of ink. This was wonderful for when they were required to draw a map of Australia **freehand** (at some schools, if you traced it you got the cuts) or write a composition — 40 lines of foolscap on a subject like *A Visit to the Country*.

Chapter sixteen

POLITE SOCIETY

Good manners

'**Don't talk with your mouth half-full. Fill it up!**' That's what fathers would say, half-jesting, to stop kids talking with a mouth of half-chewed food.

Some **table manners** which have largely disappeared:

1. Never brush your hair at the dinner table or in a restaurant or café. **It's not seemly.**
2. All gentlemen wear jackets after eight.
3. At a formal dinner, a gentleman gives most of his attention to the lady on his right.
4. It is vulgar to play with the cutlery, or fiddle with the tablecloth or the crumbs.
5. Serve from the left and take away from the right.
6. Do not look curiously at the plates of others; do not scrutinise others while they eat.
7. Never leave the table without permission.
8. No elbows on the table.
9. Put your knife and fork down on the plate while you are chewing.
10. Don't wave the cutlery around or use it to point while talking. **It's not becoming.**
11. Never lick the knife. Such people were known as **sword-swallowers**.
12. Don't laugh boisterously; **rowdiness is not mirth**.
13. Don't finger your face or hair.
14. Don't be too critical of the manners of eldery people who may allow themselves little exemptions.
15. Never reach across the table; always ask for something to be passed down the table to you.
16. Never lean across someone else's plate.
17. When asked if you want seconds, say: **I'll have just a smidgen, thank you**. Or, **No, thank you, I've had elegant sufficiency**.
18. Clear the salt before you serve the sweets. Clear away the main-course plates before you **dish up** dessert.

19. Never, ever clear the table until everyone has finished eating.
20. It's not polite to discuss sex, religion or politics at the dinner table.

But if talking politics, a mother might announce: 'The only way to vote is "**put the lion in and the tiger out**".' In other words vote against whoever is in power at the time.

MUM'S SPECIAL RULES

When having visitors:
1. Always have a tablecloth.
2. Put out forks for dessert.
3. No asking: **Can I lick the plate**?
4. Never say: **What**? Say: **Beg yours**?

When visiting: These were to ensure people didn't **frown on you**.
1. Always stand up and give your seat to an adult on the bus or train.
2. Don't go into anybody's house unless they ask you. Don't **trail behind them**.
3. Don't go **empty-handed**. (If you did, they'd be bound to tell people, '**He arrived with arms at the same length**'.)
4. Turn up on time.
5. Don't walk into someone's house with a lit cigarette in your hand.
6. **Don't prattle on**.
7. Don't ask anybody what they paid for something.
8. Don't read any documents that are lying about.
9. **Never take a shingle off another man's roof** or, **don't kill a man's pig**. If you're offered something you don't want (for example, a home-grown pumpkin) don't refuse, because you will cause offence by belittling the gift.
10. Be sure not to come to a standstill near those who are conversing

privately, and never enter a room without knocking.

11. **Don't leave like Billy the Blackfella**. Don't just wander off. Go up to your host or hostess, thank them for their hospitality, and say goodbye. (This phrase was in use in Queensland in the 1920s, perhaps because white people did not understand local Aboriginal customs, and mistakenly assumed that Aborigines were being rude when they left quietly and inconspicuously.)

12. **No picking winners**. Don't pick your nose (or clean your ears, or your nails for that matter) in public. If your father caught you out, he would infuriate you by reciting:

The boy stood on the burning deck,
Picking his nose like mad.
He rolled them into cannon balls,
And threw them at his dad.

13. While waiting to speak to someone, it is not courteous to hum, whistle or drum your fingers.

14. Don't keep your hands in your pockets.

15. Cover your mouth and turn aside when you are going to cough, sneeze or yawn.

16. If someone gives you a compliment, simply reply, '**Thank you**'.

17. **Once you give a thing you can't take it back**.

18. When there is no excuse, there is only apology.

19. Don't shake hands like a wet fish.

20. Don't use a stranger's first name. (It was only when you got to know someone that you could **dispense with formalities**.)

VIEWING THE BRIDE

If you were invited to **view the bride**, it was a polite way of saying you were invited to the church, but not to the reception.

The Matron of Honour was a married bridesmaid.

THE QUEEN'S ENGLISH

Parents and teachers were always listening to what children said, trying to correct their **bad English**. But no matter how many times they corrected kids, bad habits never died.

Can I eat some more dessert?
I'm sure you *can***, but the question is** *may* **you have some more dessert.**

I'm gonna try and ...
You mean you are going to try to ...

It's different than ...
No, it is different from ...

This is them ...
No, these are they.

I'll grab a jumper from home.
Don't say *grab***. It is bad manners.**

How are you?
Good.
We hope you're good, but are you well?

Say stomach, not stummick
Tuesday, not Chewsday
Window, not winder

Getting above your station

In the 1950s, a man could **better himself** provided he was **as honest as the day is long**. Australians admired **stickatitness**, so a man who went to do a course at night to **make something of himself** wasn't a **no-hoper**.

Of course, this was assuming that he didn't start **giving himself airs** or become **toffy-nosed** or start **looking down his nose** at everyone else.

If someone was **up themselves**, then you called them a **show-off** or a **big-noter**. If they **swanned around** boasting about their abilities or achievements they were a **skite**, or a **blowbag**, or a **know-all**, or, even worse, a **blowhard**. Such a bloke was said to be **full of himself**.

Most Australians admired people who **had no side**.

These folk didn't **put on side**, didn't **bung on side**, and definitely didn't **put on the dog**. They **stayed in their crease** — a phrase borrowed from cricket — meaning they did not try to get jobs that were above their ability. They didn't pretend to be richer or more important than you. A grocer didn't try to **puff himself up** by calling himself a small businessman; he called himself a **shopkeeper**.

But if the grocer was a snob, he would try to **lord it over** everybody else. He might even be **a social climber**, if he'd moved from Adelaide to Brisbane. He would look down his nose at the **riff raff** and the **hoi polloi**. If you were fooled by his **hoity-toity upper echelon** manners, you might call him a **toff**, or say he was very **la-di-da**.

There was no mercy for those who tried to pretend. When someone did, it was always noted that they would still end up mixing with their own kind, particularly if their own kind was of the **rough-and-ready sort**. The gossips would nod with satisfaction and say **water finds its own level**.

Women would say a **snooty** girl was **putting on airs and graces**, whereas blokes would comment amongst themselves: '**She wouldn't say shit for a shilling**.'

If your mother saw a couple overly dressed up for an occasion, she'd say: '**Who do they think they are**? **Lord and Lady Muck**?' Or: '**Who does she think she is**, **the Queen of Sheba**?' But, conversely, if your mother saw another woman trying to cut corners, such as turning over a barely soiled tablecloth to re-use it, she would joke: '**It wouldn't have done for the Duke!**' She never explained who the Duke was, but he must have been **a terrible fusspot**.

You could tell how important people thought they were by whether they asked **to spend a penny** or use the **dunny**, or the **thunderbox**, the **dyke**, the **little boys' room**, the **toot** (rhymes with put), the **lavatory** or the **bathroom**. If you went to someone's place for the whole day and never went to the toilet, you might joke, '**I've turned into a fairy**,' because you were obviously superior to mere mortals.

(In olden times on a coach journey, if a woman wanted a toilet stop, she would say she wanted to stop to **pick some flowers**.)

And you certainly knew a person wasn't pompous if they said they were **going for a bog** and needed some **dunny paper** or a **date roll**, and added, 'Let everyone know that **Parliament is in session** and I don't want to be disturbed'. In the past, torn-up squares of newspaper, and even the phone book, were used. This occasionally caused the situation where an unabashed woman might rush into the house saying: 'How can I find Mrs Marmaduke's number now? Someone has used all of the Ms!'

Young men who were starting to challenge older men were known as **smart alecs** or **smart-arses**. If a **smart alec** dressed up in a special way, talked big, or carried on in an outlandish fashion, he was **a lair**. If he was also stupid, he was **a mug lair**. A **mug** was someone who wasn't smart enough to realise he was getting **the rough end of the pineapple**.

A group of rowdy smart alecs **lairising around** were called **riffraff**, **louts**, **hooligans** or **hoodlums** by adults. Whereas a charming youth who broke some of society's minor rules was called **a larrikin**.

Mr Perfect was a sarcastic way of referring to a classmate who thought they were the **bee's knees** and always pleased the teacher.

A young worker who was always sucking up to the boss was called **Boy Wonder**.

Getting a character

Before we had human resources departments, CVs, resumés, job descriptions and performance criteria, a worker only needed a good reference to get a job.

20th December, 1954.
To whom it may concern.

This is to certify that Miss Flora Jones worked for me for one year. During that time, she displayed a sunny disposition and a sweet temperament. If charm is considered to be an asset, Miss Jones has riches.

During working hours (8.30 a.m. to 5.30 p.m. Monday to Friday, 8.30 a.m. to 12.30 p.m. Saturdays) I found her to be at all times trustworthy, honest and punctual. Her bookkeeping, typing, dictation and shorthand were topnotch.

However, her behaviour at the firm's Christmas picnic on the 11th inst. will forever be a stain on her character.

I have always subscribed to the motto 'Handsome is as handsome does', and I have never taken staff at face value.

Although Miss Jones was an ornament to the industry, and a decoration around the office, I believe it was unseemly for her to be seen cavorting with male members of staff.

It is regretful that, instead of a good name, she now takes with her a reputation and a colourful past.

I conclude by saying I was delighted to be asked to give her a character.
Yours sincerely,

Mr. Hewlett Z. Rutherforrd,
General Manager (Stores).

SALT OF THE EARTH

There was a type of man whom women admired, a man without the allure of danger. He was steady and safe, if boring. No one would ever think of running off with him, and presumably he never thought of running off with anyone either. He was unexciting and steady. Such a man was seen to have many great qualities:

- His word is his bond.
- He's as straight as a die.
- He doesn't have a mean bone in his body.
- He knows his onions.
- He's a good sort, a good type, a good stamp of a man, a good sport.
- He's a straightshooter — a plain talker, straightforward.
- He's a man of few words.
- He's worth his weight in gold.
- He's worth his salt.
- He's a good scout.
- A good doer — a hard worker, someone who puts the shoulder to the wheel, puts his back into it, pitches in, mucks in and helps.

If the **salt of the earth** was a woman, it was the highest praise, but it usually meant she was not a good sort, and therefore no threat to other women.

If she was always doing someone a good turn, you'd say she was a **good stick**, or **a good old stick**, or **not a bad old stick**. And if this good stick could be relied on in a crisis, she'd also be **a good egg**.

※

He comes from good stock.

In England, coming from good stock referred to your social class, but in Australia it meant you came from a family who worked hard and never cheated anyone, a family which had won the respect of others.

※

You're a Briton.

This is what you would say to someone who had done an especially difficult job, and stuck at it until it was done, and not complained.

※

Handsome is as handsome does.

It's all very well to have the looks, but let's see how good he is at his job, or let's see what their character is like.

※

Virtue is its own reward.

If you were good and resisted temptation, no one would ever know. So it was no good expecting accolades for doing the right thing.

※

He ploughs a deep furrow.

He takes life seriously, thinks about things deeply.

Chapter seventeen

SHOPPING

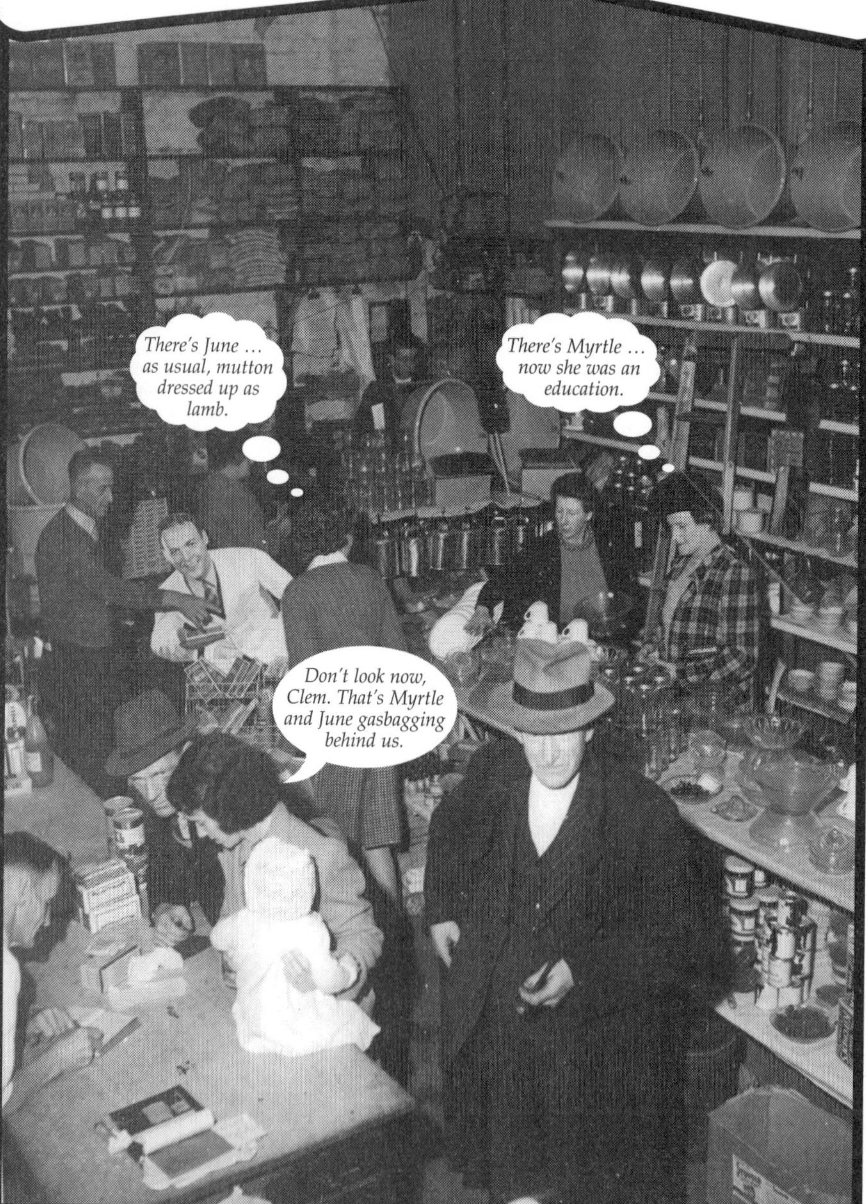

LOST FOR WORDS EPISODE 12:
Heard in the shop

Lost for Words. **The story of Bert and Grace and their trials and tribulations bringing up a young family after the War.**

Myrtle is in the draper's shop rifling through piles of buttons, cotton reels and darning wool. There are lots of ladies going through the nearby bolts of cloth, all chatting as if they are outside church on a Sunday morning.

The bell hanging over the door tinkles as June, recently widowed, marches in. She spies Myrtle.

'Myrtle! I haven't seen you in a month of Sundays.'

'June? How are you? You do look well!'

'Oh yes, Myrtle! All my prayers have been answered! Things have been soooo much better since the old man died.'

'I heard around the traps that your husband passed away some time back. Please accept my condolences, June.'

'Don't bother your pretty little head about me. I'm on clover. It's been a real shot in the arm.'

'You don't say? Your old man was in the fancy goods game, if memory serves?'

'Yes. But, Myrtle, I can tell you, I couldn't stomach him one day more. He was getting so frisky! I didn't know where to turn and, of course, divorce was out of the question. Then blow me down, he ups and dies.'

'You must still be in shock, June.'

'Oh, he'd been out gallivanting around, gadding about with Hazel Smith.'

'Now that name rings a bell.'

'The creature from the picture theatre. The usherette. Now *she* was an education. Once she got her claws into him, he couldn't escape. She'll be having conniptions now. Serves her right, the little so-and-so.'

'I can't say I'm sorry.'

'Well, as I'm fond of saying, Myrtle, *she was only a glazier's daughter — easy to see through.* She's no better than she ought to be. You can tell her type a mile off. Anyone who wears a fox fur and an orchid corsage. Common as dirt.'

'Dearie me. Tell me, June, I hear tell there was a big kerfuffle at the service.'

'You don't know the half of it, Myrtle. He'd been around the block a few times, I can tell you. There was more than the one. But I took it all in my stride. I got up at the funeral home and let him have it with both barrels.'

'What's the world coming to, June? I'm lost for words.'

'Don't be. I always told him I'm not the mothering type. I won't let the grass grow under my feet. And to think, I wouldn't have known except just after Easter I was coming home from town and I struck a woman on the tram. Hadn't seen her in the district for ages and she spilled her guts with gay abandon. Told me all about his tricks. She didn't twig I was married to him. And laugh!'

'In this day and age, too. That's a nice state of affairs. So you are staying on in the house?'

'Not on your nelly! I'm selling up. It's not a palace, but it will fetch me a tidy sum. Not to be sneezed at. So that's alright. But that tart at the picture theatre, won't she be miffed? I'd give anything to see the look on her face. She thought it was up for grabs, so she'll be having a hissy fit.'

'The awful nerve! The cheek!'

'You can say that again, Myrtle. A brassy bird. Well, she's not a brains trust, I can tell you. Now she'll just have to cop it sweet. Lord knows I put up with him for the last 24 years. My mother always told him, "Let June rule the roost", but he just wouldn't listen. And now look where he is. On the wrong side of the grass.'

'Well, June, I'll just put these buttons on tick, and then I'm off to pay the electric light bill. Not all of us have come into a fortune.'

Enid swings around with a card of bias binding in one hand and interrupts. 'That's all well and good for you girls, you lucky ducks. I've been having a bad trot lately. I'm a bit worse for wear. I've been put through the wringer. I don't know. I don't know. I could write a book about it. All this fuss has told on my nerves. I'm at the end of my tether. Only yesterday I was having a good bawl on the back porch; the tears were running down my cheeks and plopping on the newspaper.'

'What in heaven's name has happened, Enid?'

'You wouldn't read about it, Myrtle, but Clem has turned up again. Like a bad penny.'

'You should explain to June how your Clem shot through and went completely off the air.'

'Yes that's right, Myrtle, well last Saturday he turns up like a long-lost son, all palsy-walsy, making noises about moving in again with me and the nippers.'

'That's rich!'

'Too right! I told him, "*All bets are off.*" I told him, "*You were on a good wicket. But the day you walked out that front door, you shot your bolt. I wouldn't have you back now, not for all the rice in China.*" I still don't know what came over him. I said "*What did you think we were? Bottles of jam?*"'

'Did he drop his bundle, Enid?'

'No, Myrtle, but it knocked the stuffing out of him. He was beside himself. He said his whole life had gone to pot. You see, he was a Depression baby.'

'Say no more, Enid.'

'I don't know. I don't know. And now he says he needs to come back home to his family. He's even given up the grog.'

'You sure took the twist out of his tail! Did that earn him any brownie points?'

'I told him fair and square, "*That's a lot of tommyrot.*" He said, "*I've seen the light.*" So I said to him, I said, "*You started a family and then you made a meal of it. The whole idea of marriage is you scratch my back and I'll scratch yours.*" I told him, "*Never darken my door again.*"'

> 'Well done, Enid. So you kicked him out. For good.'
>
> 'Not in so many words, Myrtle. You see, Clem is generous to a fault. He'd give you the shirt off his back. And he's good with the kids. He promises that from now on, he's going to let me hold onto the purse strings. You couldn't get fairer than that, could you now? Besides, if I didn't take him back I'd never hear the end of it.'

Bargains

Money was a very scarce commodity for most Australians in the middle of last century. To protect the jobs of Australian workers from cheap imports, prices were sky high. Even **two bob** (20 cents) was considered a lot of money in the 1940s and 50s. Thus people expected a **bit of quality**, and if they didn't get it they felt **diddled**.

If a woman bought a **frock** and then discovered it was coming apart at the seams, she would soon be back in the store complaining: '**I paid good money for this**.' And if the salesgirl then tried to talk her into buying a matching **bolero**, to cover the defect, she would refuse indignantly: 'I'm not going to **throw good money after bad**.'

With little to spend, women would often go shopping for hours, but buy nothing. When a **shopgirl** approached and asked if she could help, the women would say: 'We're just **having a poke around, thanks all the same**.'

As they looked at the exorbitant prices being charged, they would say to each other: '**This is daylight robbery!**' And, '**You'd think we were trying to buy the crown jewels!**' And, '**These are as dear as poison**.'

But if she thought it was good value, the shopper would say as she handed over the money: '**Fair exchange is no robbery**.'

Occasionally, after rummaging through a lot of **cheapjack** items, the women would find a genuine bargain, saying to each other: '**It's a steal**.' Usually this meant some extras were thrown in: 'I got a second pair of trousers **into the bargain** and a good tie **to boot**.'

If she told her husband the bargains were **going for a song**, he'd be sure to say: 'Yes, dear heart, they're **giving them away**. They **saw you coming**, and they **got you coming and going**.'

At a Trash and Treasure sale, if your mother couldn't find a bargain she would complain, saying someone had **picked the eyes out of it** before she got there.

Remembering the Great Depression, people distrusted credit, loans and borrowing money. So it was a huge criticism when someone said: 'You know, they bought that lounge suite **on the never-never. They're living on the interest of what they owe**.'

There used to be a sign in shops: CREDIT FREELY GIVEN TO PERSONS OVER THE AGE OF 90, IF ACCOMPANIED BY THEIR PARENTS.

Dressing the window

Shopkeepers rarely used the cash register to add up the bill. Instead, they wrote the prices down with a pencil on a scrap of paper and added it up in their head. Occasionally, a shopkeeper might write out the bill on his palm or his wrist. But if he did this, he risked an angry customer saying: 'Is that how you **skin your customers, mate**?'

Lollies were the only item which shopkeepers put into small **white paper bags** with serrated edges. Everything else went into **brown paper bags** or was wrapped in **brown paper** and **tied with string**. There were no plastic bags. Shopkeepers cut string without scissors by winding it around a finger twice, then tugging it. The string would break because it would cut itself. Shopkeepers did this as they were talking to you, and whichever word coincided with breaking the string would be emphasised. Then they would continue on as though nothing had happened.

Shopkeepers would **dress the window**.

There were **paper shops**, not newsagencies. In Queensland, they sold tickets in the only lottery, the Casket, and the profits went to the free hospitals. Every week, every Brisbane paper shop put out a sign: **CASKET CLOSING SOON**, which used to alarm visitors from down south.

Chemist shops had large glass decanters in the window filled with coloured liquid, to show they mixed their own medicines.

Fish shops always had water running down the inside of the front window, to create a sense of cool refreshment.

The front of any **barber shop** always featured a round sign with a picture of a kangaroo: **HOP IN FOR A SPRUSO HAIRCUT**. But **California Poppy** was the most popular hair oil.

Chapter eighteen

GASBAGGING

LOST FOR WORDS EPISODE 13:
Mutton dressed up as lamb

Lost for Words. The story of Bert and Grace and their trials and tribulations bringing up a young family after the War.

It was Sunday morning when Bert and Grace sent the kids off to Aunty Myrtle's on the tram. They had settled back for a good lie-in when the front doorbell rang.

'If that's a God-botherer, I know just what to do,' Bert said, leaping out of bed. 'Kevin taught me the trick. You tell 'em, "*I'm so glad you've called, because I want to tell you all about being a Catholic.*" He swears it fixes their wagon.'

But at the door was the recently widowed June, Grace's Matron of Honour. 'Bert!' said June. 'You're still in your PJs! It's easy to see you're an owl, and not a fowl.'

'Oh it's all just go go go around here, June. Come in,' said Bert, thinking to himself: *I may be in my pyjamas, but you're dressed up like a trussed chook. You're all ribbons and bows.*

Grace emerged from the bedroom, wrapping on a dressing gown. Looking at June, all she could think was: *Mutton dressed up as lamb.* But she said: 'June, you're dressed up. I'm a bit sheepish. You've caught us at a bad moment. My get-up-and-go has got up and went.'

'Grace!' exclaimed June. 'You've got a face like a cabbie's bum! All round and fat and shiny!'

'Really? I'll just splash my face and run a comb through my hair.'

'I think you need more than a bath in a saucer of water, dear,' replied June striding off down the hallway. 'I never took you for a Canary Lil, but, never mind, you poor old thing. Don't do anything on my account, I simply can't stay. Ever since the old man died, I haven't had two minutes to rub together. It's been sooo good. I'm the Merry Widow, that's for sure. And now I'm selling up the house and the business, I'll be merrier. But of course I was well set up before I married him.'

Bert was thinking: *She's got a hide. All she brought to that marriage was her good name and her father's astrakhan coat.*

'You two will never guess who I'm lunching with today,' continued June, meandering into the kitchen and examining a pile of documents on the dresser. 'This'll knock your socks off. Remember my mother always used to say, when we were just bits of girls: *It's the ones over fifty that are the ones to beware of.* Well, I mustn't have listened to her, because you'll never guess who I'm going out to lunch with ... Alfie!'

'Now that's a turn-up for the books!' said Bert.

'Yes, and I know it's a Sunday and I should be pure, but the better the day, the better the deed, don't you think?'

'Hasn't Alfie had a bit of a chequered past, June?' said Grace, thinking: *No fool like an old fool.*

'We've been out twice before this,' said June. 'First we had a Vienna coffee in town. So that's alright. Then the next time, we had drinks at a hotel. Now don't look at me like that, Grace. Nothing untoward happened. We kept to the lounge bar, and I only had a Pimms No. 1. Or was it a shandy? And today, well, I don't have a clue where he's going to whisk me off to. Now that Alfie is a bachelor again he's quite the ladies' man, but they've all been floosies and hussies, not a true sweetheart among them, until me. Alfie swore blind he's going to turn over a new leaf.'

'Last time I saw Alfie was at the RSL,' said Bert. 'The word was he'd just spent some time at Her Majesty's Pleasure.' Bert was thinking: *He was down on his uppers then. That man has no shame. He's got more points than a porcupine.*

June looked at Bert and sniffed, then addressed Grace. 'Alfie is a true romantic. He says he follows his mother's advice. She told him: *Always look upon every girl as you would the Virgin Mary.* Alfie could have any girl for the asking, I can't think what he sees in me, but he assures me, he's been at me and at me no end, and he's very persuasive, I just melt ...'

Grace was thinking: *She's running true to form there.*

Bert was thinking: *She lays it on so thick you could shovel it. She's as tough as nails, but as soon as it comes to a man she turns to putty.*

'Cup of tea, June?'

'No thanks, Bert. Don't think me rude but I really can't stay.'

'Suit yourself.'

'Perhaps if it's fresh-made I'll have half a cup.'

'Do you want the top half or the bottom half?'

'Either or. I'm not proud. I'll drink anything. As long as it's hot and wet. Yes, one thing you can say about Alfie is he's not a stuffed shirt. He's not one to drink tea with his little finger stuck out; but his table manners are impeccable. That's the icing on the cake.'

Bert was thinking: *Yeah, the icing on the cake that isn't there.*

'Yes, Alfie is a solid citizen these days. He's the sort who loves to help others. He was telling me about this dear old biddy he's helping, I can't remember her name, it's on the tip of my tongue. Alfie has been a godsend to this old girl.'

Now Bert was thinking: *Tell me another one. I wouldn't pee in Alfie's ear if his brain was on fire. I'd like to be there when all his chickens come home to roost.*

'Alfie would give you the shirt off his back!' said June.

My foot! Bert thought.

'Please take a seat, June,' said Grace, now standing at the kitchen table, thinking: *That Alfie knows when he's on a good wicket. I bet he kisses himself goodnight.*

'Oh I don't have time to sit down, Grace, I've got to shake a leg. No rest for the wicked.'

'And less for the righteous,' added Bert, thinking: *I wonder how long before Alfie puts the fangs into June for a loan?*

'I saw Myrtle in the draper's, did she tell you? Now, I'm not a snooty-nosed woman, as you both well know, and I haven't got a sharp tongue, but your sister-in-law, she blows hot and cold. I'm the first one to notice any cold shoulder and she's such a cold fish. I know who wears the pants in that marriage ...'

'She's not everybody's cup of tea,' said Grace, 'but she grows on you.'

'I was telling Myrtle all my news. So that's alright. But she wasn't paying the slightest attention. She was just staring at me. I thought to myself: *I could talk and talk and talk until the rooks come to roost in your bum, Myrtle, and then you'd wonder how the sticks got there.* I felt like saying to her: *Yes, dear, it's the bottom jaw that moves.* I don't know why she gives herself such airs and graces. She really is a bit stuck-up, have you noticed? She's so holier-than-thou, you feel like saying to her: *You're the little white hen that never laid away.*'

Bert was thinking: *I wish you'd pretend you're a swamp, and dry up.*

Grace pulled out a kitchen chair. 'Well, June, if you're not going to sit down, I am. I'll have a cuppa. Bert, will you do the honours?'

'Though I shouldn't speak ill of those less fortunate, I'll admit not everyone has my fine English skin, not everyone can be like me, a ball of fashion, a glamourpuss, as Alfie calls me ...' said June.

Bert was sizing her up: *Beef to the ankle like a Mullingar heifer. Oh well, all cats are grey at night.*

'Now, June, be charitable,' interrupted Grace. 'None of us are spring chickens any more.'

Bert was thinking: *The more I see of people, the more I like cats.*

'And who should suddenly turn around in the draper's, we were all the time standing next to her, but Enid! It frightened the life out of me. I could have died. I was lost for words. I could have crawled under the table. I could have crawled up a hollow log and pulled the bark over me. Enid and I might be sisters-in-law one day, if Alfie plays his cards right! Because, of course, you know that my Alfie, well his brother Clem has just gone back to Enid. So that's alright. But the things she said about poor Clem, I think it was very poor ...'

So Clem came crawling back on his hands and knees, thought Grace.

'Enid is that down on him,' continued June, 'and, even so, she's holding onto him like grim death. I don't know why he went back. She gives him a dog's life. She gives me the pip. She's a street angel and a house devil, if ever there was one. I can't stand whingers.'

Bert piped up. 'I'm the same. I can't stand whingers, but somehow, they turn up on your doorstep and you can't avoid them.'

'I'm with you, Bert,' said June. 'I just lie back and let the tide wash over me.'

'But Enid hasn't got a mean bone in her body, dear,' said Grace. 'She always lets bygones be bygones.'

'You think so? Do you know what Enid does?' continued June. 'She's become friends with the owners of the Lyceum. Whenever she's in town, she drops into the picture theatre for only sixty seconds. So that's alright. She only stays just long enough to catch one particular scene in *Rebecca*. It's the part where Laurence Olivier declares: *It doesn't make for happiness, being married to the Devil.* Isn't that spooky? Why would she want to see that part over and over again?'

'Well,' said Grace. 'Enid and Clem — it's not exactly a marriage made in heaven.'

'I tell you, she's gone to the pack,' continued June. 'She never gets tarted up. She's obviously stopped caring. It's as plain as the nose on her face. And with a face like hers, well, she's got a face like the back of a bus. She's nothing to write home about, so you'd think she would put in some effort.'

Bert was thinking: *You're a mile wide and an inch deep*, but he only said, 'Enid is built for comfort, not for speed, June.'

'Oh, Bert,' giggled June, 'you're always full of funiocities. Enid has always been a bluestocking, not that all that education has done her complexion any good. But I know from Alfie she's comfortably off, she's quite well heeled ... though you wouldn't think so to look at her. I actually do feel very sorry for her.'

Yes, sorry from the teeth out, thought Bert. *Clem knows which side his bread is buttered on. He's going to stick to Enid. He's as set a jelly.*

'Now I must be off, I don't want to be late, so excuse my dust, there isn't a moment to lose. May I be so bold? Is there any more tea in the pot? That one was a bit cold. Perhaps I put too much milk in. You just can't win. Is there any cake?'

'I'm not sure, you'll have to take potluck,' said Grace.

'What's this here?' said June, pointing at a letter on the kitchen dresser.

'Have you been promoted at work, Bert? It says here on this paper ... oh don't mind me, I'm just stickybeaking. I'm just having a look-see. It's good news by the look of it. I just had a quick squiz, a screw, a gander, a gecko. I couldn't help it. You shouldn't mind, you know I don't keep any secrets from you two. But I'm going now, I don't want to be late.'

Bert was thinking: *If you were a bride you'd be sewing up your hem in the car on the way to the church.*

'By the way, Gracie,' said June at the front door, 'Strictly speaking I shouldn't say anything, and don't want to spoil your Sunday, but Janice has been going round saying you've broken a confidence. I think she's found someone else to do her books. Hooroo.'

You couldn't wait to tell me, could you? thought Grace.

Bad news will find you, always, thought Bert.

Gossips

Australians during the post-War era were often described as **laconic** — able to sum things up in few words. This hardly seems accurate, but it's true to say we had a lot of words for **gossips** and people who **never shut up**:

- She's certainly got **the gift of the gab**.
- She's **a stickybeak, a chatterbox**, or **a nosy parker**.
- He could **talk under wet cement**.
- She could **talk under wet cement, with a mouthful of marbles**.
- We can all **bubble under wet cement with a mouthful of mullet gut**.
- He could **talk under water with a mullet in his mouth**.

The language of gossip was: you **praised someone up**, but **ran them down**.

'Stop **prattling on**, you girls — it's like a Public Bar at closing time. Can you **keep it down to a dull roar**? You know what they say: **empty vessels make the most sound**.'

If people were talking a lot someone else would say: **Rhubarb rhubarb rhubarb**. What an old **windbag** he is.

He gave me such an **earbashing** — he kept talking long after I was bored with the topic. (Not the same as **boxing your ears**, which was what Grandpa threatened to do to a naughty grandson.)

He'd **talk the leg off an iron pot**.

She'd **talk to an iron pot**.

He'd **talk the leg off a three-legged pot, and on again**.

She'd **talk the hind leg off a donkey**.

The opposite to all this was: **She wouldn't say boo**.

THE DEFENCE

- We were just having a good old natter
- Having a yap
- A chinwag
- A yak
- Gasbagging
- Squawking
- Yabbering away
- Blathering on

- **Tittle-tattle**
- **A shut mouth catches no flies** — you'll stay out of trouble if you don't spread rumours.
- **This is on the QT** — a bit of gossip was then spread far and wide. Whenever gossip was passed on, the informed would say: **Fancy**, or **Fancy that**.
- **Busybody** — someone who was a **nosy parker**.
- The woman who spread all the gossip in town was called 'the bush telegraph'; hence: **The bush telegraph is working overtime**.
- Men used to say there were three ways to spread a story far and wide: *Telegraph, telegram, but best of all, tellawoman.*

- Rumours were always **scurrilous**.
- That man **has no shame** — he doesn't care what people think of him.
- **Badmouthing** — gossiping cruelly.
- She's always **running me down — slinging off**.
- Stop **bagging me** — you are putting me down.
- **In jest, in earnest** — said when someone was actually complaining but hadn't the guts to say it outright to the other person, so they pretended it was all in fun.

CONVERSATION LOLLIES

These lollies were flat, hard and round, rather like coins, in an assortment of colours, decorated with short sayings. If two people had enough lollies, they could conduct a funny conversation just by reading out the sayings:

Cutting a long story short, I wish she was here.

Don't mind me.

Have I dropped a clanger?

You could have knocked me over with a feather.

She's on my wavelength.

It's left a sour taste in my mouth.

You and me both.

She is unremittingly polite.

That's by the by.

We had words.

You don't say. (Actually means 'you do say'.)

I've been having a bad trot lately.

That's done and dusted.

The long and the short of it was ...

Can you see your way clear?

Not till Hell freezes over. She's funny.

Funny ha-ha, or funny peculiar?

Funny peculiar.

Chapter nineteen

DECENT CLOBBER

LOST FOR WORDS EPISODE 14:
Which twin?

Lost for Words. The story of Bert and Grace and their trials and tribulations bringing up a young family after the War.

💬

Doris was getting ready in her bedroom, singing tunelessly to herself as she tried on her brand-new outfit.

Her parents, Cyril and Myrtle, were sitting down the hall on the Genoa lounge suite trying to make conversation with Sandy Strong, the young lad who had turned up to take Doris out.

Another daughter, Barbara, stomped into the lounge room with the tea tray. Barbara didn't have a boyfriend, and so was doubly annoyed that she'd been caught wearing a brunch coat and jiffys in front of Sandy.

As Doris's singing became louder, Barbara called out: 'Ark ark the lark! Please give us more of your dulcet tones!'

'Did you call?' Doris said, emerging from the bedroom and sashaying around the lounge room, done up like a sore thumb, flaunting her new outfit: a mushroom-pink dress with matching hat. Doris was looking for notice, and she could expect to attract plenty of backhanders from the whole family. Particularly from her jealous older sister, Barbara.

'If she had another feather, she'd fly,' said Barbara. 'What sort of rig-out is that? What colour is it?'

'Elephant's breath, dearie,' replied Doris. 'You'd think you'd know.'

'That figures,' said Barbara, adding, 'I would say it was more of a dumduckity-mud-colour — the colour of a mouse's titty.'

'You'll be sorry on Labour Day!' chanted Doris to Barbara.

Cyril looked up, surprised. 'What did you sell? The goat?' he asked. 'Doris, why are you all gussied up? Is Sandy taking you to the Royal Ball?'

Doris was unperturbed. She tried on the large hat and recited:'*I shriek with chic! My hat of the week, is seen at the races, and all the best places.*

'Now she's gilding the lily,' said Barbara.

'That hat would have cost me four coupons during the War,' recalled Myrtle.

'I'm so glad I've had a cold-wave,' said Doris. 'It's much better than *your* old-fashioned Marcel, Mum. I don't have to have it set so often. I really should do the daughterly thing and give you fashion advice, Mum.'

'You do look very fetching, dear, when you're all spruced up,' said Myrtle.

'I wouldn't wear that hat in a fit!' said Barbara. 'And I wouldn't be seen dead in that dress!'

'Where did you get all this new clobber?' asked Sandy, giving the boyfriend's perspective.

'From "Frocks by Janice" up at the Junction,' said Doris. 'Aunty Grace told me to go there. I like Janice. You know she's nice because she has "nice" in her name. She uses rouleau cord — it's French — to decorate the pockets. And my chapeau has a pink wash. That's all the go.'

'I wouldn't go to "Frocks by Janice" in a pink fit!' said Barbara. 'I wouldn't shop there if you paid me.'

'Well, sweetheart,' said Sandy, sticking up for his girlfriend, 'let me be the one to tell you, Doris: that frock suits you down to the ground. It's you to a T.'

'It's not a frock,' said Doris. 'It's a gown. A frock is buttoned down the back.'

'I must say, she's wearing well, that Janice,' said Myrtle, wistfully, disappointed that Janice looked younger than her age, and younger than Myrtle.

'Janice certainly scrubs up well,' said Doris.

Now it was Dad's turn to be wistful. 'She's a sight for sore eyes, that Janice. She's a pocket Venus.'

'Do you think she wears falsies, Mum?' asked Doris. 'Or is it a Jezebel bra?'

'I don't think that one needs any upholstery,' said Cyril.

'I know one thing,' said Myrtle. 'Those raven locks of hers come out of a bottle.'

'No kidding?' said Sandy. 'How can you tell?'

'At school she was always a bloodnut,' said Myrtle. 'All her family are redheads. We called them the carrot tops. Her father had a florid complexion, and her mother always had rosy cheeks. But Janice herself, she had so many freckles we said she was kissed by the sun. That's why she started bleaching her skin with lemon juice, and she always puts up that parasol when she's out. She calls it her gingham.'

'By the way, Doris,' said Barbara. 'Jackie's out of jail.'

'Who's Jackie?' said Sandy.

'She means,' said Doris, hitching up her petticoat which was peeping out as a circle of white from under the hem of her skirt, 'that it's snowing down south. I'll have to adjust my straps. No looking now, Sandy. Remember it's out of bounds for boys to know anything about slips, girdles, corsets, nylons, scanties, suspender belts, step-ins, or any foundation garments really.'

'What are scanties?' asked Sandy.

'They're made from swami or charmeuse,' said Doris. 'You'll have to wait till we're married to find out more.'

'Oh, put him out of his misery,' groaned Barbara. 'Scanties are underpants with legs and lace. Swami is usually a pale coffee-coloured ribbed satin, and charmeuse is a silky lingerie fabric.'

Sandy was none the wiser.

'It's simple,' continued Barbara. 'The corsetry department is supposed to stop a girl from looking drack. They sell over-the-shoulder boulder-holders. But in Doris's case, she'd need the whole of Grace Brothers, and Allan and Starks and Myer, plus a gallon of Crème Charmosan and a bucket of Attar of Roses. Do you realise, Doris, that your hair is standing out like a birch broom in a fire?'

'Well, Miss Smartypants,' said Doris, grasping Sandy's hand, 'I'll just ask this question of our expert panel and we'll see. Which twin has the Toni?'

Daks and togs

Australians never used to have a separate set of clothes for each occasion.

Thus a woman might wear an old dress to do the housework. It might be a very formal dress which used to be saved for **best** or **Sunday best**, but is now too worn or stained to be seen outside the family.

Grandma would keep something **for good**. This meant she'd keep it forever. Or it might mean she'd keep it only for 'good' occasions.

If a child's shirt was creeping out of his duds, the kids might chorus:

Giddy, giddy gout!
Your shirt's hanging out!
Five miles in!
And five miles out!

Men would be seen working on the roads wearing a business shirt and suit — but these clothes were old, stained, darned, patched and repaired. If he had special work clothes, a man might call them his **dungarees**. Otherwise, his trousers were his **strides, britches, daks** or **duds**.

If a man wanted to wear some **decent clobber**, he would have to buy a suit, usually with an extra pair of pants since the coat would suffer less wear than the pants. Men wore **pearl tiepins** or **brass grips** to hold the tie to the shirtfront. If he worked in an office, he might wear **elastic metal shirt rings** (rather like the metallic band on a wristwatch) to stop his sleeves becoming soiled. Some office workers also wore **eyeshades**, which were much like a shiny green cap with no crown, to shade the eyes from the bright lights.

Most men wore braces, not belts. Some had a tin buckle inscribed with **Police and Fireman's Braces**. A fastidious gent would always prefer braces because they showed off the good cut of the trousers.

A man's hat had a **bash**: the crease a man, or boy, chose to have in the crown of his **fedora, panama, felt** or **pork pie** hat. Loutish schoolboys in the 1950s would give their hat a **triangular bash** — the sharper the corners the better. We used three pencils to keep the bash straight.

It was understood that men parted their hair on the left and women on the right, unless you were **as bald as a bandicoot**. If a boy's hair was half the time parted on the right, you would assume he had an older sister. Boys with an older sister were often seen as sissies. Later on, boys might favour a **ducktail haircut** that swooped down the back from both sides, then stuck out a bit at the back.

Girls desperately tried to train their hair out of its natural **cow's lick**, by having a **permanent wave** created in a salon. They sometimes resorted to the uncertainty of a **home perm**, such as the **Toni Perm** with its anodyne advertising slogan every week in the *Australian Women's Weekly*: '**Which twin has the Toni**?'

Whereas boys tried to create a cow's lick with a comb and hair oil. Or they might go for a **crew cut**, not to be mistaken for a **short back and sides**.

You might have called your shoes **beetle-crushers** or **clodhoppers** until the 1960s when everyone got **desert boots** — also known as **brothel creepers** — fawn-coloured suede ankle shoes laced with a short cord. A real **lair** might **ponce around** in a **zoot suit with a drape shape**.

Queenslanders swam in **togs**, while others swam in **cossies**, or **swimmers**, or **bathers**.

Girls wore a **muu-muu** (a sleeveless shift dress with miniature white pompoms on the hem); a **sack dress**; an **H-line** dress or an **A-line**; a **shift**; or a **ruched bloomer suit** (like a baggy swimsuit). They knew they had enough starch in their hoop petticoat when it would stand up in the corner by itself.

The main advice mothers gave their children when they were getting dressed was: **Put on something decent. Decent** meant dressed, **half-decent** meant passable.

HATS AND HANKIES

- **That's old hat** — out of fashion, the old way of doing it.
- **That went out with straw hats** — no one does that any more.
- My sponge cake will knock her scones **into a cocked hat**.
- He'd join in a fight **at the drop of a hat**.
- **I dips me lid, I tip my hat to him, I take my hat off to him**, or **You've got to take your hat off to him** — from a time when every person in town wore a hat. You took your hat off as a sign of respect, so it meant 'I want to acknowledge what he's done.'
- **I'll eat my hat** if he turns up tonight.
- **Should I throw my hat in first**? — meant 'I know you're angry at me, so you can take pot shots at my hat first before I'm game to come in the door.'
- He's **talking through his hat** — talking nonsense.
- **Keep it under your hat** — keep it to yourself; don't tell **a living soul**.
- **Don't jump up and down on your hat** — don't get too angry or excited over nothing.
- That's a **feather in his cap** — that's an accomplishment he can be proud of.

A pocket handkerchief was called a **hanky**, a **blow-nosey** or a **minky**.

Handkerchiefs had many more uses than just blowing noses.

In the heat of the sun, if they didn't have a hat, men and boys would knot the four corners of their hanky and fit it on their head like a small hat. Great at the Test cricket.

Schoolboys would tie their few coins in one corner so they didn't lose any money from a pocket, and used it as an effective weapon in a fight.

Mothers would pin a hanky to the school uniform of a young child to save them from losing it.

When about to enter a Catholic church, women who didn't have a hat would place a clean, ironed hanky loosely on their head.

Chapter twenty

GAMES

As well as walking to and from school, both boys and girls played vigorous games before, during and after. The games cost nothing and kept almost everyone very thin.

Playing fairies

Cin-der-ella,

Dressed in yella,

Went upstairs

To kiss her fella.

On the way her panties busted!

How many people were disgusted?

One

Two

Three ...

If a **nosy parker** walked past while a group of girlfriends were playing this skipping game, she might shake her hand, then point her finger at them, trilling '**Ooooowaaah! Telling on you! Telling on you!**' And if she did **blab**, like the **smartypants** she was, the girls would be called up to the headmaster's office to receive **a good talking-to**, and perhaps a ruler across the back of the legs or on the palm of the hand.

In primary schools, girls and boys played different games, and played them in separate areas of the school grounds.

Girls played **Fairies and Witches**, or **Convicts and Soldiers**, both of which involved chasing and catching. Or they played **Statues** — a hilarious game where one stood on a **form** (a long, backless stool that would seat 2–4 kids) and the others pushed her off. She had to freeze in the pose she landed in: with one foot up in the air, or almost down on her knees, or with one leg out.

As today, crazes and fads spread through schools: hula hoops, hopscotch, elastics, skipping, yoyos, jacks or knuckles, sleeping dolls, bride dolls, spinning tops, baby dolls, rag dolls and paper dolls (where girls folded paper clothes over a cardboard cut-out of a doll). No one ever knew who started each craze, or why it finished.

In skipping, most games were played with two girls turning the rope and the rest jumping in and out. They usually started with **salt**, which was turning the rope in a leisurely fashion while a girl gently skipped, and ended with **pepper**, which was brisk, growing faster and faster so the person had to jump rapidly, leaving the ground just long enough to let the rope through. Since you could skip at a slow pace indefinitely, most games ended in pepper, and you were out only when you finally stumbled — which didn't take long.

Skipping chants:
All in together,
This fine weather.
I spied a nanny goat
Putting on a petticoat.
How many layers
Did she don?
With a one, two, three ...

Two little dickybirds
Sitting on a wall.
One named Peter
One named Paul.
Fly away, Peter
Fly away, Paul.
Come back, Peter
Come back, Paul.

Over the garden wall
I let the baby fall.
The mother came out
And gave me a clout
And said she'd turn me inside out.

Salt:

How will you go to the wedding?
Go to the wedding?
Go to the wedding?

Pepper:

Coach, carriage, wheelbarrow or dunny cart?
(It was terrible if you got out on dunny cart!)

Salt and pepper
Marmalade jam
Tell me the name of your old man
P-E-P-P-E-R

Fish, fish, jump into the dish
Fish, fish, turn around in the dish
Fish, fish, jump out of the dish

Occasionally a **clapping game** would become popular among girls. Two girls slapped their thighs, then their own hands, then the opposite girl's hands in a complicated pattern (much like Bob Hope and Bing Crosby in the Pat-a-Cake scenes in their 'Road to' flicks).

My mother said,
I never should,
Play with the gypsies in the wood.
If I did,
She would say,
Naughty little girl to disobey.
Disobey. Disobey.
Naughty little girl to disobey.

In one game they sat in a circle and each girl put their fist on top of another fist while reciting:

One potato, two potato, three potato, four,
Five potato, six potato, seven potato, more.

Or,

I wrote a letter to my love
And on the way I dropped it.
One of you has picked it up
And put it in your pocket.
Not you.
Not you.
Not Y-O-U.

For a lark, girls might play **Oranges and Lemons**, where two children are chosen to be the orange and the lemon, and the rest dance through the arch of their arms. As an Australian you had no idea what it all meant, or exactly how to play; all you knew was that you didn't want the arms to come down and chop you.

Oranges and lemons
Say the bells of St Clement's.
You owe me five farthings,
Say the bells of St Martin's.
When shall you pay me?
Say the bells of Old Bailey.
When I grow rich,
Say the bells of Shoreditch.
When will that be?
Say the bells of Stepney.
I do not know,
Say the great bells of Bow.
Here comes a candle to light you to bed.
Here comes a chopper to chop off
Your
Your
Your
Your
Head!

Similarly, we had but an imperfect idea of the execution and the history of some rhymes.

Ring-a-ring-a-rosey,
A pocket full of posey,
A-tisshoo!
A-tisshoo!
We all fall down.

And it wasn't very long before I shifted,
Screaming murder, like a clown.
I was sitting, if you please, on a swarm of bumblebees.
So I shif-ted
Lower down.

AUTOGRAPH BOOKS

When a girl was leaving school, on her last day she would bring along her autograph book: a small hardcover book with each unlined page in a different-coloured paper. All her friends would write something humorous or puzzling memento to be remembered by. Someone would write on the first page:

By hook or by crook
I'll be first in this book.

Then the next person was sure to write, squeezed in above:

By pen or by quill,
I'll be darned if you will.

Then the rest would follow:

YYs U R
YYs U B
I C U R
YYs 4 me

1 1 was a racehorse
2 2 was 1 2
1 1 1 1 race
2 2 1 1 2

Time flies. So can you. But only the slowest,

Ooohey Goohey was a worm,
A little worm was he.
He climbed onto the railway track,
The train he did not see.
Ooohey Goohey!

Solomon Grundy,
Born on Mond'y,
Christened on Tuesd'y,
Ill on We'n'sd'y,
Worse on Thursd'y,
Dead on Frid'y,
Buried on Saturd'y,
And that was the end of Solomon Grundy!

New friends are silver,
Old friends are gold.
Never let the new friends
Replace the old.

One bright day in the middle of the night,
Two dead men got up to fight.
Back to back they faced each other,
Drew their swords and shot each other.
A deaf policeman heard the noise,
And came and killed those two dead boys.
If you don't believe this tale so tall,
Ask the blind man, he saw it all.

Dubbing in Dibs

Marbles was the most important game for boys in the 1940s and 50s, even ahead of cricket and footy — perhaps because it was only in marbles that boys prepared for their future corporate careers.

In other sports you collected runs or points or won a trophy. But in marbles, unlike any other game, you were **playing for keeps**. You tried to bankrupt your opposition; to grab everything he had and send him home, not just defeated, but crying and broke.

It was marbles that taught boys to be ruthless. To win **by hook or by crook**.

Wealth among boys was measured in marbles — how many, and what sort. Some boys, over the years, collected thousands of marbles of all colours and sought-after types, so many that they could never play with them all; while others stumbled around the playground every day, the cloth **marble bag** their mother had specially sewed for them blowing in the breeze.

Most boys had a homemade marble bag with a drawstring in which they carried all their marbles, like a wallet full of credit cards. Boys were so keen to play that many got to school early, and games continued through little lunch, big lunch and after school. Some played **for funsy**, but this was rare.

THE GAMES

First you had to agree which game of marbles to play. Some boys specialised in certain games which suited their favourite **tor** (their striking marble). If you didn't want to play him at his special game, to tempt you he might **dub in** a special green marble you'd always wanted, saying it was **up for grabs**. Because, once you'd **dubbed in**, your marbles became available to your opponent.

Games included:

- **Big ring:** A large circle was drawn in the dirt and each player would drop the same number of marbles, also called **dibs**, in the middle. Each player had to fire from anywhere outside the circle, and any marble knocked out of the ring was theirs. If they knocked one out and their **tor** stayed inside, they could then fire from where it stopped. Thus the first to knock a marble out could quickly clean out the ring.

In this game boys aimed for the part of the marble close to the ground, so that their **tor** was more likely to stay inside the ring. The best type of marble for this game was a ***blood alley*** — so called because it was red and white. It was a heavy marble with hitting and staying power.

- **Poison ring:** A small ring was drawn in the dirt, with marbles ***dubbed in*** to the centre. The inside of the ring was 'poison' so you had to knock the marbles out *without* leaving your **tor** in the ring. If it stayed inside, then you'd lost your marbles. The best marble for this game was a ***starry*** or ***cat's eye*** — so called because it had a beautiful burst of colour inside clear glass. It was a light marble, so if you aimed for another marble's side, both it and your starry would fly out.

- **Linesy:** You drew a long line, crossed it with a few lines, and put a marble at each cross. Starting at one end, you kept each marble you dislodged.

- **Holesy:** Three marble-sized holes were created, with one off to the side. The winner was the first to roll their **tor** into each hole. Before you shot from a hole, you spanned your hand out and around and fired from there.

Some other types of marbles were: an ***agate*** — small, hard like a rock; a ***blunderbuss*** — any marble that was huge, and good in a game of **eyedrops**; ***duck's egg*** — a despised dib that wasn't perfectly round; and ***jingers*** or ***glassies*** — glass marbles from ginger beer bottles. You had to break the bottle to retrieve them. They made a good tor.

Boys crouched down on their haunches to fire off their marbles using two different techniques: placing the marble on the thumbnail or the thumb knuckle, held by the tip of the forefinger. The firing hand was rested on top of the other hand which formed a bridge with all five fingers on the ground. The thumbnail was good for close work, but the knuckle gave the kick and power required.

No Australian children used a technique I saw in Vietnam. Vietnamese boys held the marble between the thumb and forefinger of the left hand and flicked it out with the forefinger of the right hand like an arrow. It was surprisingly effective.

THE RULES

There were some strange rules in marbles.

To stop boys creeping closer to the target, leaning their top hand forward, you yelled out '**No funking!**' Or '**No fudging!**' If they were **cribbing**, and you were quick enough, you yelled, '**Knuckle down, screw tight**' and they had to point their knuckle down into the ground.

If you wanted to **put the mockers** on them you said '**Mullygrubs**', while making a double cross in the dirt with two fingers.

Cricket

Cricketers wore a wide-brimmed, white cotton hat called a **washing hat**.

If you hit the ball hard using **the meat of the bat**, you **clocked** it, **clubbed** it, gave it **a ding**, **hoicked** it, or **took the long handle**. If you did this often while batting then you were said to **collar** the bowling. This was known as **going the slog**, giving the ball **a tonk**, having **a thrash**, **going for the doctor**, or **having a dig**.

On the other hand, someone who blocked the ball all the time was **a stonewaller** who used **a dead bat**. If you were sick of watching such a batsman you yelled out: '**Have a go, you mug!**' Whereas a batsman who tried to whack every ball for six was a **bash artist**.

To **keep your eye in**, you hung a stocking from the clothes line, put a cricket ball in it, and then hit it with your bat as it swung back and forth.

Full-size cricket bats were **six-springers**; you could see six thin bits of rubber running down into the handle. Six-springers could not be used until they had first been rubbed with linseed oil every day for two weeks. After you oiled the willow (the bat) you rolled the face of the bat with an empty soft drink bottle.

A leather cricket ball was called a **six-stitcher**, because of the six rows of white stitching that held it together.

If you dropped a **dolly** (easy catch) you had **dropsy** and spectators would be sure to yell out, '**Get a bag!**' or '**Butterfingers**'.

An unplayable, perfect delivery from a bowler was a **Jaffa** (the ball seemed to be as small as a Jaffa lolly) or a **corker**. A **donkey drop** was a slow delivery that sat up asking to be hit. A **daisy cutter** was bowled along the ground to try to get under the bat. A **mullygrubber** was when you bowled a ball that shot along the ground unexpectedly.

Batsmen **shaped up**, or **faced up** at the crease after **taking guard**.

The favourite wicket was a **kerosene tin**. No one ever had proper wickets and bails in the backyard.

Bowlers got **clobbered** by the batsman if they got **carted all over the park**. They were abused if they **pegged** the ball instead of bowled it. If a bowler tossed the ball well up to the batsman, he '**gave it some air**'.

Fieldsmen always **foxed** the ball. If you threw it back hard you **pelted it in** (as opposed to throwing bottle tops which were always **pinged**).

If you got beaten and complained, you were a **sore loser**.

To be **flogged** was to be given a **drubbing**, or a **towelling** or a **caning**, or **left for dead** — defeated by a big score. (Flogged also meant to steal, to sell something, or to drive a car or horse so punishingly you damaged it.)

If you finished last in the competition you came **stone last** or **stone motherless**. Conversely, if you won by a big margin you would skite **we beat them hollow**.

BACKYARD CRICKET

The most important rule, so you didn't lose the ball to an irate neighbour, was: **Over the fence is out**. Thus women and mothers would use the phrase: '**That's over the fence**' if you had done something and gone too far.

Tip and run — you had to run if you hit the ball, regardless. This was a fast and furious game and usually you got run out.

French cricket — your legs were the wickets; if the ball hit them you were out. You didn't have to run. The other players stood around you and threw the ball at your shins, even if they were behind you, or at the side. They usually pitched the ball into the ground, so in defending your legs you would hit the ball up in the air and be caught. Whoever hit your legs was then in, or whoever caught you was in when you were out.

This game was always played with a soft ball.

Before the contraceptive pill, boys called all balls **'pills'**, whether football, cricket or tennis balls. (Medicines in tablet form then were universally known as pills. But after *the pill* came in, women, especially Catholic women, would say they were going to take a **tablet**.)

Football

Footballers didn't kick the ball down the field. They **roofed**, **reefed** or **rooted** it.

I played rugby league at primary school in Brisbane when the forwards in rugby league were always called **the pigs**.

Rake — these days he's known as the dummy half or a hooker, but in the 1950s he was called a rake in rugby league. In those days scrums were contested so it was important to have a hooker who could rake the ball back quickly.

Leather **tags** or **sprigs** were nailed to the underside of footy boots to give you grip. Referees would make everyone stand and show him the soles of their footy boots before the match so that he could see the nails were not sticking out of the tags.

Place kick — meant kicking for goal in rugby league. A hole was dug in the ground by placing the two tags in your heel on the spot and spinning around. The point of the ball was then placed in the indentation. People on the sideline used to bet on this at A-grade games, and the men taking the bets would yell, **'I'll back it in'** or **'I'll back it out'**.

Coathanger — tackling someone around the neck with a **stiff-arm** tackle.

Force-ems-back — played in schoolyards. The idea was to force the other fellows back to the other end of the field by kicking over their heads or away from them. If the ball was caught on the full you were allowed to take three giant strides forward before kicking.

Important rules to remember in football were:

1. Always turn side-on to catch the ball (so if you drop it you don't knock on).
2. Tackle low: they can't run without their legs.
3. Never let them know they've hurt you.

Players injured in the second half were always bandaged up and sent back on, because in the 1950s no replacements were allowed after half-time in rugby league or rugby union.

If someone played brilliantly he was said to have **played out of his skin**.

Supporters in Australia **barrack for** their favourite team. But in England to barrack a team means to jeer and heckle, so this is done to the opposition.

Party games

CONSEQUENCES

Everyone sits in a circle armed with a sheet of paper and pencil.

First, each participant writes, on the very top of their paper, a man's name (whether their father, or Augustus Caesar or the Dunny Man or King Kong). Then they fold the paper over so no one can see the name and *pass it on* to the person beside them.

The next person writes down a woman's name. *Pass it on.* Where they met. *Pass it on.* He said to her … *Pass it on.* She said to him … *Pass it on.* And the consequences were … *Pass it on.* You try to make your little story quite cogent and sensible.

By the end of the game, each story has been impossibly mixed up with every other story. Finally, each person reads out what is on the sheet in their hand. It might come out something like this: The Dunny Man met the Queen of Sheba on the Bondi tram. He said to her: 'It doesn't quite fit.' She said to him: 'I've always found that Buckley's Canadiol Mixture does the trick.' And the consequences were: Bob Menzies was declared the winner!

BILLY JOHNSON'S BLACK PIG WITH THE DIRTY SNOUT

If you are **It**, you have to answer every question by saying: 'Billy Johnson's black pig with the dirty snout', without laughing.

The family tries to trick you with embarrassing questions, such as:

Who are you in love with?

Who helped you in your exam?

Who is the Prime Minister of Australia?

Who did you back in the Melbourne Cup this year?

Who are you taking to the pictures tomorrow night?

Who asked you out last week?

Who do you think you look like?

What did we eat for dinner today?

Remember: you are forbidden to laugh. Or, in the case of little girls, you are not allowed to cry.

VAMPING

Everyone at the party, including the children, does a performance on spec, without any preparation. It might be singing, reciting a poem, playing the piano, or acting a scene. It is made up as you go along, usually a poem with a slightly risqué repeated chorus, for example: 'I'm very fond of the parson's nose, but don't stick it out like that'.

RECITATION

Adults might recite from their favourite poems.

From *Ned Kelly*

> *... and Dan, the most religious,*
> *Took the Sergeant's wife to mass ...*

... I will not surrender,
To any coat of blue.
Or any man
Who wears the crown
Belonging to your crew ...

From *Ben Hall*

It took ten men
To take Ben Hall
When he was fast asleep

A SINGSONG

After lunch, someone would say: 'Give us a tune', and the piano accordion would be strapped on. Or the best musician in the gathering would open the piano, get out the sheet music from under the piano seat, and the rest of the family would sit or stand around it and sing along.

Bless the Lord
How we roared
In our old-fashioned Ford
Along the road to Gundagai.

With the radiator hissin'
And half the engine missin'
Beneath that sunny sky.

There was water in the petrol
And sand in the gears
Hadn't seen a garage
In over forty years.

Bless the Lord
How we roared
In that old-fashioned Ford
Along the road to Gundagai.

Or a tune made famous by tenor John Charles Thomas, around World War II:

I'm as free as the breeze,
I can go where I please.

Or a tune your mother would sing:

Go home to your mother,
You red-headed bugger.
You don't belong to me.

Chapter twenty-one

OLD TECHNOLOGY

On the wireless

SERIALS

In the 1930s, 40s and 50s Australians sat around large timber cabinets in their lounge rooms and stared into the green glow emanating from the cabinet's glass face, as they listened carefully to **the wireless**. The face contained all the country's radio station names embossed on the front: 4BC, 2UE, 3AW etc. A large white needle, operated by turning a knob, led to the station you were after.

Like TV today, everybody had their favourite wireless programme which they would rarely miss: it was usually a fifteen-minute serial. The name of the serial, and its catchphrase, let you know exactly what to expect:

- **When a Girl Marries**. 'For all those who are in love, and all those who can re-mem-ber.'
- **Jeffrey Blackburn Adventures**
- **Biggles Sweeps the Desert** and **Biggles Flies East**. Kids used to joke there was **Biggles' Fly's Undone**.
- **Mary Livingstone, MD**
- **Portia Faces Life**. 'The story of the only woman who ever dared to love com-pletely.'
- **You be the Detective**. In police dramas the cops always caught the crooks **red-handed**.

Some serials went for a decade. **Blue Hills** had run for so long that everybody called it **Flu Pills**.

CRICKET

The same blokes used to do the ABC (which was then the Australian Broadcasting *Commission*) radio commentary for the cricket, decade after decade. One bloke used to often make a comment, and then say to his colleague: 'What do you think, Arthur?' It happened so often that people in conversation would suddenly say: **'What do you think, Arthur?'**

When you listened to cricket or football broadcasts from overseas it sounded like there was a cyclone happening in the background as the sound rose and fell. You had to sit close to the receiver with your ear up against the speaker trying to catch the words while the wireless howled eerily.

ADVERTS

The wireless was filled with catchy advertising jingles that went something like this:

Breakfast time is Breakfast Delight time,
Eat it up and be strong,
Start your day right with some Breakfast Delight,
And you'll last all day long.

A road safety message played each morning was:

I've a tale to tell
All you little boys
And little girls as well.
When you leave the schoolyard
And go out to play,
Don't run into danger,
Think of what I say:
Look to the right
And look to the left
And you'll never, ever get run over.

How can you be sure there are no white ants in the floor?
Borers in the door?
Silverfish galore?
Get a Flick Man,

That's the answer.
Remember, one Flick
And they're gone!

Kinkara Tea — good to the last (ding-dong) drop.
Fourex Beer — It takes one X to mark the spot, but it takes four Xs to mark ... the
Perfect Spot.
The time, by my Wallace Bishop Loyal watch, is half past seven.
Come naked to Coolangatta, and let Bev Stafford dress you!
It's ten o'clock, and the Commonwealth Bank is now open for business.
Mr Max Factor, of Hollywood, now makes this promise to you:
I promise you
That my new powder,
Cream Puff,
Will make you lovelier than ever before.

In the absence of: pathology offices in every suburb, CAT scans, MRIs, whole body scans, colonoscopies, endoscopies, laparoscopic surgery, statins and vacuum cleaners to suck out earwax ... Australians took headache powders. Lots of them. Advertisements for these dominated the airwaves and shop windows.

There were four main headache powders, all wrapped in paper. At any hour you could see someone with their head tipped back, shaking the powder from the folded paper directly into their open mouth.

1. *Take Sitruc or suffer*. (Sitruc was Curtis, the name of the creator, spelt backwards.)
2. *B–E–X. Bex. Bex is Better*.
3. *Take Vincents APC with confidence and a hot bath*. (Small boys hearing this advertisement had visions of a happy smiling woman swilling a bathful of hot water down her throat.)
4. *ASPRO will ease it*. (Or a Bayer's Aspirin.)

The common preference was for *a cup of tea, a Bex and a good lie down*.

Telegraph

TELEGRAMS

In the days before telephones were commonplace, people kept in fast contact with little bits of yellow paper. These bits of paper arrived in a pouch on the hip of a **telegram boy** who rode a bicycle around the suburbs from the nearest post office. You would go to a post office and fill in a form, clearly printing your message. There was a basic charge for 12 words including each full stop (which counted as one word) and any additional words would cost **a pretty penny**. So everybody cleverly tried to get their news across in as few words as humanly possible. You handed your form over to the post office clerk, who checked it and charged you. Then your message went out the back to be sent.

Sometimes people would combine two words into one, or use initials, or drop unnecessary prepositions, verbs and pronouns. **'Meeting cancelled stop arriving 6pm train stop need taxi stop love Jack.'** There was a famous story where two mates wanted to back a horse. Only one of them, Willy Fennel, could get to the track. They put all their money on it. Willy sent a cryptic telegram to his mate because he had spent all his money on the horse. The message read: **SFSFWIRYWF**. Finally when Willy got back, his mate complained that he couldn't understand the telegram.

'But it's simple!' said Willy. 'The message reads: **Started favourite, slipped and fell. Wouldn't it root you, Willy Fennel.'**

TELEPHONES

Everybody who was lucky enough to have their own telephone in the house had a queue of neighbours, friends and acquaintances forever dropping in and saying **'May I use the phone?'**

Before **public phones** became **payphones**, and before the advent of Gold Phones and Blue Phones and phone cards and mobile phones, it was considered **the height of bad manners** to refuse access to such a sought-after and necessary convenience. So everyone who had a phone kept a moneybox next to the telephone, often with a sign pointing to its presence. Anyone who made a phone call was supposed to put in the normal fee: tuppence, fourpence or sixpence as prices went up over the years.

The moneybox next to someone's large, heavy black phone might be a red and white tin saying, **Aid The Spastics** (those with cerebral palsy) with a picture of a laughing girl in a cardigan and callipers. Or it might be the bronze and green **Commonwealth Bank moneybox** in the shape of the eight-storey Sydney **bank headquarters** building. Or it might be a green moneybox in the shape of a thick bank **passbook**.

A moneybox in the shape of a passbook was very reassuring. Long before it was privatised and sold on the Australian Stock Exchange, the Commonwealth Bank was trusted by almost all Australians. Every home contained at least one grey linen Commonwealth Bank passbook. Many schoolchildren even had an account into which they deposited a little bit of money each week.

People only used the telephone for relaying an important message: an arrival time, news of a sick relative, or to wish someone Happy Birthday. A telephone was considered too important to play around with.

Sometimes when you got on **the blower**, you had a bad line and could hardly hear, so it was a common thing to say: 'I'll hang up and try again for a better line.' You also often got **crossed lines**: you picked up the phone and you'd hear a couple of people talking to each other so you'd hang up and try again. But if you asked someone to **drop you a line**, it meant you wanted them to write you a letter.

Because all long-distance calls were handled by operators called **switchgirls**, whenever you made a phone call to another town or state, the operator would say: 'Hold on' and 'Connecting.' Almost no one phoned overseas before the 1970s because it was just too expensive. I lived overseas for seven years from 1964 to 1971 and never received or made a phone call home. I wrote aerograms — letters on thin blue paper which when folded and stuck down did not require an envelope.

For long-distance calls, you could talk only in three-minute blocks, and towards the end of your three minutes the operator, who was watching the clock, would come on the line and say: '**Are you extending?**' If you said yes she would disappear for another three minutes before breaking into the conversation again: '**Are you extending**?' This was called **a trunk call**.

Each time you agreed to extend you had to remember it would cost you more money. Thus people often asked the operator to **reverse the charge**. She would ring up and ask the person you were calling if they would accept a reverse-charge call from you. To try to save money, in case the person you wanted to speak to wasn't home, when making a long-distance call you asked the operator for a **person-to-person trunk call**. Then, if someone else answered the phone, the operator would come back on the line and say '**The party isn't available**', and so, since you didn't talk to them, it didn't cost you anything.

If you wanted someone to ring you up, you'd tell them: '**Give me a tingle some time**.'

In the old money

What's the damage? I hope it's not too much.

That's two and fourpence all up.

Crikey, I've only got some coppers.

Don't worry. Your money's no good here. Put it back in your skyrocket.

But you've totted up the bill.

**Forget it; it's just a piddling amount. It's not worth a cracker, not worth
tuppence, so you can have it for nix.**

Gee, thanks, mate, but you know what they say, every mickle makes a
muckle. If you save the small coins, you'll end up with big ones. Look
after the pennies and the pounds will take care of themselves.

Well my motto is penny-wise, pound-foolish.

I'm not so sure about that. I'm only paid a pittance at work.

**You poor wage slave. And look at me. Already this week I've lost a packet
on the races, and I'm not complaining. I wouldn't be dead for quids.**

You should remember that money is made round to go around, and made
flat to stack.

**Well it burns a hole in my pocket. You see, my wife has got champagne
tastes on a beer income. That's why I follow the gee-gees. In for a penny,
in for a pound I say. If you are going to get into something, then you
might as well do it properly, go the whole hog. I won a motza last month.**

I would never be allowed to gamble. My wife is so stingy she reads the
menu from right to left. She's as mean as cat droppings. She's a
tightwad skinflint. You could turn her upside down and shake her, and
tuppence wouldn't fall out. She still has her first lunch money. If she
opened her purse the moths would fly out.

You should tell her to take the death adder out of her purse.

If she owned the town hall clock she wouldn't tell you the time, and if
she owned the ocean she wouldn't give you a wave. She's so mean
she'd skin a flea for its hide. She wouldn't give you the dirt from under
her fingernails. She wouldn't give you last year's calendar.

But gambling on the gee-gees is easy money, old son, if you know what you're doing.

Yeah, but I can't even afford to bet pin money. I've already forked out for a set of false teeth. And I had to take money out of our radio licence account in order to pay our electric light bill, so I'm already robbing Peter to pay Paul. I thought I was going to get ahead this week, but all my savings have been mizzled away. I'm stony-broke. I'm so broke, I can't afford to buy a mozzie a pair of leggings.

I'm sorry to hear you're down on your luck.

All our money is tied up in the house.

I thought it was tied up in the rafters! C'mon, relax! Come with me to the races tomorrow and invest a pound, it's money for old rope, money for jam. I can give you a dead set cert. If you do your dough and have to shell out, well, it's only a miserable ten quid. No one ever went broke for the want of ten pounds.

I'm skint. I'm feeling the pinch. I'm finding it hard to keep my head above water as it is. I'm only just making ends meet. I'm into hock up to my eyeballs now. I'm hanging on like grim death, just trying to make a quid, make a crust. I haven't got two pennies to rub together. I'm very low on the old LSD.

But what about that car you're driving? That would have cost an arm and a leg. It must have cost a poultice. I bet it cost a bomb. Don't tell me you got it dirt-cheap. You must have shitloads.

That's not my car, it's my uncle's. I'm looking after it for him.

And what does he do for a crust?

He makes money.

Where there's muck there's money.

Yeah, he's got money to burn. He's got more money than sense.

If I had a quid for every time you said that, I'd be rich.

He's as rich as Croesus. He's loaded. He's raking it in, hand over fist. He's got more money than the Queen. He's rolling in it like Uncle Scrooge in the Donald Duck comics. He's worth a mint.

From what you've told me, he sounds like a money-grubber; always

wanting to make money out of everything he does. It's always the way.
Much wants more.

Yeah, he is a moneybags. But he's not quite the full quid. He's a few bob
short of a quid, a bit whacky-the-noo.

Then all the better. Get in for your chop, put the bite on him for a loan.

That's no-go. I'm not going into hock for anybody. Anyway, he thinks I'll
blow the lot — he reckons I'll spend it on grog, gambling, and women.
Last time I asked him for a loan, he said: 'What do you think I am? Made
of money?' He said he was bleeding at the eyeballs. He always reckons
he's going slowly broke, but, more precisely, he's just not going to lend
me any more money. He never splashes the moolah around. He just does
everything to suit himself. I wouldn't get a brass razoo out of him.

Well, can I put in my two bobs' worth? You are trying to make an honest
bob, and your uncle, who's worth a bob or two and is not short of a
bob (but is silly as a two-bob watch) thinks you're not worth two bob,
and he obviously likes to have two bob each way.

Right.

Tell him it's his turn to dub in.

LOOT

Grandad would say: 'Money is a necessary evil,' or, 'It's love of money, not
money itself, that is the root of all evil.' Then he would give you a penny or a
ha'penny and say as a joke: 'Don't spend it all at once,' or 'Don't spend it all
at one shop.' Or he might say: 'Here's threepence. Now when you get to town,
take this threepence out of your pocket, look at it, and then put it back in your
pocket. That way, you'll always have it.'

The symbol for a pound was a curly L with two short horizontal lines through
it, representing libra, the scales; the symbol for a shilling was s, which is
logical; but then the symbol for a penny was d — thus, LSD.

- To spend a penny — meant going to the toilet
- Penny for your thoughts?
- Then the penny dropped — I twigged
- He hasn't got a penny to his name
- He hasn't got a penny to bless himself with
- People would turn up unexpectedly and unwanted, **like a bad penny**
- Bright as a brand new penny — or a button
- Coppers — pennies and ha'pennies
- Triddley-bit or trey-bit or trey — threepence
- Zac — sixpence
- A one-bob bit — a shilling
- Deaner — a shilling
- A two-bob bit — two shillings, or a florin
- A guinea — 21 shillings
- Any paper money was always referred to as **a note**: a ten-shilling note, a pound note, a five-pound note
- **I wouldn't miss it for quids** — said when someone was very enthusiastic about something, a quid being a lot of money. Sometimes a man might say it sarcastically, referring to the church fete for example.
- Cabbage
- Dibs
- Dough
- Dosh
- Filthy lucre

I've got sixpence,
Jolly, jolly sixpence,
Sixpence to last me all my life.
I've tuppence to spend,
And tuppence to lend,
And tuppence to take home to my wife.

Keeping the time

Few people owned watches. When out of the house, most people kept time by the town hall clock or the clock on the GPO. Thus **keeping the time** was not an exact science, as the language showed ...

- **In this day and age** — now
- **In a sec** — very soon
- **In a jiffy** — several seconds
- **Any tick of the clock** — at any moment
- **I'll be there directly** — not right now
- **This arvo** — later today
- **It's about time** — at last!
- **A fair while** — a large amount of time
- **For a good while** — for months, if not years
- **Tomorrow never comes** — because by the time tomorrow has arrived, it's today!
- **The other day**
- **Slow as a wet week** — seems like a very long time
- **A month of Sundays** — years
- **Once in a blue moon** — not very often
- **Since pussy was a cat** — for a long time
- **For yonks** — a long, long time
- **Donkey's ages** — even longer
- **Early in the piece** — at the start of this time frame
- **From way back** — early on in life (She's a con artist from way back)
- **For old time's sake** — almost a lifetime
- **For the duration** — seems like forever
- **Since Adam was a boy** — longer than you can remember
- **Since the year dot** — since the start of keeping time
- **Out of the Ark** — since the world began
- **Don't hold your breath** — it's going to be a long wait

People who were in a hurry were **pushed for time**. Watching the clock was different from **getting clocked**, which was being whacked in the head. If people got up early, they were **up at sparrow's**.

- Wait a sec
- Wait a mo
- Wait a few shakes
- I'll be there in a jiff
- I'll be back in two secs
- I'll be there in two shakes of a lamb's tail
- I'll be there shortly
- I'll be there directly
- I'll be there before you can say Jack Robinson

Measurements

The bush in Australia was such a huge place that there was barely any need to measure things exactly. So Australia's system of measurements was expansive, to say the least.

DISTANCE, SIZE AND NUMBERS

You needed a **yardstick** before measuring something. Many distances were measured in **chains** (22 yards) because it was the length of a cricket pitch, and everyone in Australia had a good idea approximately how long that was. **The sun has only 2 chains to go till sunset. He could throw a rock four chains. The shop's about 20 chains down the dirt road.**

- Not within **spitting distance** — about a **chain** away
- You could **spit across it** — a narrow creek
- Just **a hop skip and a jump** — not far

- **A stone's throw** — people often picked up a stone and threw it — at a tin or a snake. So they knew the limit.
- **Not within cooee** — nowhere nearby
- **Not within a bull's roar** — out of sight and sound
- **A country mile —** not within **shooting distance**
- **Not by a long shot**
- **A fair hike** — a long hard walk
- **Woop Woop** — as far away as you could imagine
- **By a whisker** — a tiny margin

- More kangaroos **than you could poke a stick at**
- More than you could **shake a stick at** — even more
- They're **coming out of the woodwork** — more again
- **Big mobs** — a huge amount
- **Oodles** — almost too many
- The place was **lousy** with cats
- There were **droves of them**
- **In the old money** — to say 112 degrees Fahrenheit, 4 feet 7 inches … you're talking **in the old money**. 'That'll be 10 stone in the old money.'
- **Small beer** — a trifle

- He was **hard to fathom** … but I got his measure
- I've washed my hands for **the umpteenth time**
- I'm taking them all to the shop, **bar one**
- That's quite a few, in **anyone's language**
- The **whole shooting match**, the **whole kit and caboodle** — everything
- There was **bags of room**

Weather

Before weather girls on TV, Australians had their own way of describing the weather. After World War II they would blame the heat on the **atomic bomb**, and after 1969, on man **landing on the moon**.

- Isn't it funny how in winter, it gets late early
- There's a nasty nip in the air
- It's as cold as a witch's tit
- It's fairly freezing
- It'd freeze the fleas off a mongrel dog
- It'd blow a dog off the chain
- It's as dry as a dead dingo's donger
- It's as dry as a wooden god
- It's as dry as chips
- It's as hot as a sausage
- It's hellishly hot
- It's a real stinker
- I'm just a grease-spot
- It's very close
- It's shabby weather
- It's as black as a nun's habit
- The heavens opened
- It's bucketing down
- I'm as wet as a shag
- If the dog's wet, it must be raining
- If there's enough blue sky to make a sailor's pants, then it will fine up

Chapter twenty-two

ANIMAL TALK

Raining cats and dogs

- *Mean as cat droppings* — miserly, hidden away, rarely seen.
- It would make *a cat laugh* — no one has ever heard a cat laugh, so it must be pretty funny or ridiculous.
- There's more ways than one to *skin a cat*.
- Not enough room to *swing a cat*.
- *Cat-burglar* — a very quiet thief.
- You think you're *the cat's whisker* or *the cat's meow* — you think you're something special.
- She's the *ant's pants, the bee's knees, the cat's pudding, the cat's pyjamas*.
- *Cat got your tongue?* — Why aren't you answering me?
- You look like something the *cat dragged in* — dishevelled. Or, *Look what the cat dragged in!* — if you turned up unexpectedly and people were either delighted to see you, or they actually weren't.
- *A cat can look at a king* — I'm allowed to stare at you if I like.
- A *cat's eye* marble had a small sliver of colour in the middle, like the slivered pupil of a cat's eye.
- Let the *cat out of the bag* — reveal the secret.
- You're a *scaredy-cat*.
- *A catnap* — having *forty winks, a lie-down*.
- You've got more cobbler's pegs, customers, or takers *than hairs on a cat's back*. Or, the weeds are coming up *like hair on a cat's back* — there's millions of them.
- He was *like the cat that swallowed the canary* or *the cat that got the cream* — he was looking very pleased with himself.
- Every little bit helps, said the tomcat as he did a wee-wee in the sea.
- *All cats are grey at night* — don't choose a wife for her looks alone.
- If you were getting upset, they'd say you were *having kittens*, or *having fluffy pups*.
- Don't call me she. She's the *cat's mother* — something your mother would say.

- **Pussyfoot** around — creep unnaturally softly around so you don't upset someone.
- I'm **full up to pussy's bow** — I've eaten till I can eat no more.
- The kids were fighting like **Kilkenny cats**, and they fought till only their tails were left!
- **Curiosity killed the cat. Information brought her back!**

or

- **Curiosity killed the cat. Information took care of that.**

- Fighting like **cats and dogs**.
- It's raining **cats and dogs**.
- He's a **fox terrier** — he goes into a room and starts an argument or a fight, and then gleefully watches everyone from the safety of the sideline. Similar to **putting the cat among the pigeons.**
- He's **gone to the dogs**.
- It fits **like a sock on a dog's nose** — what a workman would say when he was proud of a job he'd just finished, or what a husband might say when asked what he thought of his wife's new hat.
- **I'm as happy as a dog with two tails.**
- **Every man and his dog was there.**
- Everybody knows **hair of the dog**, but in past times the whole expression was used. The cure for a hangover was another drink: **a hair of the dog that bit you**. A bit of sympathetic magic.
- This medicine **would kill a brown dog**. There was always a brown dog about, and they were mongrel and hardy. They were also called **bitzas** because they had bits o' this breed and bits o' that breed in them.
- He's **lying doggo** — he's pretending to be asleep, hurt or dead in order to surprise; he's **playing possum**; he's **foxing**. Someone who might be pretending to be asleep so they won't be asked to mow the lawn. Or they might be **foxing**, pretending to practise or train.
- **Barking mad** — crazy.
- **Even the dogs are barking it** — you think something's a secret, but actually

everybody, even the dogs, knows.

- **Dog's disease** — a cold or flu.
- **Dog-tired** — dogs ran around all day because they were never fenced or chained.
- This composition looks like **a dog's breakfast** — it's a mess, all over the place. Not to be confused with **a dingo's breakfast**.
- **The night's a pup** — it's early in the evening, let's party.
- **No use having a dog and barking yourself**.
- **Dog in the manger** — someone who wants to keep whatever he's got for himself, even if he doesn't really want it or value it. Like a dog who hangs onto a bone even though he doesn't want to chew on it.
- Dog — a **pan-licker**.
- It's **an old dog for a hard road** — if it's a tough job, you'll need someone with experience.

Horses, snakes and other assorted beasts

HORSES

Australians lived much closer to the bush in the 1940s and 50s, even if they were in the suburbs of major cities. Australia was said to be a country where **a dark horse could be a fair cow**. Large areas of creek and bush were still untouched; they were too difficult to develop with shovels and picks. So we had much more contact with animals and nature. It was only when giant bulldozers arrived that city gullies, creeks and hills could be levelled and all plant life removed. Thus many of the sayings of my time related to horses, snakes and other animals. For example, it was not at all uncommon in Brisbane in the 1950s and 60s for a stray horse to wander into your backyard, in the inner suburbs of Annerley and St Lucia. Australians always said they **rode the bus**

to work. You never knew your luck until **a dead horse kicked you**.

If someone wouldn't give up on a failed project, they were **flogging a dead horse**. If they wanted to **get cracking**, they were **champing at the bit**. Some people were said to have **more hide than a highwayman's horse** — very game, cheeky and disrespectful. Hence, **the hide of him! The nerve**. However, if you had **the hide of a rhinoceros** it meant something quite different: you were not easily insulted or dissuaded.

- **I'm so hungry I could eat a horse and chase the rider.**
- **Don't get on your high horse** — don't start acting righteous and important and insulted; don't get uppity.
- **Radish** — the red horse in the Sunday coloured comics, was an old nag who every year tried to win the Melbourne Cup, but never even arrived at the track in time because something always happened. He had no hope anyway. Hopeless horses were sometimes called **a Radish**.
- **Hold your horses** — hang on a minute, you're rushing into something.

- That's *a horse of a different colour* — you were not comparing like with like. Similar to: *that's a different kettle of fish*.
- *Home, James, and don't spare the horses* — what your father said as a joke to the bus driver.
- A *dark horse* — much more effective or faster or better than everyone thinks.
- *Horseplay* — when children were overdoing it and getting too excited.
- *Horse feathers!* — nonsense!
- *Never say die till a dead horse kicks you.*
- She changed her mind so often that *every horse she bred was a jib* — a jib is one who baulks and won't go forward, is indecisive.
- *Home and hosed* — we've nearly finished this assignment, and all that's left to do is small jobs, like hosing down the horse after a long ride.
- If someone was really angry with you they'd say: *You should be horse-whipped!*

SNAKES

- *The black snake bites the hand that feeds it.* Your mother would say this if you didn't stick up for her in a family argument, meaning you were ungrateful. If you live in the bush and a black snake moves into your shed, you don't kill it, because of the old bush lore that says if there is a black snake about, you won't get any browns or other deadly snakes. But, despite living under your merciful protection, it proves itself ungrateful, and will bite you all the same. It's venomous too.
- *Don't stir up more snakes than you can kill* — don't start arguing on all fronts, making enemies all over the place, or you'll get yourself into trouble.
- There were *more snakes than you could poke a stick at*.
- She turned out to be *a snake in the grass*. If you have ever tried to watch a snake moving through grass you'll appreciate this phrase. You never realised she was out to get you; it all seemed transparent, there seemed to be no camouflage, yet she tricked you all the same.

- **Don't get snaky** — don't get silently angry or sour.
- **Mad as a cut snake** — angry. Anyone who has chopped a snake knows what this looks like.
- In some Aboriginal cultures, it was said that the **death adder**, reputedly deaf, had symbols written on its stomach which read: 'If I could hear as well as I can see, neither man nor beast would pass by me.'
- **Hoop snakes** — a mythical snake that puts its tail in its mouth and rolls after you. Told to **new chums** (newcomers, especially from England) and tourists.

CHICKENS AND OTHER BIRDS

- A **shot duck** — you've had it.
- A **dead duck** — the same.
- **Not this little black duck** — there's no way you're getting me to do that.
- **Like water off a duck's back** — immune to criticism.
- Your **goose** is cooked — you're **for it.**
- **Stop playing ducks and drakes** — stop being evasive and not saying what you really mean.
- I felt a bit of a **galah**, a bit of a **goose,** when I forgot his mother's name.
- I'm **a bit of a bowerbird** — the bowerbird collects blue things that no one else wants, and decorates his bachelor pad with them to attract girls. Mothers who said they were like the bowerbird collected cuttings from people's gardens, recipes from other women, and scraps of useful material.
- As **scarce as lark's tongues**.
- He's as **dead as a dodo** — it didn't mean he was dead. It meant he was not the life of the party.
- I feel like I've got **an eagle on my shoulder** — you're worried that some enemy is keeping an eye on you, is going to defeat you very soon.
- It's as wet as a **shag's** arse.
- **Don't count your chickens before they're hatched.**
- She's **flown the coop**. She's **shot through.**
- He's running round **like a chook with its head chopped off**. Because many

people had a chook pen in the backyard, they would have to kill their own fowls. When you chopped the head off, or broke the neck, the body would run off wildly around the yard. This saying meant you were frantic, panicking, not actually getting anywhere fast, just like the chook.

- Do you like this dress?
- **I wouldn't put it in the henhouse to frighten the chooks into laying.**
  It's enough to put the chooks off laying.
  Hang it in the henhouse.

Because many people had chooks or pet birds, feathers were a part of everyday life, and thus were a part of everyday language.

- People who had no money would say: '**I haven't got a feather to fly with.**'
- If a husband wasn't allowed to go to the races he'd say: '**So here I am with clipped wings and frozen tail feathers.**'
- If a woman was overdressed, other women might say: '**If she had another feather, she'd fly!**'
- If a woman thought something was **a load of old nonsense** she might exclaim: '**Horse feathers!**' Or if she was completely taken aback by some unexpected news she would say: '**You could have knocked me over with a feather.**'

PIGS, GOATS AND DONKEYS

- She **squealed like a stuck pig**.
- **Happy as a pig in mud**.
- Why don't you go **the whole hog** and move to Sydney?
- I'm **sweating like a pig**.
- He's **on the pig's back** — doing well.
- He's **living high on the hog** — after the experience of the Depression, it was considered a bit of a sin to be conspicuously wealthy or spending too much; the implication being that it won't be for very long.
- **You can't make a silk purse out of a sow's ear** — you can't turn an uncouth person into a cultured one.

- **You've bought a pig in a poke** — it didn't live up to expectations, wasn't any good.
- He's an **ugly old goat** / You **silly old goat** / Stop **getting on my goat** / Stop **acting the goat** (carrying on in a silly way).
- If someone was spending up big, Grandad would say, '**They must have sold the goat.**'
- A cure for depression was to buy a goat; then after a few months **get rid of the goat**, and you are so relieved you feel happy with your lot.
- That was **donkey's years ago** — a long time ago.
- Haven't laughed that much **in donkey's ages**.

RABBITS AND LAMBS

During the Depression people lived on rabbits and scrub turkeys. **Rabbits** were called **underground mutton**.

- He took off like **a scalded rabbit** — when rabbits got too plentiful, people tried to eradicate them by pouring boiling water down the burrows.
- **Mutton dressed up as lamb** — mutton is grown-up sheep, and not as tender as lamb. A butcher might try to pass off mutton as lamb, just as an older woman might think she looks younger if she wears lots of make-up and clothes that only suit young girls. But, like the butcher, she doesn't get away with it.
- **I might as well be hung for a sheep as a lamb** — if I'm going to get into trouble for pinching one lolly, I might as well take a dozen, because the punishment is not going to be any worse.
- I'll be there **in two shakes of a lamb's tail** — soon.
- You might be **quiet as a lamb**.

BULLS AND COWS

- He wouldn't get **within a bull's roar** of winning the match — it's a big distance so there's no chance.
- He's **as useful as tits on a bull**. Even ladies would say this! He couldn't **train a choko vine over a dunny**.
- **Bull's wool** — balderdash.
- It was **a cow of a turn-out** — the dance or the party was no good, terrible.
- **It's a fair cow** — the whole situation is bad.
- **The cow that hollers the loudest forgets the soonest.**
- They were wandering along **like Brown's cows** — slowly, dawdling, or, as some said, **like brown scours**.
- You can try to move that stump **till the cows come home**, but it won't budge. If you've ever lived near a dairy farm, you'll understand this. It means you can do that all day, until 4 p.m. or so, when the cows actually do come home to be milked. They come home in single file, walking very slowly, stopping to look over gates and at people on the way.
- Stop going at things like **a bull at a gate** — rushing into a job without planning.
- Mad as **a bull stung by a bee**.
- **No bull** — it was ridgy-didge!

FISH AND INSECTS

Don't just sit there like **a stunned mullet**, do something. You fish for mullet by going into a muddy creek at night and shining a torch. The mullet fairly leap into your boat and flap around till you bop them on the head to stun them. So this phrase means you have been left speechless with embarrassment or shock.

- It's better than being **hit in the belly with a wet fish**.
- **House guests are like fish** — after three days they stink.
- Throw a **sprat** to catch a **mackerel** — offer a small cheap bargain out the front of a shop and customers might then come in and buy something

expensive. Or, give a concession and they might come to the party on the main sticking point in a deal.

- We've got **bigger fish to fry** — don't get stuck on this little problem, concentrate on the main job.
- **Strain at a gnat, and swallow a camel**. Today we would say 'Don't sweat the small stuff'. **Don't fuss about nothing**; take it in your stride.
- She's got **a bee in her bonnet** — she's got a favourite gripe she goes on and on about.
- There's no **flies** on him — he's smart, not easily fooled.

OTHER ANIMAL SAYINGS

- He's **as cunning as an outhouse rat**.
- **I smell a rat** — I'm suspicious that everything is not as it appears.
- I've got **a frog in my throat** — a sore throat.
- **She's got more points than a porcupine** — she's clever, cunning, full of tricks.
- **God stiffen the wombats!**
- **I'm blind as a bat**.
- **Well I'll be a monkey's uncle** — I'm surprised.
- She woke up all **bright-eyed and bushy-tailed** — alert.

Chapter twenty-three

ANGRY and REFLECTIVE

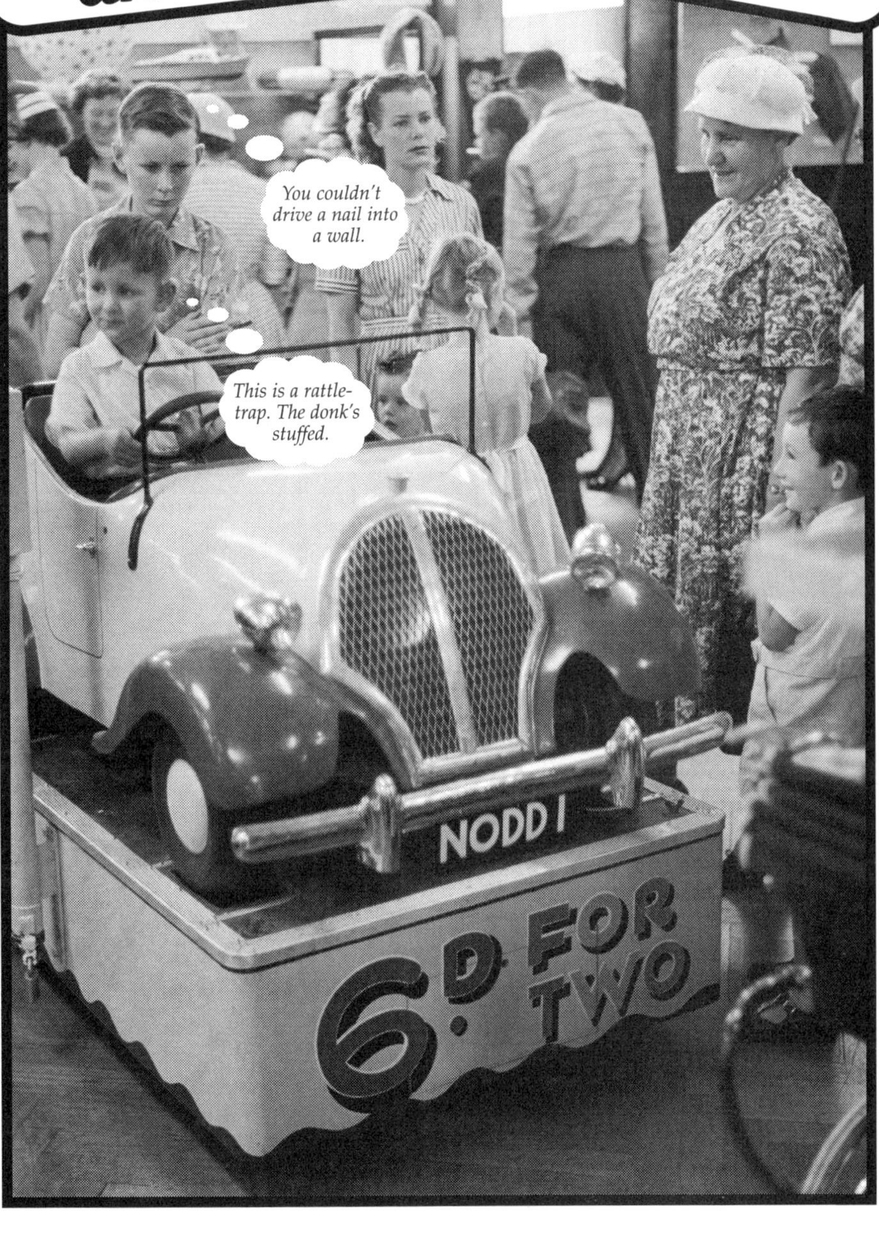

Blastbuggerbitchbum

- -

Most men used language **that would make a bullocky blush**, but not if they were **in female company**. So if a man wanted to warn a woman that he was about to swear, he would say: '**Well, to put it in the vernacular** ... ' or, '**Pardon my French** ...'

- Your brains are in your arse
- I slipped and went A over T
- Shit a brick!
- Damn and blast!
- Jesus wept!
- By the Lord Harry
- Bloody hell!
- Hell's bloody bells!
- Bullshit!
- Get rooted!
- Piss off!
- I'm pissed off with you!
- The dirty bastard!
- Pig's arse! (Pig's bum! If in female company)
- Come on, don't get shirty
- He's built like a brick shithouse
- It's a pain in the rear end!
- That's heifer dust!

Stinking, blasted, flamin', blinkin', blessed, bloomin', bleedin' and jolly were all used instead of **bloody**. Those **stinking** wild passes/the **flamin'** mower/the **friggin'** government/the **blasted** clothes line/this **jolly** hardwood/the **bloomin'** neighbours, the **bleedin'** obvious.

Before anti-bullying legislation, bosses would say: '**That's a blithering excuse! I'll have your balls for a necktie.**'

Bugger was perhaps the most widely used swearword, since no one had any idea what it meant. Extensions of this included: **Bugger me dead, I'm buggered, bugger that for a joke, be buggered! Go to buggery! Stop buggerising around!** Or, **that other bugger down the road**.

If a man was asked how much he made out of a job, he'd probably say: '**Sweet FA**' or '**Sweet Fanny Adams**' or '**Bugger-all of nothing.**'

And Grandma would always say: '**I've never heard such language**.'

A RORT

If someone announced '**I've been plucked**' it meant they'd been **fleeced, skinned, rooked, dudded**.

- They'd been the victim of some **jiggery-pokery**.
- They'd been **diddled** because someone pulled **a rort**.
- It was a **shady deal**.
- It was **a stew** — a fix
- **It stinks.**
- **He put one over on me.**
- So that's how you **skin** people.
- There are a lot of crooks around, and **I've struck the lot**.
- The perpetrator is on a **good lurk**, a **cushy little number**.

ARGY-BARGY

If you were involved in a bit of **argy-bargy**, having a **barney**, a **yike**, a **blue**, an argument, a bit of negotiation, you would be going at it **hammer and tongs**, pretty fierce and spirited. You had to be tough, so that when it was **all over bar the shouting**, you could leave with your pride intact.

Stop sitting there like a stunned mullet.

Well you've gone and upset my equilibrium.

You have to cop it sweet.

But I can't get a word in edgewise.

Well what do you think it is? Bush Week?

Fair suck of the sarsaparilla! Fair suck of the sav!

If your brains were dynamite, they wouldn't blow the wax out of your ears.

Fair crack of the whip! You're laying it on a bit thick.

Well, you're in cloud-cuckoo-land. You're being naïve. You're off with the fairies.

I don't believe anything I hear, and only half of what I see.

You mean you're blind in one eye and deaf in the other. Do your eyes deceive your ear-sight?

Are you having a lend of me? Are you taking the mickey?

I don't want to cast any nasturtiums on your mental faculties, but you wouldn't know if the town hall fell on you.

That's a load of bunkum, hogwash, rubbish, codswallop, claptrap, nonsense, poppycock and humbug.

Keep your hair on, keep your shirt on. Don't bite my head off.

But I got the rough end of the pineapple.

Don't get your knickers in a knot, or in a twist.

It's a free country.

Don't get your dander up.

Go tell Aunt Fanny!

Don't get on your high horse.

Go tell that to the marines!

Don't stand on your dignity.

Well fair's fair.

Don't go getting shit on the liver. You'll bust a valve. You don't look a pretty sight when you're sulking and miffed.

See if I care.

You're like an accident looking for somewhere to happen, so why are you hanging around here?

Pardon me for living.

Alright, let's iron out our differences.

I couldn't give a tinker's cuss, or a tinker's curse, or a rat's.

I'll believe you, thousands wouldn't.

Oompah! Oompah! Shove it up your jumpah! I've had enough of this!

Alright, alright, don't make a federal case out of it. Try to keep a civil tongue in your head.

That's rich! I will if you stop pooh-poohing my argument.

Your argument has been shot down in flames because it doesn't hold water, when all's said and done.

That's drawing a long bow. That's a sweeping statement. You're jumping to confusions.

Like it or lump it.

You're hard to toss.

You hit the nail on the head.

You don't say.

I don't like to argue the point.

Now that's a moot point.

Get off your soapbox, pal.

What's that got to do with the price of eggs?

Buggered if I know.

My big fat aunt!

Yeah, and I'm a monkey's uncle. You'd do a lot with a stick and a bucket of eggs.

Shut your gob.

I'll go through you like a packet of salts.

Shut your neck.

The country's buggered for the want of a Catholic King and a Protestant Pope. Play that on your piano! Put that in your pipe and smoke it! I'm going home.

That suits me down to the ground. Best suggestion to date. If I never see you again, it will be ever so much too soon.

Hell to pay

Whenever Mum said she was **as mad as one thing**, you knew there'd be **hell to pay** if you hadn't collected the eggs from the **chook pen** by dinnertime.

Or if you and your brothers arrived home late, Mum would announce she was **as mad as a hornet**. 'OK, you've **done your dash**. You're all **in strife**, you're **in hot water**,' she would say. '**There'll be fireworks** if you get home late for tea again. **I'll take it out of your hide**. You kids better learn to **toe the line, or else**!'

Or else was code for **you'll get a belting** or **you'll taste my stick**.

Mothers didn't hesitate to hit kids if they felt the kids deserved it. But they usually gave umpteen warnings first: Just because your father lets you **get away with murder**, don't think you won't **come to grief. You'll cop it if I catch you. You're incorrigible. You'll come unstuck. I'll give you curry. I'll blow my stack. I'm going to blow my top in a minute. I'm going to read the riot act**.

Depending on what sins you were committing Mum would say:

- **Stop that malarky**
- **Stop playing silly buggers**
- **Stop being obstreperous**
- **Stop that growling**

Things only got really serious if a child started being cheeky and **answering back**:

Tidy up your room.

What for?

I'll give you **what for**!

Normally mothers just threatened their kids with **a good tongue-lashing** or **the edge of my tongue** or **a piece of my mind**. Her favourite warning when out was: **Behave yourself.** But if this didn't work she tried: I'll put you in a **home for delinquent children**. I'll give you **paddywhack the drumstick. I'll box your ears**.

Any insolence or disrespect was **over the fence** and upped the ante straight-away. **Don't be impudent, you ungrateful pup**, a mother would say. **Don't you raise your voice to me**. To shut you up mid-sentence if you were attempting to argue your way out of trouble, your mother would say: '**Alright, Mouth Almighty**', or '**Alright, Know-all-Not!**' '**OK, Smarty-pants**.'

Mothers could be moved to increasingly unlikely threats, half said in jest:

- **I'll slap you with a wet tram ticket**
- **You need a good belting**
- **I'll tan your hide**
- **I'll give you a good flogging**
- **I'll thrash you to within an inch of your life**
- **I'll wring your neck**
- **I'll skin you alive**
- **I'll spiflicate you**

When a Mum was really angry she **did her lolly, did her nana**, was **out of her tree**, was **very scotty**.

Beltings were usually accompanied by explanations of the effect they would have on the child. **This will shake up your liver bile. This'll give you something to think about. This'll give you something to be going on with.**

But if a mother was feeling put upon and powerless, particularly when frustrated by a naughty daughter, she might say: **I could murder you. I could kick you, you wilful child. I should throttle you.**

The child took this for what it was. A totally idle threat.

Scariest of all for most kids was: **Wait till your father gets home**.

When they did get home, fathers would use boxing parlance to threaten their kids: **I'll give you a clip over the ear. Do you want a lift under the lug**?

If they were really angry, fathers might also say: **Do you want a boot up the arse? Don't fool. I'll knock your block off, you blockhead.** I'll have your **guts for garters**. Don't **play silly buggers** with me. Stop carrying on **like a man possessed**.

When this didn't work, fathers often resorted to getting a **switch** (a whippy twig from perhaps the guava tree) to hit kids with. Some fathers would instruct their children to go outside and break off a switch from the tree — to fetch their own implement of terror. Then the switch would be used to punish the child by whipping on the hand or bottom.

GETTING BLOWN UP BY MUM

- You're for it
- You'll get your pants blown off
- You'll have to smoodge up to Mum to get out of this
- Mum will blow us up
- Mum will be spitting chips
- Mum will go off her rocker
- Mum will go ballistic
- Mum will scream blue murder when she finds out
- Mum will rouse on you
- Mum was spewing
- Mum went crook
- Mum blew her lid/top/stack
- Mum blew her top
- Mum lost her block
- Mum burst her boiler
- Mum cracked a darkie
- Mum hit the roof

- I was ticked off
- I got into strife
- She caught me red-handed
- She copped me
- I got pinged breaking the window
- She had me on toast
- She came down on me like a ton of bricks
- I copped it from her
- I've had the royal order (I've had it; I'm in deep trouble)

LOST FOR WORDS EPISODE 15:
Fishing friends

Lost for Words. **The story of Bert and Grace and their trials and tribu-lations bringing up a young family after the War.**

Bert and his good mate Kevin are on the end of the pier fishing. They were expected home some hours ago. They know what awaits them, so they linger even longer.

'I'm gonna come in for a lot of stick when I get home,' says Bert.

'You think you're in the gun,' says Kevin as he wets his line again, hoping not to go home empty-handed. 'I'm in more trouble than Flash Gordon. I promised my sister-in-law I'd look after the kid tonight.'

'Oh, you mean Little Lord Fauntleroy,' said Bert. 'I thought she never let him out of her sight.'

'She wants me to hold the fort while she ducks out tonight,' said Kevin. 'I'll be in more trouble than Ned Kelly. I'm a shot duck. I'll be hauled over the coals. I'll be hung, drawn and quartered.'

Bert starts playing an imaginary violin, as though he is providing the sad music for a pathetic character in a silent film.

Kevin refuses to rise to the bait. 'Alright, Bert, quit while you're ahead, you won't get a rise out of me. I agree that we're both up the pole.'

'Yeah, in the wars again.'

'We've made a meal of it.'

'We haven't made a good fist of it.'

'I'll say. It's a real dog's breakfast.'

'It's enough to tear the fork out of your nightie.'

'It's bad enough to rot a rabbit rissole.'

'It'd rot your socks.'

'There's no point screaming about it. If we growl all day, we'll be dog-tired by night.'

'We'll all be ru'ned said Hanrahan.'

'We'll be caught fair and square.'

'In the pooh.'

'Yeah, up shit creek without a paddle in a barbed wire canoe.'

'She'll give me some curry.'

'I'll be a sorry sight. I'll have to go to my kennel.'

'They'll be complaining to me left, right and centre. I was supposed to run the cutter to the shops.'

'We're both under the thumb, Bert.'

'They know not what they do, Kevin.'

'Yeah, I'm the man who needs to be told. Are you going to the Royal Show?'

'No. I'm waiting for the musical.'

Kevin offers a bag of peanuts. 'Give sweets to the sweet. Have a nut, Bert,' he says.

'In jest, in earnest,' replies Bert, getting snaky. 'You know they're not actually nuts, Kevin, they're legumes.'

'Intelligence is rife. Have a legume then.'

'You'd think we'd get something on the line, we've been here all day,' says Bert.

'Rome wasn't built in a day,' says Kevin. 'It took a thousand years.'

Bert looks up with a grin and replies, 'It must have been a government job well.'

'That joke is so old it's got whiskers,' says Kevin.

'You gotta laugh, or you'll go mad,' says Bert.

'Like another beer, Bert?'

'Kevin, you're a scholar and a gentleman. I could go a round or two for a pound or two.'

'You know I'm not a betting man,' says Kevin. 'I'll give you odds on that I catch a fish in the next hour but.'

'You're on. I'd like to be as sure of winning the lottery. I'm sick of watching you drown worms. I shall await with bated breath!'

'Alright! Stand back and let the dog see the rabbit. How come the fish are as scarce as hen's teeth? They're as scarce as rocking horse manure. Maybe it's a bit sharky around here.'

Bert looks around in the gathering dark.

'The boss has been on my tail over that last big order being late,' Bert says. 'He likes to get his pound of flesh. He fair put the wind up me, Kevin. He's a hard task-master.'

'Well, why have a dog and bark yourself?'

'He's driving me dingbats well. Lord knows I'm always there when the chips are down. But those apprentices he's given me are a pack of useless no-hopers. I wouldn't give any of them a guernsey if it was up to me.'

Kevin responds:

Little fleas have smaller fleas
Upon their backs to bite 'em,
And smaller fleas have lesser fleas,
And so on, ad infinitum

'The mind boggles! Kevin, I think you're talking a load of balderdash. A load of codswallop. You've got the wrong end of the stick.'

'Well, Bert, have you tackled the boss about it? Crossed swords with him? Told him a few home truths? He'll probably go to water. Why don't you give him a piece of your mind? Get my drift?'

Bert breathes a sigh as he baits another hook: 'Now that's a different kettle of fish. That's a horse of a different colour. It wouldn't be any use. He just expects everyone to kowtow. It sticks in my gizzard.'

'Well, then, rise above it. On Monday, check out the lie of the land, then get stuck in and knock everyone else into a cocked hat. Make him eat his words. Then later in the week, put the hard word on him for a rise.'

'Better you than me, Kevin. I've found it well nigh impossible to get anywhere with him.'

'I had a good powwow with him the other week, Bert. He told me all about the dignity of labour.'

'And did you get the rise you wanted?'

'Well, no, not yet.'

'Strikes me, Kevin, that our mutual boss tried to soft-soap you. I wouldn't give you tuppence for any boss. I've never met one who would do a hand's turn. I don't think our boss is worth his salt.'

'Still and all, Bert, in the long run, he provides the job and we provide the labour. It's better than a kick in the backside. It keeps us out of mischief.'

'Don't give me that! We're the wage slaves for the Tories. It's a rum deal. All the pushy people get the cushy jobs.'

The two men sit in silence for a time, and then Bert speaks.

'You know, Kevin, what I'm on about is that Grace and I need a bigger house or a smaller dog. I'm on a hurdy-gurdy, in the hurly-burly. Every morning, Monday to Saturday, Grace comes in with a cup of tea and says, "Wake up, Australia! Your King and country needs you." And when I get up, I say to Grace, "I think today's the day I'm gonna die." Then I put on my badge of servitude, saddle up and box on. I work all day flat strap, flat chat, flat out. And if I didn't we'd all end up in the poorhouse. I'm on penal servitude, Kevin. I think I've run out of puff. I'm fed up. It's the last straw. I'm at the end of my tether. For two pins, I'd throw it all in as a bad lot. That's why I love fishing on this pier with you every Sunday, even when there are no fish.'

'Bert,' says Kevin, 'I'm lost for words.'

Picture credits

All pictures reproduced in *Lost For Words* are reproduced courtesy of the National Library of Australia.

nla.pic-an24296103 — After Sunday morning mass at St Ita's, Drouin, Victoria, c. 1944, photo by Jim Fitzpatrick, 'Drouin town & rural life during WWII' collection, National Library of Australia (page 52)

nla.pic-an24358529 — Mrs Josephine Smith and an unidentified man in Connolly Colquhoun's butcher shop, Drouin, Victoria, c. 1944, photo by Jim Fitzpatrick, 'Drouin town & rural life during WWII' collection, National Library of Australia (page 105)

nla.pic-an24206325 — Unidentified woman testing the heat of her iron, Drouin, Victoria, c. 1944, photo by Jim Fitzpatrick, 'Drouin town & rural life during WWII' collection, National Library of Australia (page 120)

nla.pic-an24296089 — Unidentified family having a meal, Drouin, Victoria, c. 1944, photo by Jim Fitzpatrick, 'Drouin town & rural life during WWII' collection, National Library of Australia (page 127)

nla.pic-an24295922 — Three unidentified women clearing the table after a meal, Drouin, Victoria, c. 1944, photo by Jim Fitzpatrick, 'Drouin town & rural life during WWII' collection, National Library of Australia (page 128)

NAA Image no. : A1200, L79215; Barcode : 11245735; A large crowd of young schoolchildren drinking 1/3 pints milk outside a Melbourne milk bar , 1969, National Archives of Australia (page 134)

NAA Image noL A1200, L19964; Barcode: 11656750; Bill Denby, oldest local resident, spinning yarns to youngsters, Talbingo Station picnic race meeting, 1956, National Archives of Australia (page 140)

nla.pic-an24190156 — Chairman of the Council, Edward Porter gives instructions to Bill Pertzel, Council worker, Drouin, Victoria, c. 1944, photo by Jim Fitzpatrick, 'Drouin town & rural life during WWII' collection, National Library of Australia (page 148)

nla.pic-an20865637-30 — Robert Gotts and Philip Gotts, 10 Ballarat St, Brunswick, 1940. Playing in the backyard with billy cart, C.R. Gotts collection of family photographs, National Library of Australia (page 152)

nla.pic-an24207635 — William Russell putting the four gallon monthly ration of petrol into a customer's car, Drouin, Victoria, c. 1944, photo by Jim Fitzpatrick, 'Drouin town & rural life during WWII' collection, National Library of Australia (page 154)

NAA Image no. : A1200, L58778; Barcode : 11397355; Child receiving a spoonful of medicine to protect against poliomyelitis. Lyneham School, Canberra, 1966, National Archives of Australia (page 157)

NAA Image no. : A1200, L43413; Barcode : 11223334; Small patient gets attention, Canberra Hospital, 1963, National Archives of Australia (page 172)

NAA Image no: A1200, L22678; Barcode: 11397298; Children being vaccinated against tuberculosis, 1957, National Archives of Australia (page 175)

nla.pic-an24358358 — Mothers and babies attending the Drouin Infant Welfare Centre, Victoria, c. 1944, photo by Jim Fitzpatrick, 'Drouin town & rural life during WWII' collection, National Library of Australia (page 176)

nla.pic-an24174781 — John H. Lowin, who delivers Drouin's mail, has a letter for Mrs Leslie Allison of Drouin, Victoria, c. 1944, photo by Jim Fitzpatrick, 'Drouin town & rural life during WWII' collection, National Library of Australia (page 180)

nla.pic-an24355689 — Drouin Newsagency, Victoria, c. 1944, photo by Jim Fitzpatrick, 'Drouin town & rural life during WWII' collection, National Library of Australia (page 183)

nla.pic-an24366026 — Farewell presentation to Father Edward Hynes of St Ita's Catholic Church, Drouin, Victoria, c. 1944, photo by Jim Fitzpatrick, 'Drouin town & rural life during WWII' collection, National Library of Australia (page 189)

nla.pic-an24358545 — The choir at the Methodist Church in Drouin, Victoria, c. 1944, photo by Jim Fitzpatrick, 'Drouin town & rural life during WWII' collection, National Library of Australia (page 191)

nla.pic-an24220186 — Mrs Robert Wharton making a cake in her kitchen, Drouin, Victoria, c. 1944, photo by Jim Fitzpatrick, 'Drouin town & rural life during WWII' collection, National Library of Australia (page 195)

nla.pic-an24345274 — Unidentified man and boy preparing a meal, Drouin, Victoria, c. 1944, photo by Jim Fitzpatrick, 'Drouin town & rural life during WWII' collection, National Library of Australia (page 206)

nla.pic-an24229656 — On the way home from school, Drouin, Victoria, c. 1944, photo by Jim Fitzpatrick, 'Drouin town & rural life during WWII' collection, National Library of Australia (page 212)

nla.pic-an24358189 — Unidentified woman and child buying shoes in the shoe section of Bell and Macaulay's Store, Drouin, Victoria, c. 1944, photo by Jim Fitzpatrick, 'Drouin town & rural life during WWII' collection, National Library of Australia (page 217)

nla.pic-an24280499 — Drouin schoolboys playing, Drouin, Victoria, c. 1944, photo by Jim Fitzpatrick, 'Drouin town & rural life during WWII' collection, National Library of Australia (page 225)

nla.pic-an24229822 — Teacher and children in the classroom at Drouin State School, Drouin, Victoria, c. 1944, photo by Jim Fitzpatrick, 'Drouin town & rural life during WWII' collection, National Library of Australia (page 239)

nla.pic-an24229798 — Children at Drouin State School listening to a story, Drouin, Victoria, c. 1944, photo by Jim Fitzpatrick, 'Drouin town & rural life during WWII' collection, National Library of Australia (page 244)

nla.pic-an24295904 — Afternoon tea with the Hamley family and visitor June Wellwood, Drouin, Victoria, c. 1944, photo by Jim Fitzpatrick, 'Drouin town & rural life during WWII' collection, National Library of Australia (page 254)

nla.pic-an24144981 — Drouin Shire Secretary Thomas J. Ryan (behind desk) talking to Councillor Frederick Lilley, c. 1944, photo by Jim Fitzpatrick, 'Drouin town & rural life during WWII' collection, National Library of Australia (page 261)

nla.pic-an24358165 — Grocery section, Bell and Macaulay's Store, Drouin, Victoria, c. 1944, photo by Jim Fitzpatrick, 'Drouin town & rural life during WWII' collection, National Library of Australia (page 269)

nla.pic-an24358225 — Customers in the hardware section of Bell and Macaulay's Store, Drouin, Victoria, c. 1944, photo by Jim Fitzpatrick, 'Drouin town & rural life during WWII' collection, National Library of Australia (page 264)

nla.pic-an24295002 — Shopping in Main Street, Drouin, Victoria, c. 1944, photo by Jim Fitzpatrick, 'Drouin town & rural life during WWII' collection, National Library of Australia (page 271)

NAA Image No: A1500, K1220; Barcode: 11697818; 1952 Miss Pacific finalists Mary Clifton Smith, Pamela Jansen and Judy Worrad, stand in front of surfboards on Bondi Beach, National Archives of Australia (page 280)

nla.pic-an24358132 — Ladies clothing section, Bell and McCauley's Store, Drouin, Victoria, c. 1944, photo by Jim Fitzpatrick, 'Drouin town & rural life during WWII' collection, National Library of Australia (page 285)

nla.pic-an24280176 – Drouin schoolboys playing cricket, Drouin, Victoria [1], c. 1944, photo by Jim Fitzpatrick, 'Drouin town & rural life during WWII' collection, National Library of Australia (page 225)

nla.pic-an24340468 — Drouin Railway Station interior during world War II, Victoria, c. 1944, photo by Jim Fitzpatrick, 'Drouin town & rural life during WWII' collection, National Library of Australia (page 305)

nla.pic-an24358494 — Unidentified women shopping with coupons during world War II in Drouin, Victoria, c. 1944, photo by Jim Fitzpatrick, 'Drouin town & rural life during WWII' collection, National Library of Australia (page 308)

nla.pic-an24340489 — The Station Master in his office, Drouin Railway Station, c. 1944, photo by Jim Fitzpatrick, 'Drouin town & rural life during WWII' collection, National Library of Australia (page 320)

nla.pic-an24212077 — Ethel McDonald (farmer's wife) ties her horse in Main Street, Drouin, Victoria, c. 1944, photo by Jim Fitzpatrick, 'Drouin town & rural life during WWII' collection, National Library of Australia (page 324)

NAA Image No: A1200, L29771; Barcode:11377724; Scene at a Sydney toy store, Christmas 1959, National Archives of Australia (page 331)